Boatowner's Guide to Marine Electronics

3rd edition

Gordon West
and
Freeman Pittman

with illustrations by Jim Sollers

International Marine
Camden, Maine

Published by International Marine®

10 9 8 7 6 5 4 3

Library of Congress Cataloging-in-Publication Data
West, Gordon.
    Boatowner's guide to marine electronics / Gordon West and Freeman
Pittman; with illustrations by Jim Sollers. —3rd ed.
        p. cm.
Rev. ed. of: The straightshooter's guide to marine electronics. 2nd ed. 1987.
    Includes index.
    ISBN 0-87742-342-3 (pbk. : alk. paper)
    1. Boats and boating—Electronic equipment. 2. Consumer education.
    I. Pittman, Freeman. II. West, Gordon.
Straightshooter's guide to marine electronics. III. Title.
VM325.W46 1993
623.8'504—dc20   93-17489
                        CIP

Questions regarding the content of this book should be addressed to:
    International Marine
    P.O. Box 220
    Camden, ME 04843
Questions regarding the ordering of this book should be addressed to:
    The McGraw-Hill Companies
    Customer Service Department
    P.O. Box 547
    Blacklick, OH 43004
    Retail customers: 1-800-822-8158
    Bookstores: 1-800-722-4726

This book is printed on acid-free paper.

Printed by R.R. Donnelley, Crawfordsville, IN
Design and Production by Faith Hague
Edited by J.R. Babb, Tom McCarthy, Dorathy Chocensky

Contents

Preface

Welcome to the world of marine electronics! Whether you are a sailor or a powerboat operator, and whether you are technical or non-technical, we will present to you the very latest in marine electronic technology. Our goal is to give you the information you need to judge what is out there and what is compatible with your boat and your purposes. Along the way we will explain the operation, capabilities, and limitations of each instrument.

If you are a professional marine electronics installer you will learn some new "trade secrets" that may allow you to squeeze out every last bit of performance from a particular piece of marine electronics and do things with these sets that you might not have known possible.

We will help you decide whether to buy from a local marine electronics specialty dealer (who probably will install the equipment as part of a sales package) or a mail-order discount house (which will simply give it to you in a big white box).

We will discuss some procedures for maintaining the equipment and for troubleshooting malfunctions. Too many mariners are frightened into inaction by the complex circuitry contained in most instrument housings. Better than 50 percent of all marine electronic malfunctions could be fixed by anyone with a little patience and some common sense, and by maintaining your own equipment and doing the simpler repairs yourself (as well as the installation, tuning, and calibrations, when possible), you will save money, avoid the inconvenience of equipment downtime, and become a more skilled and knowledgeable operator.

We will talk about what equipment you can legally install yourself without an FCC license, such as marine VHF and radar, and which installations still need to have a technician sign off the log book, like your marine single sideband.

This book will also tell you what is the best piece of marine electronics for *your* boat. No, we won't tell you the best brand name to buy, nor the exact model number—but we can tell you how to select the piece of equipment that will best meet your cruising requirements.

Never before have we had so much good marine electronic equipment to choose from. This equipment is much smarter, more compact, and in many instances *less* expensive now than it was just a few years ago. Not surprisingly, the process of shopping for gear is correspondingly more complicated. We hope this guide helps.

              Gordon West   Freeman Pittman

CHAPTER 1

The Marine Electronics Marketplace

by Gordon West

Probably the most frequently asked question in the marine electronics business is, "Which unit is best?" It's a good question, but there is no one right answer. The question should perhaps be rephrased as, "Which marine electronics are best for my particular application?" To answer this properly, the marine electronics seller would need to ask you many questions about your boat, your intended cruising or fishing area, your experience in operating electronic equipment, and the level of sophistication you desire. If any seller tells you which unit is best without interrogating you first, look for another place to shop.

Deciding Where to Buy

There are four major avenues of distribution for marine electronic equipment:

1. The traditional marine electronics dealer
2. Marine electronics catalog houses
3. Marine hardware stores that also sell electronics

4. Boat dealers who include built-in electronics with new or used boat sales

There is no love lost between the specialty dealers and the catalog houses. The sales and servicing of marine electronics have traditionally gone exclusively to the former, but the catalog houses have recently made major inroads on the dealers' sales.

Most specialty dealers have elaborate showrooms with examples of every type of marine electronic gear hooked up and operating. This allows you to hear, manipulate, and get the feel of any type of equipment you may be thinking of purchasing, and there is no substitute for this. Most dealer showrooms also stock an ample supply of literature for each piece of equipment that is on display, as well as some that are not.

The specialty dealers hire the cream of the crop when it comes to qualified sales personnel. Many of the men and women who make up their sales forces are qualified not only to recommend gear but to give you a fairly technical overview of any piece of equipment in their showroom. In addition to these sales personnel, a dealer usually employs three to eight FCC-licensed technicians who possess marine electronics technician certificates; these are the top experts in their field, and many of them have had extensive additional factory training on specific products. (Equipment manufacturers spend thousands of dollars training technicians on the installation and operating techniques and the servicing of particular pieces of equipment.) If you have a question that the dealer's sales force can't answer, they can often bring out the technician "from the back" who will answer your query in detail. The dealer also can provide you with a custom installation aboard your boat or assist you with a do-it-yourself installation.

The marine electronics specialty dealers also offer factory-authorized warranty repair. Thus, if your new piece of gear should fail, it may be fixed for free by the dealer. Sometimes the equipment must be taken back to the shop for service, but in other cases the fix can be accomplished aboard the boat. Troubleshooting of equipment aboard your boat is another unique feature of a specialty dealer. They have the portable equipment to do it. Labor rates are high if not covered by warranty, but usually are worth every penny. (More about warranties shortly.)

Specialty dealers have united with manufacturers to form a trade organization called the National Marine Electronics Association (NMEA). The NMEA has a code of ethics that all member dealers must meet; if a dealer sports the NMEA logo, you can be sure that he is indeed a specialty dealer who has met the membership requirements.

Marine dealers normally sell their equipment at the manufacturers' suggested retail prices. They are not known for heavy discounting, for they must maintain a minimum markup in order to cover the showroom, the trained sales personnel, and the expensive service equipment. It is for this reason that catalog sales of marine electronic equipment have been growing so strongly in recent years.

Marine catalog houses that sport exciting color brochures and even more exciting discount prices are indeed doing well. These relative newcomers to the world of marine electronics got their start when gear that could be user-installed became more common, and when the manufacturing of marine electronic gear began to overwhelm the available avenues of distribution. Twenty years ago most marine electronic equipment was American-made, and production was just right to support the specialty dealers. There was no such thing as too much gear to sell, and discounting was taboo. Now U.S. manufacturers of marine electronics are importing a huge portion of their gear from the Far East. In doing so, however, the domestic manufacturers have lost control of production volume. The Oriental manufacturers don't and won't slow down on production, so alternate sources of fast distribution are necessary to keep the pipeline clear. The name of the game for the marine electronics catalog discount house is quick sales, which they achieve with low prices. Some very aggressive promotional work is carried on by the marine electronics discount catalogs and showrooms. Their creative marketing skills leave the specialty dealers in the dust. Manufacturers must surely be impressed with their sales figures, as well as their promotional ideas.

If you plan to install your equipment yourself and you know what you want, discount houses and catalogs might be a good way to go. But don't expect many catalog houses to give you an hour or two of their time going over a particular piece of marine gear. Their toll-free numbers are for placing orders and their personnel, though they may indeed be knowledgeable about marine electronics, are not on the phone to plan your entire marine electronics system. Be advised, too, that discount and catalog houses frequently don't tune or repair the equipment they sell, and most don't offer any installation service at all. Advice, yes; service, no. If your equipment breaks, most catalog houses will tell you to ship it back to the manufacturer for repair. This "we sell it, they fix it" approach may not be popular with manufacturers, but when a lot of units are sold through these houses, they don't have much choice.

Purchasing a piece of marine electronics through a discount house, having it fail, and then taking it to the marine electronics specialty dealer down the street for repair may cause hard feelings, especially if the specialty dealer took the time originally to tell you which piece of equipment to buy. Some dealers might throw you out the door. Others, if they have a repair shop, may fix your unit, but most will take their sweet time if you bought it elsewhere.

A few marine electronics discount organizations do possess service as well as installation facilities. These are rare, however, and you should carefully check out such an organization before buying equipment from it. Even if a discount house staffs two or three technicians, they are probably unable to keep up with the repair work generated by the discounter's large volume of sales. As a general rule, when you buy equipment from a catalog house, you will encounter less delay and frustration if you send it directly back to the manufacturer for repair.

Buying electronics in a marine hardware store is another option. But what you might find is a gaggle of equipment sealed under the glass in the showroom counter. Sometimes it is hooked up, and hopefully the hardware store personnel know something about it.

Buying marine electronic equipment with a boat and having it installed by the boat dealer is another proposition. Most boat dealers will subcontract the installation to local marine electronics specialists, so you can get a good deal in a packaged boat sale. Just be sure to find out who's going to do the installation of the equipment, who will service it, and who is going to show you how to run it. Most boat dealers are specialists in boats, not electronics.

If you are buying a boat that already has marine electronics aboard, make a list of the gear and take it to a local marine electronics specialist to find out how up-to-date it is. The better marine electronics specialists will give you a fair answer, but you may want a second opinion. New boats with built-in marine electronics may be a very good deal if the electronics are exactly what you are looking for. The more serious mariner or marine electronics enthusiast, however, will specify certain pieces of equipment. If such a request can be honored, make sure a qualified technician will do the installation.

The retail margin from the manufacturer to the seller of marine electronics averages about 40 percent. On large equipment such as radars, water makers, and sonars it is usually less, and on smaller pieces of equipment such as VHF transceivers, depthsounders, and GPS the margin can be as much as 50 percent. Marine antennas may go as high as 60 percent. Keep this in mind when you are offered a percentage discount off the manufacturer's suggested retail price.

Marine electronics specialty dealers like to operate at a 20 to 30 percent margin, while the catalogs can operate as low as 10 to 15 percent above cost if they move large quantities. Boat dealers that offer marine electronics as a package may sometimes break even—the marine electronics will help them sell the boat, and that's their main interest. This gear will not be too heavily discounted, however, since the boat dealers buy from another distributor rather than directly from the manufacturer. The hardware stores, too, usually buy from distributors, the distributor making about 10 percent and the hardware store hoping to sell the gear at a margin of 20 percent.

Summing up, if you want a turnkey operation and the ability to put your finger on one person to select the appropriate equipment, install it, and show you how to use it, the marine electronics specialist is a good way to go. If you want the best buy for the least money and you plan to install and tune everything yourself in your spare time, you might want to buy your gear through a discount house or catalog.

If it's your wife's birthday and a Sunday to boot, and she absolutely has to have that marine VHF handheld radio, and you spot it in an open marine hardware store, then go ahead—pay the retail price, get your set, and hope it doesn't break.

If the boat price is no longer negotiable but you can get the dealer to throw in a bucketful of marine electronics, have at it.

Equipment installation is an important factor. Unless you're a confirmed do-it-yourselfer or an electronics hobbyist, for example, you're probably going to want to have your radar system, single sideband station, or automatic direction finding station professionally installed aboard your boat. If you buy the equipment from a mail-order house and then ask a local marine electronics dealer to do the installation, you'll be charged on a time-and-materials basis. Using SSB radio as an example, a typical installation takes two days or more, and at $75 per hour plus materials you would be facing an additional out-of-pocket expense of at least $1,200. If, after the unit was installed and certified, you were not satisfied with its operation, the additional grounding or other recommended remedy would cost you more money still. If, on the other hand, you buy the SSB radio (or radar, or ADF station, or loran, or . . .) from the local dealer, you can have the price of the installation included as part of a sales-and-service package. Have this agreement drawn up beforehand, in writing, and insist that it permit you to call back the technician *without additional charge* if you are not happy with the initial installation. An installation included as part of a sales agreement should cost substantially less than one contracted on a separate, time-and-materials basis.

Probably the best approach is to buy larger, hard-to-install, hard-to-remove gear from the marine electronics specialist and smaller, removable equipment from a discount house. If the big stuff breaks you can bring the specialist aboard to fix it. If the little stuff goes sour you can unplug it and either take it into the discounter's local repair depot or ship it back to the factory. The discussions of individual instruments in this book will give you a feel for which ones you may safely buy from a discounter.

The most important thing to remember, no matter where you buy your equipment, is not to trust anyone who says, "This equipment is best for you" without first finding out how you plan to use it. Take time to look at your options when buying marine electronics, and always play fair—don't pick the brain of the marine electronics specialist only to turn around and buy your gear through a discount house. Stay honest with the people you are dealing with, and you may find that they will meet you halfway when you tell them what you want to put aboard and what your budget is.

One further warning: No matter who you buy from, you are definitely taking a chance when the new equipment you buy is delivered in a carton that has been previously opened without any documentation having been added. Few sellers check out and certify equipment before selling it, but if this was the case, that's fine. But demand their certification sheets on the equipment in the preopened box. Otherwise, you may be getting a unit that has already been sold once. It is not unusual for a buyer to return a unit to a dealer complaining of one defect or another. If the dealer can't find the defect on the test bench, he may decide the buyer was mistaken, repack the unit, and sell it to the next customer, who might be you.

Warranties

Warranty periods for free repair and possible retuning of the equipment you buy may be as short as ninety days or as long as three years. Study the warranty before you buy.

The manufacturer's warranty is expressed clearly enough in the paperwork that comes with each piece of equipment. If you take the unit off your boat and send it back to the manufacturer (who is in reality the American importer if the unit is manufactured in the Orient), they will fix it free of charge provided the warranty has not expired. You pay the shipping charges, however. Most factories will get the unit back to you within three weeks. But if it's not convenient or even feasible to return a piece of gear to the manufacturer for repair, you will be dependent on a factory-authorized, licensed repair facility, and here you may encounter delays or frustration.

As discussed, not all sellers of marine electronic equipment are licensed repair facilities. If you buy from a discounter, for example, you may have to go somewhere else to have the unit repaired or tuned. If that somewhere else is a specialty dealer, he may or may not do the repair, and he will almost certainly put your gear at the end of the line behind any equipment bought directly from him. He will probably refuse to honor the factory-authorized warranty if you do not have proper sales slip information, so do send in the warranty cards and do keep accurate purchase records.

Marine electronics specialty dealers and a few discount catalog sellers will service everything they sell and are factory-authorized to do so. They will give you a written statement on the terms of their free service, and they may have extended-service options as well. These written statements should be examined carefully. While manufacturers will often pay dealers to service your equipment when it is under warranty (many demand that the more complex units, such as GPS receivers, be returned to them for repair), they may not pay a technician's travel expenses to your boat. Will a dealer pay for that service if you buy the unit from him? Find out beforehand; a permanently installed radar unit would not be convenient to dismantle and return for service.

Remember, too, that even if a discount catalog seller is factory-authorized to service and repair the equipment, you will usually pay the shipping charges, and you would probably get your equipment back sooner were you to ship it directly to the manufacturer.

When you buy equipment, ask what will happen should your gear fail in a distant port. Can the seller or manufacturer supply you with a list of authorized service facilities that will honor your warranty? For reasons already stated, this is particularly important when you buy mail-order equipment, but it applies when you buy from a specialty dealer, too. Although specialized marine electronics dealers are united through the NMEA, a dealer 1,000 miles away from where you bought the unit will not necessarily honor the warranty and fix your set for free.

Get your warranty claims in writing, and more important, find out exactly what the local marine electronics dealer will do to back up the manufacturer's warranty. Some enterprising dealers will exchange any item that fails within the first ten days of operation. That's a nice feature to look for.

Comparing Models

The National Marine Electronics Association gives annual awards to the "best piece of marine electronics" in several categories, and these awards are decided by the dealers. But although the quality and capabilities of the equipment are weighed in the selection process, the dealers may be biased toward units that give them a good profit margin, and the awards are thus, in part, a popularity contest. Also, marine electronics dealers have been slow to accept new and innovative designs, preferring to wait as long as several years while the designs prove themselves. Ten years ago, when the first keyboard-entry VHF marine radio was introduced, it represented a breakthrough, but it won no industry awards or accolades, partly because the marine electronics specialists simply didn't trust a radio without knobs and partly because they wanted a more favorable profit margin on the product. It is true that new designs sometimes need a year or two to stabilize and have their bugs worked out (and you can use this as a criterion for selection if you don't mind buying last year's technology), but there are nevertheless new instruments each year that deserve awards but garner none. The NMEA awards may signify marketability first and foremost, and true excellence only incidentally.

The quality of the instruction manual is a good clue to the quality of the marine electronics unit you may be planning to buy. Better units will have a more complete instruction book, and some units will have an additional service manual that may be purchased separately. If you can't quite decide which piece of electronics to choose, ask the dealer for a peek at the instruction book.

A technical service manual is a boon if you plan to have the equipment serviced by different dealers along the coast. This eliminates the age-old problem of dealers telling you they can't fix your equipment because they don't have the appropriate service manual. The service manual might also give you some basic troubleshooting guides to follow should your equipment go on the blink. Again, generally, the more complete the service manual, the better the equipment.

Most important, however, the best electronics are those that fit with greatest precision your installation and operating needs. Again, if a seller recommends a particular model before asking you any questions about how you plan to install and use it, he or she is only selling equipment, and not a service. Don't decide on the name brand until you have seen them all and reviewed the capabilities of each.

Buyer's Checklist

Is the marine electronics seller you are considering characterized by the following?

- Factory-authorized service approval
- Sells marine electronics as its major business
- Buys directly from the manufacturer
- Offers trained salesmen to spend up to one hour with you in planning your system
- Has demonstration equipment on the floor
- Offers catalog sheets for you to study at home
- Has a licensed technician available for consultation
- Offers installation and service aboard your boat
- Possesses the necessary technical equipment and personnel to calibrate, tune, test, and FCC-certify all equipment
- Offers a selection of equipment
- Stocks the popular accessories for each unit

- Boasts factory achievement certificates of technical merit for technicians

Here are some other questions to ask:

- Is the equipment sold to you in factory-sealed containers, or is it "demo gear" previously taken home by someone else?
- Can the seller modify the equipment to meet particular installation needs?
- Will the seller replace dead-out-of-box equipment?
- Will the seller loan you a piece of equipment while your new piece is being fixed?
- Can the seller provide a custom installation, such as cabinetry, for your equipment?
- Is the seller a member of the NMEA?
- Is the showroom or catalog tidy, complete, and professional?
- Has the seller been in business for more than a few years?
- Can your purchased equipment be fixed in any other cruising area in the United States or the world?
- Is the pricing competitive?

If you can answer "yes" to most of these questions, you have found a good, safe place to buy. For small pieces of equipment, if you know what you want, you can accept "no" answers to more of these questions as you gravitate toward reputable discount houses in search of a better price. If you do buy from a dealer, demand the strong warranty backup for which you're paying, and demand that the loran-C receiver, SSB radio, GPS receiver, radar set, autopilot, or automatic direction finder be properly tuned, calibrated, tested, installed (if dealer installation is part of the package), and, if necessary, FCC-certified.

CHAPTER 2

Depthsounders

by Gordon West

There have been huge advances in depthsounder technology in the last five years. Foreign and American depthsounder manufacturers are battling it out to see who can come up with the most features at the best price, and we consumers reap the benefits. The latest generation of depthsounders will work at higher boat speeds, suffer less ignition interference, ignore swiftly passing air bubbles, and stay locked onto the bottom for up to five seconds when your boat pops completely out of the water at fifty knots. Yet prices are lower than they have ever been. Two distinct types of depthsounder have emerged, one for navigation and one for locating fish. This chapter covers both.

How They Work

The principle of operation behind echo sounding hasn't changed over the last sixty years. A depthsounder beams pulsed sound waves down toward the bottom, then picks up the weak echoes and converts this information into bottom and fish readout information, which is displayed on the indicator. While variations in water temperature, salinity, and density affect the speed of sound somewhat, acoustical pulses normally travel at about 4,945 feet per second in water, compared with 1,117 feet in air. If it takes two seconds for a pulse to leave the underwater sender/receiver unit, bounce off the bottom, and return to the unit, the depth of water must be 4,945 feet.

Depthsounders consist of three components:

1. The *transducer*. This is the underwater device that translates pulses of electrical energy into acoustical vibrations, directs these toward the bottom, receives the echoes, and converts them back into electrical impulses. The transducer case may be all plastic or bronze with a plastic face, and it is mounted with its face in the water and pointed downward.

2. The *amplifier*. Located inside the depth indicator unit, this component actually comprises three subcomponents: an oscillator to produce electrical impulses of a uniform frequency; a transmitter amplifier to step up the impulses before sending them to the transducer; and a receiver amplifier to pick up the faint return echoes and convert them into strong, usable signals that are fed into the display or indicator circuitry. Bigger and more expensive transmitter amplifiers give stronger signals to reach extremely deep bottoms.

3. The *indicator*. Take your pick! Chart recorders, flashing neon bulbs, liquid crystal displays, video presentations, color scopes, and other readouts are available for the indicator unit. This is the device that translates the transducer input into a readout form— graph, digital, or analog—that you can understand and interpret. When you select one of the several types of sounders, what you are really choosing among is the various types of indicator units.

The transducer is a critical part of your depthsounder assembly. Many different types are available with any one type of sounder, and the one you choose must fit your particular echo sounding needs. A transducer is a ceramic element, or several ceramic elements in a "phased array," encapsulated in a suitable housing. When a voltage pulse is applied to the element, it will vibrate at its designed frequency. The vibration is called a piezoelectric oscillation, and it can be made to recur many hundreds of times per minute through the application of alternating voltage between two metal plates that sandwich the crystal. In the majority of depthsounders the quartz oscillates at a frequency of 200 kHz, or 200,000 cycles per second, well above the range of human hearing. Depthsounders that need to send a signal extremely deep will use a lower frequency crystal, usually at 50 kHz (50,000 cycles).

These sonic waves are aimed downward, reflect off the bottom or from fish, and then reenter the underwater transducer assembly, which picks up

Cross section of a through-the-hull transducer mounting, showing the fairing blocks that must be hand-carved to fit the hull shape precisely while keeping the transducer in a vertical position.

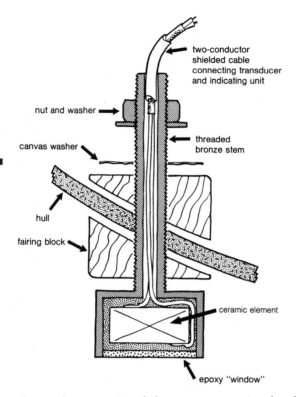

two-conductor shielded cable connecting transducer and indicating unit

nut and washer

threaded bronze stem

canvas washer

hull

fairing block

ceramic element

epoxy "window"

the weak return signals between transmitted pulses. The incoming echo strikes the element (also called a "plate" or "crystal") and applies a tiny mechanical stress that travels to its opposite face; the crystal is set vibrating mechanically for an instant, and in doing so generates an alternating voltage between its two faces. The vibrating sound pulses are thus turned back into electrical energy that is then fed through the metal plates and back to the receiver amplifier. Shallow-water sounders may generate up to 25 watts of peak power (from the transmitter amplifier) so that the sound pulse will strike the bottom with enough force to return a substantial echo. In deep-water units, over 100 watts of power must be used to pick up the distant bottom, this power applying more than 400 peak volts to the transducer's piezoelectric mechanism.

The pulse repetition rate will vary between and within echo sounders depending on how deep they are intended to sound. On shallow sounding units, pulses are transmitted and received up to 1,500 times per minute. On deeper sounding units, more time is needed for the echo to be returned, so the pulse repetition rate may be as low as 60 times per minute. This lets the receiver section listen for the weak echo before the transmitter section fires off another ping. Shallow sounders will also transmit short pulses, and deeper sounders will transmit longer pulse lengths. For an analogy, imagine yourself in a boat in the fog, giving blasts on a foghorn and listening for echoes from a distant shore. Because the sound may be scattered by the shore and the fog and intermittent background noises may intrude, you'll stand a better chance of picking up the echo of a longer blast. On most sounders offering more than one depth range to select from, pulse length and repetition rate are both set automatically when you "dial" the depth.

A 200 kHz transducer can be used for fishing, navigating, or both. Like transducers of other frequencies, it sends out a cone of acoustical energy that gets wider as it goes deeper, the usual beam width at 200 kHz being 9 to 15 degrees. (Beam widths up to 45 degrees are available for shallow-water fishing.) With a 9-degree beam, a 200 kHz transducer is effective at depths up to 600 feet; at 100 feet, it will "see" a circle about 14 feet in diameter, giving quite a detailed picture of the ocean floor. If fish are right under you— even individual fish of moderate size—the 200 kHz, 9-degree transducer will pick them up quite nicely. Most digital indicators (which are used strictly for piloting) and flashers (which have some fishfinding capability) use 100 to 200 kHz transducers.

For a larger picture of the ocean floor you need a physically larger, lower-frequency transducer. The 50 kHz transducer may have a beam width of up to 54 degrees, covering a 100-foot-diameter circle in 100 feet of water. This lets you see fish activity off either side of your boat, and the lower frequency enables you to sound much deeper bottoms (3,000 feet or more, depending on the transmitter power). You lose a bit of definition, however; you won't be able to pick out those small rocky protrusions on the ocean floor, as you can with a tighter beam angle, and small fish may escape detection. For somewhat improved resolution at depths beyond the reach of a 200 kHz sounder, a 50 kHz transducer with a narrower beam width (as narrow as 16 degrees) might be a better choice. Regardless of beam angle, however, no 50 kHz transducer will provide the shallow-water resolution of a 200 kHz transducer. The 50 kHz transducer is commonly used where both navigation and deep-water fishfinding capabilities are desired.

If you want the best of both worlds, choose a depthsounder with two transducers—perhaps a 200 kHz transducer with a wide cone angle for shallow-water fishing, and a 50 kHz transducer with a narrow cone angle for deep-water fishing and sounding. You can use a transducer switch box to select between them. Fishfinders frequently use this configuration.

A recent innovation in underwater sounding for fishfinding is the transducer assembly that may scan a large portion of the ocean floor ahead, to the sides, and astern.

First attempts at this feat were to mount a small transducer on a steerable arm, and to electronically or manually rotate the transducer to pick out fish to the side. This is sometimes referred to as "side-scanning." While this works, it doesn't work well as you get more horizontal with the surface of the water. Trying to scan out to the sides will lead to false echoes from the mirrorlike water all around you.

A transducer with several fixed elements might allow you to first look port, then straight down, and then starboard—and electronically, it would sweep from left to right, giving you a wide-angle look at fish below and at the sea floor. While this worked, it still didn't meet the demands of fishermen looking for a high-resolution picture of the bottom.

Then came a period of three-dimensional sounding. Instead of seeing the bottom from just one aspect, the sea floor would show up as pinnacles on your LCD or CRT screen. Some manufacturers tried this out, but quite frankly, I think they may have had so much information on the display that the average fisherman became befuddled about what he was looking at. But there are some fishermen out there who swear by the enhanced three-dimensional display. Check it out for yourself—you'll either like it or hate it.

But the biggest breakthrough was from ultrasound technology, proved in the medical field and brought into the world of sportfishing for the first time. A transducer, comprised of multiple crystal elements, allows for a very smart head unit to phase the individual crystal elements for a steerable look at the bottom. Phased array scanning has been done for many years in radar, as well as out on research vessels—this is the first time that it has been made affordable for the small-boat operator.

The use of a phased array transducer, and a special beam-former design in the head unit, allows this setup to steer an acoustic beam electronically in any of sixty-four directions. This creates an amazing lifelike image on the display. Because of the ultrafast electronic scanning, moving fish and other objects seem to come to life on the display. Fishermen can now see the bottom contour as never before, finding submerged objects, dropoffs, and other fishing hotspots.

The transom-mounted transducer is compact and about the same size as a standard triducer—speed, depth, and temperature. The phased array system will show fish and bottom at much higher speeds due to its fixed transducer. The phased array also allows you to direct the beam in different directions almost immediately, thanks to its matrix of electronically controlled elements inside the transducer housing. This would allow a simultaneous split-screen image of a wide angle—up to ninety degrees—and a conventional straight-down reading on a super-twist LCD screen.

But phased array technology is in its infancy. The transducers are now available, but manufacturers are still refining the head display units for better resolution. But we know the system works when we take a look at some of the graph recordings from phased array systems aboard ocean research vessels. It's a whole new type of technology getting scaled down for the small-boat market.

Check with the local fishing community to see what type of transducer they are using for a particular fishing area. If you already own a depthsounder, you can switch transducers providing you match the new transducer frequency and impedance with the frequency and power of your depthsounder transmitter. Check your instruction manual for the operating frequency of your sounder. The converse is also true—you can replace your indicator unit with a "smarter" or more sophisticated unit (from a different manufacturer if you desire), yet keep the old transducer. Again, you must ensure that the frequency and power of the depthsounder transmitter matches that of the transducer. If the transducer is physically small in size, it could be damaged by an extremely high-powered transmitter. High-power, low-frequency transmitters, such as those used for extremely deep sounding, require massive transducer systems and will not be compatible with the typical 200 kHz transducer. With this exception, however, mixing and matching components is quite feasible and certainly advantageous, since transducers seldom wear out. You may not get a discount on the indicator unit by telling the seller you don't want the new transducer, but at least you'll have a spare transducer, and you'll save the hassle and expense of another transducer installation.

Transducer Installation

The transducer must be in contact with the water for best performance, and proper location and fairing of the installation is critical. On larger vessels, power or sail, the transducer is usually mounted through the hull. Although manufacturers' instruction manuals for other types of marine electronic equipment usually offer complete installation directions, this often is not true of depthsounder transducers mounted through the hull, because the manufacturers assume, wisely, that you will leave the job to a boatyard. If you do decide to go it alone, however, the key to good depthsounder performance is to find a spot where no aeration will disturb bottom soundings.

The placement in a sailboat must be far enough from the keel that signals are not deflected when the boat is heeled. To get around this you can mount a transducer on each side of the keel with a gravity switch automatically selecting between them. Many available depthsounders can be modified for this system.

The transducer is mounted through the hull using a special fairing block that will keep it pointed directly down toward the ocean floor when the boat is on an even keel. These are streamlined to minimize drag and to shield

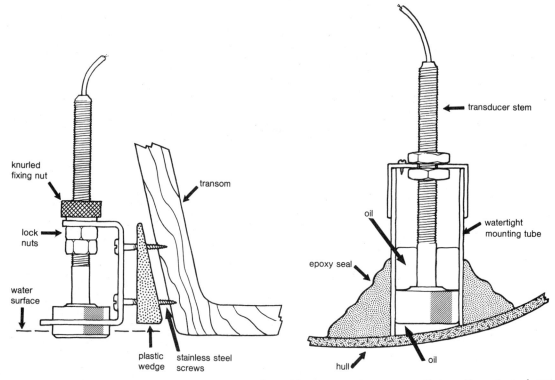

Transom-mounted transducers are subject to erratic operation caused by air bubbles flowing off the boat's bottom. They are practical for slow-speed boats where the transducer is totally submerged at all times, but on planing hulls they may provide only intermittent information. Some brackets are gimballed, and by pivoting the transducer it is sometimes possible to find a position that will minimize erratic readings.

There are various means of mounting a transducer inside the hull, but the installation must almost always be custom fitted. The transducer must be positioned vertically and the face of it submerged in oil to exclude any air between it and the hull. Any transducer with a threaded stem can be installed in such a watertight compartment.

the transducer from turbulence, bubbles, and damage. Sounders that are professionally placed through the hull usually give superb performance, and if you are into serious long-distance cruising, this is the only way to go. Transducers *can* be mounted by a scuba diver with a minimum amount of water let into the bilges, but if you want to try this trick, get an experienced diver. It would be much better to have the transducer mounted during your next haulout.

Most manufacturers supply a transom bracket for small boats that allows you to mount the transducer off the stern (but still underwater), and some such brackets allow the transducer to self-adjust its orientation depending on your speed through the water. A slight miscalculation of transducer

In waters where there is a heavy growth of barnacles it is sometimes necessary to remove the growth from the face of the transducer to keep it operating properly. Special through-hull fittings are available that permit withdrawal of the transducer into the bilge for cleaning. One must screw a cap over the fitting when the transducer has been removed. A small amount of water will rush into the hull during the moments the transducer is being withdrawn and before the cap is screwed down.

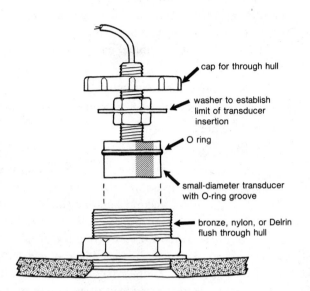

cap for through hull

washer to establish limit of transducer insertion

O ring

small-diameter transducer with O-ring groove

bronze, nylon, or Delrin flush through hull

placement can seriously compromise readings even at moderate speeds, however, and on planing hulls the readings may be intermittent.

On some boats you can mount the transducer inside the hull and sound through the wood or fiberglass. The accuracy of readings will not be affected, but the maximum sounding depth will be reduced by as much as 75 percent or more, and the ability to find fish may be all but eliminated. This system will not work at all with most cored hull constructions or when the laminate has local voids.

If you decide to try an inside-the-hull mounting of the transducer, follow the manufacturer's instructions precisely. The usual first step is to try out the transducer at different points below the waterline. The face of the transducer must be flat against the wood or fiberglass hull and covered with water or oil. Putting your boat in fairly deep water, move the transducer around in the bilge and find a spot where you get a solid reading of the bottom. If you find the results satisfactory, you can spring for one of the commercially available kits designed specifically to mount any type of transducer to the inside of your hull.

One further note: The marine electronics specialty dealers do many installations, but they will *not* install transducers. This job is usually done at a boatyard.

The transducer assembly is linked to the depthsounder equipment by a two-conductor coaxial-type cable. This cable should never be nicked or cut. Allowing moisture to enter a crack in the outside black sheath could damage the entire affair. Since this cable is carrying both transmitted and received signals, it must be shielded from external noise. *Never* route it beside the primary wires in your ignition system, and while you *can* run the cable beside other electrical wiring for short runs, it's best to keep it as far away from them as possible. Here are some examples of wires you want to avoid:

- Wires to fluorescent lights
- High-voltage wires from your SSB radiotelephone antenna circuit
- Satellite antenna wires
- Bait tank wiring

The transducer cable usually contains an outside braid to keep static out and the signal in. Should the cable be severed, you must carefully reattach all of the wires, making sure that the braid covers up the entire works.

The end of the transducer cable simply plugs into the back of your depthsounder. Watch this connection! If neglected, it may become loose, corroded, and then intermittent. Make sure also that none of the wires pull free from the chrome connector collar. Intermittent bottom readings at slow speeds are sometimes the result of a loose or poorly connected transducer plug.

An inexpensive digital sounder that does one thing and does it well.

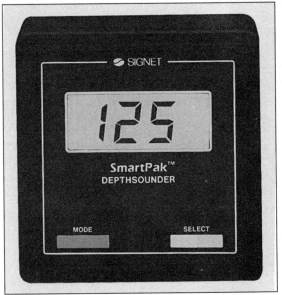

Digital depth indicators will neither show fish reliably nor indicate type of bottom holding ground. However, built-in anchor alarms are a handy feature.

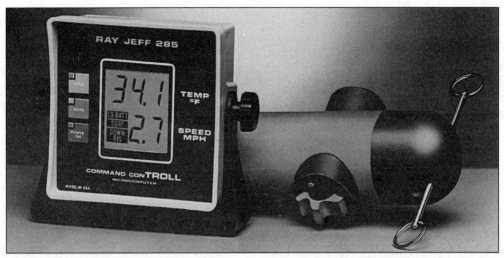

This indicator is matched to a "triducer," a through-hull pod housing an impeller and a temperature sensor in addition to a depth transducer. This seems to have been accomplished without noticeably affecting the efficiency of the individual sensors.

Indicator Units

Some manufacturers refer to their depthsounders as "sonars," but this is really not accurate. A true sonar is a device that sends out energy horizontal to the surface of the water, while a depthsounder, of course, directs its energy perpendicular to the water's surface. Sonars are very expensive pieces of equipment designed for commercial fishing applications—spotting large schools of fish, rocks, or obstructions on either side, astern, and ahead of the vessel. Depthsounders won't do this. Even if you turn a depthsounder's transducer horizontal to the water it won't do it, because it does not possess the right type of transducer and associated circuitry to scan horizontally without picking up the water surface as a false target.

Manufacturers have developed extremely powerful transmitters and extremely sensitive receivers to be housed in the indicator unit, but don't be overly influenced by advertised transmitter powers. Since these claims may refer to peak watts, peak-to-peak watts (a highly inflated figure), average watts, or useful watts, comparisons are difficult. For better or for worse, the better indication of the performance of a sounder is its price tag; the higher the price tag, the more watts in the transmitter, and generally the greater the sensitivity—that is, the ability to see weak echoes in the receiver.

The difference between a depthsounder and a fishfinder lies in the indicator unit and the microprocessor circuitry associated with a particular type of display.

Digital readout indicators are best for anchoring and handy for piloting, and they are the frequent choice of cruising and racing sailors and other consumers whose concern is depth in feet, fathoms, or meters, not where the fish are or what the bottom is like. Manufacturers are getting away from duller, light-emitting diodes (LEDs) to the more brilliant liquid crystal display (LCD) readouts, which can be seen easily in direct sunlight and are backlighted for night viewing. The LCD readout also draws less current, so your depth indicator can operate off portable dry-cell batteries. These readouts are reliable and efficient and are now considered "state of the art." Light-emitting diodes are fast disappearing.

Digital sounders and meter-movement (also called "analog") sounders are both easy to read. In addition, digitals have no motors or moving parts, so they operate silently and effectively. Some digitals sport innovative features such as depth alarms and anchor alarms, products of microprocessor technology. You need only predetermine at what depth or depths you wish the alarm to sound. If you aren't watching the unit and get too close inshore, your alarm will let you know immediately. If you're asleep at night and are blown offshore or onshore the alarm will sound, letting you know you have exceeded a minimum or maximum preset depth setting. Sounders offering this feature differ widely in the available range of depth alarm settings. "Forward looking" sounders will even keep track of the rate of change in depth, giving a warning alarm when the water shoals rapidly toward a critical depth. Digital indicators with averaging circuits are advertised, and these will ignore wildly errant, ephemeral readings caused by debris or bubbles, or by a powerboat's hull momentarily lifting from the water at a high speed. Some digital sounders will automatically adjust raw depth readings (which, by definition, indicate depth below the transducer) to depth below the keel or below the water's surface. Some units are wired to speakers and programmed to deliver vocal depth reports.

Flashing indicators or flashers utilize a neon bulb or LED mounted on a rotating disk that is driven by a constant-speed motor. On each rotation a switch is magnetically activated, causing the transmitter to send an electrical pulse to the transducer. When the weak pulse from the returning echo is amplified, the bulb or LED is lit up and displayed against a circular calibrated scale. Because the disk rotates at a constant rate, the arc swept by the bulb in the time between outgoing and returning pulses is directly related to the depth as read off the scale. The disk rotates so rapidly that the flashes appear motionless but for changes in depth. Random flashes usually indicate fish, and if you watch a flasher closely you can see the return echoes of even one or two large fish just off the bottom. Flashers are sometimes used by sportfishermen because they are inexpensive and they work well, providing you keep your eye on the dial. Most flashers give you a num-

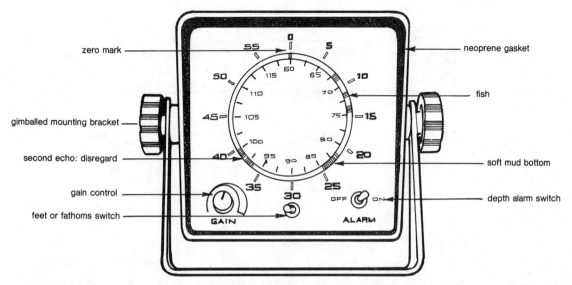

A flashing indicator is inexpensive and provides both bottom and fishfinding information. The price range **with transducer is $100 to $450, and a typical size is 8½ inches high, 6½ inches wide, and 4 inches deep.**

ber of depth ranges to select from. In making a selection you are in actuality adjusting the speed of the disk's rotation, with slower speeds being required for greater depths.

Flashers will also indicate the type of bottom below you. If you receive a broad bottom flash, it's probably mud. A sharp bottom flash is likely to be hard sand or rocks, and an irregular bottom would probably show up as a very broad bottom flash that changes in width.

The latest innovation in flashers is a no-moving-parts liquid crystal display. The round dial remains, but the LCD black lines take over for the rotating disk and its mounted display lamp. The same LCD display can also give you (with separate sensors) water temperature and boat speed; digital depth displays and predetermined depth alarms are possible, too.

A flasher should have a gain control knob on the front panel with which to adjust the sensitivity of the receiver circuitry. Tuning this efficiently takes practice. Too much gain causes loss of target discrimination and may even cause false targets to appear; too little gain will cause weakening or loss of bottom echoes.

If you are really into serious fishfinding, you'll want a graph paper or graph LCD depthsounder, also known as a fishfinder. There are two types— *graph recorders* and *video* or *CRT* (cathode ray tube) *recorders*. Graph recorders are excellent, and they are quite useful in navigating in deep or shallow waters. The chart paper or LCD readout will give you an accurate view of the bottom and everything in the water column. A typical reading

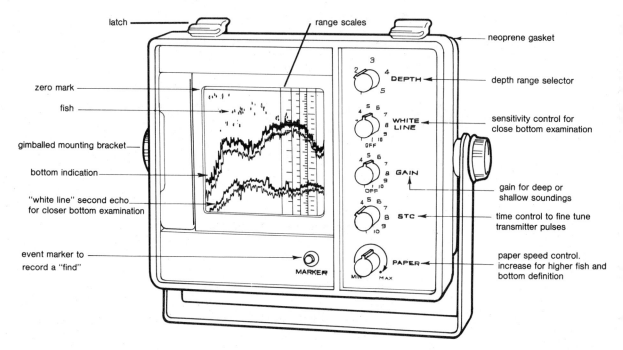

Labels on the diagram:

latch — range scales — neoprene gasket

zero mark

fish

gimballed mounting bracket

bottom indication

"white line" second echo for closer bottom examination

event marker to record a "find"

MARKER

DEPTH — depth range selector

WHITE LINE — sensitivity control for close bottom examination

GAIN — gain for deep or shallow soundings

STC — time control to fine tune transmitter pulses

PAPER — paper speed control. increase for higher fish and bottom definition

A chart recorder. This type of sounder is a favorite among fishermen, offering a tremendous amount of bottom and fish information. It is extremely useful in navigation as well as fishfinding. The price range with transducer(s) is $150 to $1,000, and a typical size is 9½ inches high, 12 inches wide, and 4 inches deep.

might depict your downrigger being brought up from 70 feet for a lure change, large fish feeding off the bottom, game fish just below the surface of the water, and a well-defined wreck or obstruction on the ocean floor that might be a great candidate for skin-diving exploration. Graph recorders will also assist you in following charted bottom contours to find your way home in the fog, and they will let you see the trend of a shoaling channel as you reenter a harbor.

Chart or graph recorders are also getting smarter, so if you're going to get a graph recorder, get a smart one. You can now adjust a dial to zoom in on the exact depth you want to examine. Want a closer look at that possible game fish at forty fathoms or the ocean floor beneath you? Zoom in and take a long gander. And if you need to mark a spot on the chart where your downrigger hit a snag, push a button and there it is!

Many recorders feature bottom definition circuitry, variously referred to as "white line," "gray line," or by one of several other monikers. By purposely reducing bottom echo, this circuitry isolates fish that are floating just off the bottom. Some graph recorders will allow you to change display speed, too; a faster display speed yields better bottom definition, "definition"

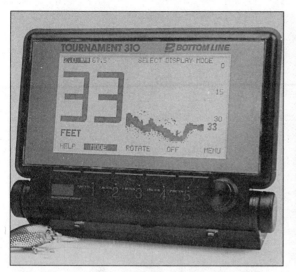

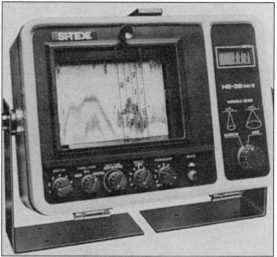

Here a high-resolution LCD display illustrates both recorded bottom contour and easy-to-see depth range. Look closely for mph and water temperature, too.

This chart recorder is matched to two transducers contained in one pod, so a narrow or wide cone angle can be selected as desired.

implying the ability to detect small targets and deep bottoms (sensitivity) and to separate crowded targets (resolution). All of this is available in the more sophisticated depth recorders that offer variable display speed, variable pulse length, and a combination of switchable transducers in addition to power and gain controls.

Another innovation in depth recorders is the super-twist liquid crystal display, in which the LCD imagery is so sharp it looks like chart paper! These units are usually completely waterproof, and they'll let you see up to 32,000 bits of information at one time. You can recall one full screen of past information by pressing a single button, and an auxiliary tape recorder will allow you to record the digital information for later replay. The super-twist LCD readout is ten times more detailed than your digital watch, so you can imagine the precision of each target. The only characteristic you must get accustomed to is that every target is a miniature square, as opposed to a faithful reproduction of what the transducer is "seeing." An ascending bottom line that would appear smooth on a chart recorder will look like miniature ascending steps on the LCD readout. The better the resolution, the less noticeable each pixel square. The more pixels per inch, the more money the unit will cost.

A new feature of LCD graph recorders is the multicolor pixel display. Recent innovations in LCD readouts now allow manufacturers to develop

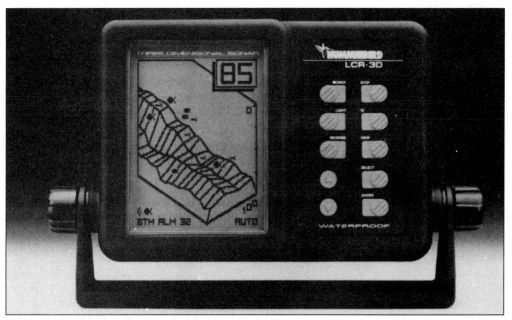

A three-dimensional look at bottom contours has now been made possible with multi-element underwater transducers. This emerging technology may also use phased array transducer elements.

colors that represent different echo intensities. The LCD color display will indicate extremely strong echoes as red pixels, while echoes with slightly less strength may show up as yellow or green. Some manufacturers claim that certain colors indicate given species of fish, but this is a little hard to swallow. Echoes return quite as nicely off kelp, for example, as off fish between the surface of the water and the bottom.

A drawback to the color LCD recorder is its requirement of direct viewing and the right amount of light for best color discrimination. If you don't have ideal light, or if you are positioned a little to the left or right, the colors are very hard to discern. Take a close look in the showroom before you get caught up in the enthusiasm for color LCD recorders.

Video sounders represent another area of rapid development within the depthsounder field. Actually, monochromatic (black and white) and color video are not new to commercial fishermen. Video sounders and video sonar have been part of their fishing arsenal for years. Only since 1985, however, has digital computer technology allowed this equipment to be manufactured smaller, more powerful, and at lower prices. One commercial fisherman of my acquaintance, operating out of San Pedro, California, has been using color video for ten years and claims to be able to identify fish species by their echo colors. Years of experience in his home waters have given him this

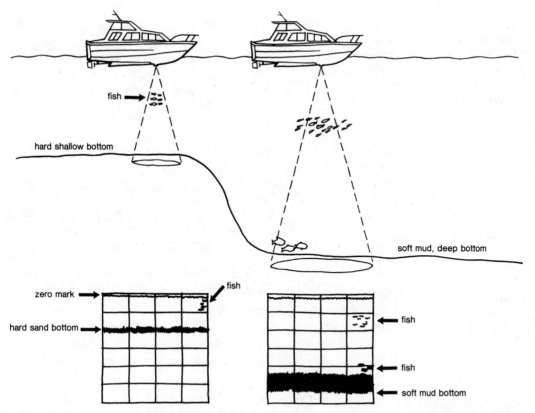

fish →

hard shallow bottom

soft mud, deep bottom

zero mark →

fish

hard sand bottom →

fish

fish

soft mud bottom

Vertical lines on a recording sounder's display represent time that has elapsed as the display moves **from right to left, and the horizontal lines represent depths in feet, fathoms, or meters.**

ability; in different waters, with different species of fish, he would have to teach himself all over again by consultation and by trial and error.

The new megabyte computers inside video sounders will catalog returning echoes by their intensity, the relative sizes of the targets, and their depths. Thousands of bits of information can be processed and then presented on a ten-inch screen. The first low-cost video sounders were monochromatic—black and white, amber and white, or gray and black. These are amazing machines because of their wide dynamic range, enabling them to pick out weak echoes close to the bottom and strong echoes near the water surface simultaneously. This is a feat beyond the capability of a chart recorder, on which the gain would need to be set so high to pick up a tiny bottom target that anything near the surface would be obliterated.

The monochromes sell for between $300 and $1,000. Multiple levels of quantization allow these hardworking units to elicit five to nine different shades of intensity to differentiate among large and small targets (strong

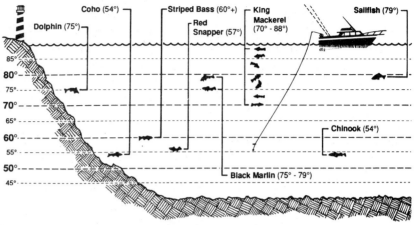

Ocean cross section. If the ocean were to stratify in increments of 5 degrees, the fish would stack up as shown here.

OCEAN CROSS SECTION

and weak echoes). Just as there are still black and white televisions and viewers who swear by them, monochromatic videos will not be completely superseded by the smarter, color videos that are taking their place aboard the boats of serious fishermen.

The color videos usually incorporate a ten-inch television-type display. Here is an example of the display colors and what they may represent:

Color	Meaning
Red	100% relative echo return
Orange	85% relative echo return
Yellow	70% relative echo return
Dark Green	55% relative echo return
Light Green	40% relative echo return
White	25% relative echo return
Light Blue	10% relative echo return
Dark Blue	No echo return

It takes a day or so to begin to figure out what's going on below the water and what you are actually seeing as color-coded information. A hard, rocky bottom will show up red, while a bottom with kelp or mud might show up as red overlaid by orange. Large fish with big air sacs will cause strong echo returns and may show up as orange, yellow, or green targets. A school of fish or shrimp rising off the bottom might show up as green or white. Every species of fish has its own color characteristics, and once you learn your machine, you can interpret what's down there with good accuracy.

The dynamic range and sensitivity of a color video is so sharp it may also show up thermoclines (density stratifications in the water caused by sharp variations in temperature). Since certain fish like to feed in thermoclines, the video sounder adds one more fishfinding tool to the electronic tacklebox.

As in a color television set, the images on the screen of a video sounder are well defined at a distance. At close range, however, rows of tiny dots (usual resolution 256 x 256 dots across the screen) are visible. The color sets can change the color of an individual dot to any one of eight to sixteen hues. The following display controls may be available on a color video:

- Depth range
- "A" scope readout
- Zoom minimum and maximum
- Screen speed indication
- Loran information (when interfaced)
- GPS information (when interfaced)
- Boat speed
- Speed log
- Water temperature
- Digital bottom depth
- Depth in feet, fathoms, or meters
- Noise rejection indication
- Percentage of gain
- Alarm modes
- Variable range marker line

The transducer offers discrete shallow- and deep-water frequencies, a speed sensor, and a water temperature sensor in an assembly that is hardly larger than older, conventional transducers. (It is possible to mate your existing transducer to a video sounder if you can find a video indicator having the same frequency and power as the indicator you're replacing. In this instance, however, resolution will probably be better if you buy the transducer recommended by the video manufacturer.)

The digital logic of the video sounders allows you to freeze pictures, store up to ten displays in memory and later compare them with a new display, split the screen, or lock on the bottom. If you are sounding at 400 feet and spot something just off the bottom, you can zoom into the bottom area—perhaps with the 380-foot contour at the top of the screen and 410 feet at the bottom of the screen. Targets within those depths are then enhanced, and you get a close-in look at the ocean floor.

Another feature is an audible fish alarm. Set your desired maximum or

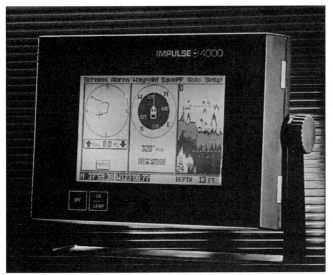
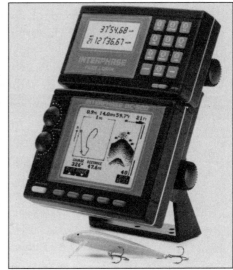

Two LCD depth recorders, each with multiple displays. The high-resolution LCD screen can do a lot more than just show you bottom contours.

minimum depth range, turn on the alarm, and wait for it to be triggered, indicating yellowtail at the selected depth.

Videos are best operated in the shade, so you can see what's happening on the screen. Sun can easily wipe out the colors when a screen is viewed on a bright flying bridge. These units will also create some video interference to a loran set if not properly grounded. Their horizontal sweep can easily knock out weak loran signals, so make sure the video installation is well grounded and that all wires are properly shielded.

If you are already equipped with a video sounder, you may wish to add a speech synthesizer device, which simply plugs in between your transducer and the video display unit. This device won't affect the video readout at all, but it will speak out depths less than 100 feet in plain enough English. The idea is that you won't have to study the screen to see what the depth is before anchoring; just listen for the spoken word. Although there's no change in tonal inflection when a boat rapidly approaches grounding (no trace of panic!), the unit is useful when you've got your eyes on the bow and want to know your depth in feet or fathoms.

Before you purchase a depthsounder, consider whether or not you need one that is waterproof, or at least weatherproof. Manufacturers are giving us completely waterproof sounders that can be hosed down after a day of fishing, and if you're going to be running your depthsounder in an open cockpit, then by all means select a unit that will take this type of punishment.

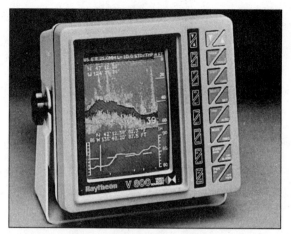

Raytheon V-800 Color Fishfinder with split-screen standard and temperature graph displays.

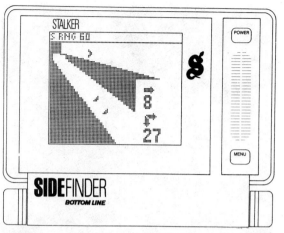

Side-scanning techniques utilizing transducers with crystal elements set at an angle.

Installation of the indicator unit is straightforward, and you can accomplish it yourself. The units don't draw much current, and manufacturers usually suggest No. 10 wire for the positive and negative leads. This wire for voltage goes over to a switch panel, and there is nothing tricky about it—red to hot, and black to negative. Most sounders don't require an additional wire to ship's ground, but it's a good idea, helping to reduce static. A single No. 12 wire from the ground post on the sounder (or under any screw) should be run to your ship's ground plate or any common ground. Ground to your engine if nothing else is available.

Preventive maintenance involves cleaning the power connection, the transducer plug, and other connections regularly and making sure the unit is firmly in its mounting bracket. There is little to do inside the unit; sounders seldom require recalibration.

It is recommended that you paint the face of the transducer with antifouling paint. Usually one thin coat of bottom paint will keep the barnacles from forming on your transducer. Go with the bottom paint, not the barnacles. (If you should ever encounter growth of any kind on your transducer, take great care in removing it. That quartz crystal is protected only by a thin layer of plastic, and if the plastic gets gouged it skews the acoustical energy in different directions.)

Depthsounder malfunctions are usually traceable to the indicator unit, not the transducer, and the unit can easily be removed and sent back to the dealer or manufacturer for repair. Rarely do well-installed transducers go bad unless they have been physically damaged. If you treat your equipment properly, your depthsounder should work flawlessly for years.

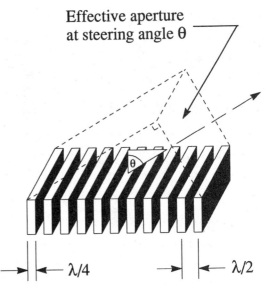

Effective aperture
at steering angle θ

λ/4   λ/2

The phased array transducer assembly may contain as many as fifteen individual crystal elements, electronically steered for a graphic presentation of the sea floor below. This same transducer may also contain a water temperature pickup, plus a paddle wheel for boat speed. (Courtesy Airmar Technologies Corp.)

Finally, let's talk about something you might not have known a sounder is capable of—and that's serious navigation. For example, you can tell what type of bottom you are over from a recorder, video recorder, or flashing indicator, though not from a digital. Over a sandy bottom, you will see a hard bottom indication, while kelp on the bottom will appear as a broad bottom signal. If you are cruising in unknown waters and following charted depth contours, remember that charts are based on mean low water. You can safely navigate around islands by following bottom contours and watching the chart. Unsure what island you are going around? Look for underwater hills and valleys by cruising in a straight line alongside the island, and match the depth configurations you see to the chart. In similar fashion, with a chart, dividers, a stopwatch, and a little mathematics, it's possible to use a depthsounder for determining speed over the bottom. Watch those bottom contours—charts are quite detailed for this purpose. Your charted depth contour can also constitute a line of position to substantiate bearings from a radio direction finding station.

Buying Tips

The information contained in this chapter may be used as a springboard for the examination of manufacturers' literature and advertising claims. By now, you probably have a good idea as to what kind of depthsounder best meets your particular needs.

A depthsounder may be a logical piece of equipment to purchase from a catalog discount house or a specialty dealer, because you're not giving up much in the way of service in order to save some money. Marine electronics dealers will install the indicator unit in your boat, but that part of the installation you might easily do yourself. They will *not* install the transducer, so you'll have to pay a boatyard to do that or struggle through it yourself in any case. Finally, if the indicator unit does malfunction, it will be easy to disconnect and ship directly to the manufacturer for repair.

Type of Depthsounder and Suggested Use

Type of Depthsounder	Navigation in Small Boats	Sport Fishing	Large Motor Yachts	Trailerboats	Sailboat Cruising	Sailboat Racing	Freshwater Fisherman	Powerboat Racing (high performance)	Commercial Fishing
Digital	✓		✓	✓	✓	✓		✓	
Flasher	✓	✓							
Paper Chart Recorder		✓	✓		✓				✓
LCD Graph		✓		✓			✓		
Video, monochromatic		✓			✓				✓
Video, color		✓	✓						✓
Sonar, phased array, and multiple transducer units		✓			✓				
Sonar, color (full set)			✓						✓

CHAPTER 3

VHF Radio

by Gordon West

Marine VHF radio enables you to communicate with other vessels up to 20 miles or more away, or with shore stations at greater distances. The VHF signals, having a short wavelength, are not much affected by local weather conditions, so VHF radio is a very reliable mode of marine communication. Before any other marine radio can legally be carried in your vessel, you must have a marine VHF transceiver aboard.

Most VHF radios are manufactured in the Orient. State-of-the-art sets are synthesized—that is, they employ a single crystal that can be split by means of factory-programmed microprocessor circuits to transmit and receive on any existing marine VHF channel. The more traditional crystal sets cannot cover all the channels without employing multiple crystals, a more ponderous and expensive approach. Crystal sets are still being manufactured, but these generally offer only 12- or 24-channel coverage. Some 55-channel synthesized sets cost less than 24-channel crystal sets.

Armed with a basic understanding of the available VHF channels and a few simple rules to follow when choosing an antenna and a transceiver, you can put together a VHF station that suits your boat and satisfies your requirements. When you do, remember that perhaps the biggest problem facing marine VHF radio is the abuse of broadcasting protocol by pleasureboat operators. Mariners should learn and adhere to the standard marine VHF procedures.

The Channels

The marine VHF (very high frequency) band is centered around 156 megahertz (MHz), between Channels 6 and 7 on your television set. It is a group of frequencies standardized throughout the world by international agreement of the World Administrative Radio Conference (WARC). The band encompasses approximately 78 25-kHz channels between 156.050 MHz (Channel 1) and 157.425 MHz (Channel 88A) for ship transmitting; certain public telephone shore stations will also transmit on frequencies from 161.800 MHz (Channel 24 receive) to 162.025 MHz (Channel 88 receive, not applicable in the United States). The VHF band also includes several national weather transmitting frequencies centered around 162.550 MHz (Weather Channel 1 receive). Those frequencies between the ship transmit and shore transmit channels are allocated to other radio services (157.450 MHz to 161.595 MHz).

The number of channels that a mariner has access to in the United States is actually no greater than 55, some channels being paired differently with shoreside channels in other countries. Examples are Channels 23A and 88A. The letter "A" after any VHF channel indicates that the channel has a split capability, being used in the United States for simplex (same frequency)

Frequency Allocations

Cellular Phones	850 MHz
406 EPIRBs	406 MHz
Channel 7 (Television)	179 MHz
Very High Frequency (VHF) Radiotelephone	156.00-162.55 MHz
EPIRB (Class C)	156.8 MHz
EPIRB (Classes A and B)	121.5 MHz
Omni/VOR	108.0-118.0 MHz
FM Radio	88-108 MHz
Channels 2-6 (Television)	54-88 MHz
Citizen's Band (CB) Radiotelephone	26.9-27.3 MHz
High Frequency Single Sideband Radiotelephone	4.0-26.0 MHz
Medium Frequency Single Sideband Radiotelephone	1.6-3.5 MHz (1,600-3,500 kHz)
AM Radio	530-1,800 kHz
Marine Radio Beacons	190-400 kHz
Loran-C	100 kHz
Decca	70-130 kHz
Omega	10.2-13.6 kHz

transmitting and receiving, while having another use elsewhere. Channel 23A might be used by Coast Guard auxiliary members (with special permission from local Coast Guard units) to communicate with Coast Guard vessels. Channel 88A is used in almost all areas of the United States for ship-to-ship simplex commercial communications as well as for fish-spotting by aircraft. In other countries, such as Canada, Channel 23 (without the "A" designation) is used for communications to a shoreside marine telephone service where the transmit and receive frequencies are different (a duplex split of 4.6 MHz). In the Great Lakes, mariners use Channel 88 (no "A") in the duplex mode to place telephone calls with shore stations that transmit on a different frequency (4.6 MHz higher) than the ship stations.

Modern VHF sets have programmed microprocessor circuits that tell them on what channels to operate simplex and when to switch automatically to duplex (different receive). Since on the "A" channels (and only on the "A" channels) this may vary by country, sets are usually factory programmed for use either in the United States—designated as the "United States" or "domestic" mode—or elsewhere—the "foreign" mode. A few sets offer a manual override for switching modes. Apart from these few exceptions, no matter where you cruise throughout the world, all VHF channels are the same.

The most important channel is 156.800 MHz, Channel 16, the international distress and calling frequency. Every VHF radio must have this channel installed in it, and it must be monitored at all times when your set is turned on, except when you are operating on another frequency. The U.S. Coast Guard and other rescue agencies worldwide monitor this channel 24 hours a day, and it is also monitored by orbiting search-and-rescue satellites that will retransmit the distinctive sounds of an emergency position indicating radio beacon (EPIRB) signal, along with its approximate location, when one is received. This channel must be used only for distress and safety calls or establishing communications with another vessel before switching to a working channel. You are not allowed to talk for more than 59 seconds on VHF Channel 16 unless you are making an emergency communication.

VHF Channel 6 is the safety channel, to be used only for intership communications relating directly to the safety of vessels. Use this channel to communicate priority or urgent traffic to another vessel. Every VHF set must have Channel 6.

There are six pleasureboat ship-to-ship communications channels: 9, 68, 69, 71, 72, and 78. Use any of these to communicate with other boats in your area. The messages you transmit must relate directly to the operation of your vessel, and all communications must be kept to a minimum, since other vessels in your area may wish to use the same frequencies. Yacht clubs,

Suggested Channel Distributions for Pleasure and Commercial Craft

Channel Numbers	Type of Communication	Suggested Channel Selection		
		Recreational Vessels		Commercial Vessels
		6 ch.	12 ch.	12 ch.
16	DISTRESS, SAFETY & CALLING, ALT CH. 9 calling	*	*	*
6	INTERSHIP SAFETY Intership. NOT to be used for non-safety intership communications	*	*	*
22A	Communications with U.S. Coast Guard ship, coast, or aircraft stations	1	1	1
1,5,65A,66A, 12,73,14,74, 63,20,77	PORT OPERATIONS Intership & ship to coast	1	2	
13,67	NAVIGATIONAL Intership & ship to coast	1	1	
68,9,69, 71,78A,72	NON-COMMERCIAL Intership & ship to coast	1	3	
72	NON-COMMERCIAL Intership	2		
1,7A,9,10, 11,18A,19A, 79A,80A,63	COMMERCIAL Intership & ship to coast	3		
67,8,77, 88A	COMMERCIAL Intership	1		
24,84,25, 85,26,86,	PUBLIC CORRESPONDENCE	2	2	2
27,87,28 70	Ship to public coast Intership & ship-to-coast selective signaling only. No voice communications.			
***88				
162.400 (WX-2)	NOAA WEATHER SERVICE	**	**	**
162.550 (WX-1) 162.475 (WX-3)	Ship receive only			

*These channels are REQUIRED to be installed in every ship station equipped with a VHF radio.
**The weather receive channels are half-channels (receive only) one or more of which are recommended to be installed in each ship station. Many manufacturers include one or more of these channels in their sets in addition to the normal six or twelve channel capacity.

ship supply stores, and fuel docks may also use Channels 9, 68, 69, 71, and 78 to communicate with ships.

VHF Channel 70 (156.525), once available for voice communications between pleasureboats, is now reserved exclusively for digital selective calling (DSC). Digital selective calling is new to the marine radio service but old technology to land services. The DSC system allows shore stations to call silent ship receivers digitally to alert them of waiting messages. It might also be used to alert groups of stations that calls are holding.

Digital selective calling is relatively new for the United States VHF and SSB radio service. In Europe, DSC equipment is commonplace. Most commercial and passenger boats in Europe are equipped with exotic DSC systems.

Here in the United States there are only a couple of marine radio manufacturers offering DSC as a built-in feature. Quite simply, the reason there are no big DSC systems aboard boats is because there are few DSC systems ashore. What a pity—think of the possibilities with DSC:

- Placing a radiotelephone call with DSC requires a single push button. A data burst signals the VHF or SSB marine operator that your particular vessel is on frequency, wishing to place a call. Within this data burst is your vessel registration information, your billing information, and a digital request that they acknowledge that your call is on frequency. In less than a second, their digital acknowledgment is received by your set, and you push a single button for a prestored phone number. In less than 10 seconds you hear the phone on the other end of the radio circuit ringing. All this, using DSC, without having to go through the traditional marine telephone operator.

- You finally found *the* hot fishing spot. A DSC call to your buddies on VHF digitally (no voice to be eavesdropped on) alerts everyone, as a group, that you've hit fish, and your latitude and longitude is automatically transmitted to them. Each of their sets confirms the reception of your DSC "packet," and all this in less than a couple of seconds, all without saying a word.

- Yikes, you have water up to your ankles, and your boat is sinking fast. You push your red VHF or SSB DSC button, and your call to the Coast Guard is completed. On the screen, they see your vessel registration information, plus they also see your latitude and longitude. Help is on the way.

Your radio equipment receives latitude and longitude information from a tied-in loran or GPS set. It is automatically stored in your DSC buffer for immediate output. In fact, if your friends with DSC equipment know your particular DSC number, they may poll your vessel and know exactly where you are located without you having to do a single thing! Everything is done on VHF Channel 70, including the possible command that switches you over to a VHF or SSB working channel to carry on using voice.

The U.S. Coast Guard is just beginning to set up shore stations with VHF DSC equipment. Their first installation is in Tampa Bay, Florida. And it's the same thing with the marine telephone service—they, too, are looking at DSC as a possible life ring to help save their sinking VHF radiotelephone business. Cellular has stolen much of VHF phone traffic, but possibly DSC may get them back in business again. No one likes talking credit card numbers over the air, and DSC would allow a non-voice data burst to the marine operator, giving him everything he needs to know about who you are, where to place the call, and who to bill.

Keep your eyes on DSC equipment innovations—but unless you have fellow mariners with the same type of DSC gear, or a local shore station with DSC equipment, I'm not sure I would jump right into a more expensive DSC set this year.

Pleasureboat operators are not allowed to use commercial frequencies, nor may commercial vessels use noncommercial frequencies. Of course, while it's illegal for pleasure-boat operators to transmit on Channel 88A, for example, there is no harm in monitoring this channel to get the latest scoop from commercial fish spotters! Marine Channel 9 is shared by both commercial and pleasureboats, so if you wish to talk to a commercial fishing boat, first call him on 16 and then switch to 9.

When you hear the distinctive warbling sound of an emergency position indicating radio beacon on Channel 16, it means that someone in your area is in distress. The Class C EPIRB will alternate automatically between Channel 16 and the adjacent Channel 15. EPIRBs are only one-way transmitters, so you won't be able to establish communications with the vessel in trouble. Your role is to contact the Coast Guard on Channel 16 immediately and let them know that you hear an EPIRB in your area. Call the Coast Guard when the EPIRB switches from Channel 16 to Channel 15 so you can hear their response. They may ask whether you have direction-finding capability, and if so, what bearing the EPIRB is from your computed location. Unfortunately, Class C EPRIBs will soon be discontinued, and you should *not* buy one.

The table lists several channels used for placing phone calls to marine telephone operators ashore. It's best to register ahead of time with your local marine operator before you attempt to place a phone call through their service. This is easily accomplished with a shoreside call. Marine electronics specialty houses may also have marine operator registration forms for specialized phone services not listed with your AT&T operator. Many of these

FREQUENCIES (MHz)   CHANNEL USAGE

Channel Number	Ship Transmit	Ship Receive	Intended Use
1	156.050	156.050	PORT OPERATIONS AND COMMERCIAL (Intership and ship-to-coast). Available for use within
3	156.150	156.150	the U.S.C.G. designated Vessel Traffic Services (VTS) area of New Orleans, and the
63	156.175	156.175	Lower Mississippi River.
5	156.250	156.250	PORT OPERATIONS (Intership and ship-to-coast). Available for use within the U.S.C.G. Vessel Traffic Services radio protection areas of New Orleans and Houston.
6	156.300	156.300	INTERSHIP SAFETY. Required for all VHF-FM equipped vessels. For intership safety purposes and search and rescue (SAR) communications with ships and aircraft of the U.S. Coast Guard. Must not be used for non-safety communications.
7A	156.350	156.350	COMMERCIAL (Intership and ship-to-coast). A working channel for commercial vessels to fulfill a wide scope of business and operational needs.
8	156.400	156.400	COMMERCIAL (Intership). Same as channel 7A except limited to intership communications.
9	156.450	156.450	COMMERCIAL AND NON-COMMERCIAL (Intership and ship-to-coast). Some examples of use are communications with commercial marinas and public docks to obtain supplies or schedule repairs, and contacting commercial vessels about matters of common concern. **Secondary calling channel in U.S.A.**
10	156.500	156.500	COMMERCIAL (Intership and ship-to-coast). Same as channel 7A.
11	156.550	156.550	COMMERCIAL (Intership and ship-to-coast). Same as channel 7A. It should be noted, however, in certain ports channels 11, 12, and 14 are to be used selectively for the Vessel Traffic Service now being developed by the United States Coast Guard.
12	156.600	156.600	PORT OPERATIONS (Intership and ship-to-coast). Available to all vessels. This is a traffic advisory channel for use by agencies directing the movement of vessels in or near ports, locks, or waterways. Messages are restricted to the operational handling, movement and safety of ships and, in emergency, to the safety of persons. It should be noted, however, in certain ports 11, 12, and 14 are to be used selectively for the Vessel Traffic Service being developed by the United States Coast Guard.
13	156.650	156.650	NAVIGATIONAL (Ship's) bridge to (ship's) bridge. This channel is available to all vessels and is required on large passenger and commercial vessels (including many tugs). Use is limited to navigational communications such as in meeting and passing situations. Abbreviated operating procedures (call signs omitted) and 1 watt maximum power (except in certain special instances) are used on this channel for both calling and working. For recreational vessels, this channel should be used for listening to determine the intentions of large vessels. This is also the primary channel used at locks and bridges.
14	156.700	156.700	PORT OPERATIONS (Intership and ship-to-coast). Same as channel 12.
15		156.750	ENVIRONMENTAL (Receive only). A receive only channel used to broadcast environmental information to ships such as weather, sea conditions, time signals for navigation, notices to mariners, etc. Most of this information is also broadcast on the weather (WX) channels.
16	156.800	156.800	DISTRESS, SAFETY, AND CALLING (Intership and ship-to-coast). Required channel for all VHF-FM equipped vessels. Must be monitored at all times station is in operation (except when actually communicating on another channel). This channel is monitored, also, by the Coast Guard, public coast stations and many limited coast stations. Calls to other vessels are normally initiated on this channel. Then, except in an emergency, you must switch to a working channel.
17	156.850	156.850	STATE CONTROL. Available to all vessels to communicate with ships and coast stations operated by state or local governments. Messages are restricted to regulation and control, or rendering assistance. Use of low power (1 watt) setting is required by international treaty.
18A	156.900	156.900	COMMERCIAL (Intership and ship-to-coast). Same as channel 7A.
19A	156.950	156.950	COMMERCIAL (Intership and ship-to-coast). Same as channel 7A.
20	157.000	161.600	PORT OPERATIONS (Ship-to-coast). Available to all vessels. This is a traffic advisory channel for use by agencies directing the movement of vessels in or near ports, locks, or waterways. Messages are restricted to the operational handling, movement and safety of ships and, in emergency, to the safety of persons.

Marine VHF Channel Allocations

FREQUENCIES (MHz)			CHANNEL USAGE
Channel Number	Ship Transmit	Ship Receive	Intended Use
22A	157.100	157.100	COAST GUARD LIAISON. This channel is used for communications with U.S. Coast Guard ship, coast and aircraft stations after first establishing communications on channel 16. Navigational warnings and, where not available on WX channels, Marine Weather forecasts are made on this frequency. *It is strongly recommended that every VHF radiotelephone include this channel.*
23A	157.150	157.150	U.S. GOVERNMENT ONLY.
24	157.200	161.800	PUBLIC CORRESPONDENCE (Ship-to-coast). Available to all vessels to communicate with public coast stations. Channels 26 and 28 are the primary public correspondence channels and therefore become the first choice for the cruising vessel having limited channel capacity.
25	157.250	161.850	PUBLIC CORRESPONDENCE (Ship-to-coast). Same as channel 24.
26	157.300	161.900	PUBLIC CORRESPONDENCE (Ship-to-coast). Same as channel 24.
27	157.350	161.950	PUBLIC CORRESPONDENCE (Ship-to-coast). Same as channel 24.
28	157.400	162.000	PUBLIC CORRESPONDENCE (Ship-to-coast). Same as channel 24.
65A	156.275	156.275	PORT OPERATIONS (Intership and ship-to-coast). Same as channel 12.
66A	156.325	156.325	PORT OPERATIONS (Intership and ship-to-coast). Same as channel 12.
67	156.375	156.375	COMMERCIAL (Intership). Same as channel 7A except limited to intership communications.
68	156.425	156.425	NON-COMMERCIAL (Intership and ship-to-coast). A working channel for non-commercial vessels. May be used for obtaining supplies, scheduling repairs, berthing and accommodations, etc. from yacht clubs or marinas, and intership operational communications such as piloting or arranging for rendezvous with other vessels. It should be noted that channel 68 is the most popular non-commercial channel and therefore is the first choice for vessels having limited channel capacity.
69	156.475	156.475	NON-COMMERCIAL (Intership and ship-to-coast). Same as channel 68.
70	156.525	156.525	Intership and ship-to-coast selective signaling only. No voice communications.
71	156.575	156.575	NON-COMMERCIAL (Intership and ship-to-coast). Same as channel 68.
72	156.625	156.625	NON-COMMERCIAL (Intership). Same as channel 68, except limited to intership communications.
73	156.675	156.675	PORT OPERATIONS (Intership and ship-to-coast). Same as channel 12.
74	156.725	156.725	PORT OPERATIONS (Intership and ship-to-coast). Same as channel 12.
77	156.875	156.875	COMMERCIAL (Intership). Same as channel 7A except limited to intership communications.
78A	156.925	156.925	NON-COMMERCIAL (Intership and ship-to-coast). Same as channel 68.
79A	156.975	156.975	COMMERCIAL (Intership and ship-to-coast). Same as channel 7A.
80A	157.025	157.025	COMMERCIAL (Intership and ship-to-coast). Same as channel 7A.
81A	157.075	157.075	U.S. GOVERNMENT ONLY.
82A	157.125	157.125	U.S. GOVERNMENT ONLY.
83A	157.175	157.175	U.S. GOVERNMENT ONLY.
84	157.225	161.825	PUBLIC CORRESPONDENCE (Ship-to-coast). Same as channel 24.
85	157.275	161.875	PUBLIC CORRESPONDENCE (Ship-to-coast). Same as channel 24.
86	157.325	161.925	PUBLIC CORRESPONDENCE (Ship-to-coast). Same as channel 24.
87	157.375	161.975	PUBLIC CORRESPONDENCE (Ship-to-coast). Same as channel 24.
88A	157.425	157.425	COMMERCIAL (Intership). Same as channel 7A, except limited to intership communications and between commercial fishing vessels and associated aircraft while engaged in commercial fishing vessels and associated aircraft while engaged in commercial fishing.
WX1	—	162.550	WEATHER (Receive only). To receive weather broadcasts of the Department of Commerce, National Oceanic and Atmospheric Administration (NOAA).
WX2	—	162.400	WEATHER (Receive only). Same as WX1.
WX3	—	162.475	WEATHER (Receive only). Same as WX1.

offer terrific telephone service, including message handling and conference calling. A marine telephone service is a great bargain. There is no monthly fee if you don't use their service. You're only charged for the phone calls you place, and if you sit the winter out and never make a call, you are not billed. The average price of a three-minute call to a local shoreside station is generally less than two dollars. Some phone companies may charge a one-time registration fee or a small yearly renewal fee.

Some marine telephone operators announce traffic lists on VHF Channel 16 on the hour. Due to tremendous traffic on Channel 16 during the summer months, however, you may wish to monitor, with a second VHF set, your marine telephone channel to receive phone calls the second they are placed to your vessel from a shoreside station. You can do this with a small handheld transceiver.

Since telephone channels are separate transmit and receive frequencies, it's impossible to transmit ship-to-ship on vacant phone channels. You simply won't hear the other ship station respond because your receiver is tuned 4.6 MHz higher than your transmitter. If you wish to establish ship-to-ship communications through a telephone operator, however, because the two of you are well beyond VHF line-of-sight range, the phone company will patch you in together. Your signals will boom in loud and clear thanks to the phone operator "repeater." You could be as much as 1,000 miles apart yet still stay in contact. There is a charge for the service.

The other channels are described briefly in the accompanying table and are explained more fully in VHF owners' manuals, in piloting books, and in the *Marine Radiotelephone User's Handbook,* put together by the Radio Technical Commission for Marine Services in cooperation with the FCC. A copy can be purchased from the RTCM, P.O. Box 19087, Washington, D.C. 20036.

Range

VHF radio waves travel over the water on a line-of-sight basis plus a mere 22 percent over-the-horizon allowance for "super-refraction"; that is, the VHF waves, being only about two meters long, will not bend around the horizon to any great extent. Ultimate range is determined by the height of your antenna over the water and by its gain. The Coast Guard and marine operators often use well-elevated shoreside antenna locations to offer excellent range to ship stations. (They also frequently use remote receivers that pick up distant calls.) The usual range to any Coast Guard station or marine operator is in excess of 50 miles from any good VHF 25-watt station. If you use a handheld VHF, your range may diminish to a maximum of 35 miles, but output power on a clear channel is not of primary importance to the ultimate range of a VHF signal.

The maximum range of ship-to-ship communications is substantially less because neither station has any appreciable height over the water. Average ship-to-ship communications are limited to 15 to 20 miles on most days. Given the heights of both antennas, specific maximum ranges are easily calculated: An antenna 10 feet off the water "sees" the horizon at four miles, and two such antennas will "see" each other at eight miles. Adding the 22 percent factor for refraction of VHF radio waves over sea water gives us a maximum communications distance of 10 miles. Going to higher power levels will add no more than a half mile or so.

You might occasionally establish ship-to-ship communications between vessels up to 50 miles apart as a result of "tropospheric ducting." This most often occurs when a high-pressure system slips over your local cruising area and there is little wind. A temperature inversion forms at an altitude of approximately 1,000 feet, trapping VHF radio signals below it. In Southern California the "smog belt" at 1,000 feet sometimes carries VHF signals up to 300 miles away, ship-to-ship. These are not "skip" signals—rather, they are signals experiencing an intense super-refraction. Communications with shoreside stations over 400 miles away may be possible on rare occasions.

Antennas

The VHF antenna is an extraordinary setup of phased vertical elements within a fiberglass shaft, or a precision-wound coil topped by or built into a fiberglass or stainless steel stinger. It is, in effect, a complete system, because there is no need to develop a ground network below the antenna itself—the ground plane is built in.

The most basic VHF antenna, rarely seen because of its odd shape, consists of an 18-inch vertical spike with four 18½-inch radials protruding at a 45-degrees-down angle from the base. The entire system is a half wavelength long with respect to marine frequencies at 156 MHz, as indicated by the formula:

$$\frac{468}{\text{frequency (MHz)}} = \text{Length in feet}$$

This half-wavelength ground plane made up of a quarter-wavelength vertical radiator and quarter-wavelength radials offers a feedpoint impedance ("feedpoint" meaning the point of entry of the coax cable into the antenna) of 50 ohms—exactly what your radio and coaxial cable would like to see. If we were to bend the radials straight down, the impedance would be 70 ohms and a mismatch would occur. Mismatched impedances cause reflected power and power losses.

All antenna performances are rated against this half-wavelength antenna system, which gives a zero decibel gain. In other words, 25 watts into the antenna will give 25 watts effective radiated power out of the antenna, and weak incoming signals will sound like weak signals at the receiver.

You won't find many spider-type ground plane antennas on recreational boats. But you will find base-loaded VHF antennas that offer good performance at masthead heights yet give only small amounts of actual gain. These three-foot whips, usually base-loaded (only two models have the loading coil partway up the whip rather than right at its base), in either ½-wave or ⅝-wave configurations, are often referred to as 3 dB or 6 dB gain antennas, when their actual gain is closer to ½ dB. Despite their minimal gain characteristics, however, these antennas hoisted aloft provide outstanding performance compared with higher-gain antennas mounted on deck. Providing a base-loaded whip is fed with low-loss coaxial cable (described later), its performance is excellent.

Base-loaded imported whips that closely resemble domestic antennas have recently flooded the U.S. market, carrying retail prices that look very attractive. Their reliability and durability is suspect, however. An evaluation performed by Metz Antennas, a U.S. antenna manufacturer, revealed that the coil section of imitation antennas featured extremely small loading coil wires, and the entire assembly was sealed in wax rather than a hard epoxy compound. When the antenna heated up from long transmissions the coil would begin to deform, and the antenna characteristics could change enough to damage a VHF set. According to the report:

> Our Metz antenna is developed around a stainless steel shell that encompasses our DC shunted coil wrapped around a form. Each of our coils is precisely tuned for proper resonance. This imported look-alike antenna features a chrome outside shell that resembles ours, and they even copied our whip post mounting assembly. Field strength tests of these imported units indicated greatly diminished radiation and receive capabilities as opposed to our domestically made halfwave antennas. We also found that these imports used PVC molds that could distort in heat on the masthead, diminishing performance.

While the ⅝-wave and ½-wave base-loaded whips look similar to one another and exhibit almost the same amount (½ dB) of gain over a dipole, their radiation characteristics are slightly different. The halfwave antenna requires no ground plane beneath it. It also features a slightly higher angle of radiation, which works out well in those areas of mountain peaks that the Coast Guard and marine operators favor for antenna locations.

The ⅝-wave base-loaded marine whip requires a metallic ground plane (such as a mast) directly below its base for proper radiation characteristics. This antenna has a slightly longer whip and its radiation is slightly lower to the horizon, favoring distant ship stations. Halfwave and ⅝-wave antennas perform almost identically when mounted properly at masthead heights.

A 3 dB gain is a twofold power increase, so a 3 dB gain antenna has the effect of doubling your transmitter power to stations miles away. The 3 dB antennas are constructed of fiberglass within which halfwave vertical elements—usually two of them—are stacked end to end to form a colinear array. This configuration takes some of that otherwise-wasted skywave energy and flattens it out closer to the water. The 3 dB gain antenna is approximately 54 inches long and may also feature a decoupling section, which prevents radio energy from traveling back down the coax cable as wasted power. Quality 3 dB gain antennas use brass rods for the radiating elements inside the fiberglass shaft. I received this report from a representative of the Shakespeare Antenna Company:

> We tore open a cheap imported 3 dB gain antenna, and all we found was coax cable stripped back as the radiating elements. We also found no decoupling circuit, which allowed this inexpensive antenna to radiate some of the signal back down the coax line. With any type of vibration, one could easily expect the coax assemblies to break apart on the inside.

In actual sea tests, I have found little difference between domestic 3 dB antennas and inexpensive imports. During survival tests, however, which included vibrating antennas and banging them against bridge overpasses when left upright aboard a trailer boat, I found that only domestic models survived without breaking. In other words, the less expensive antennas may work just about as well, but only when not subjected to the rigors of the environment.

A fourfold power increase on both transmit and receive is achieved with a 6 dB gain antenna. This antenna is approximately 10 feet long and contains up to four halfwave colinear elements stacked vertically on the inside. Again, almost all domestic antenna manufacturers use brass elements for many of the vertical sections, whereas the inexpensive imports use coaxial cable held together by solder. Again, in tests I helped conduct, initial performance of both antennas was almost identical, but in surviving water

A 6 dB antenna (nine-foot whip) mounted on the side of a pilothouse. The objective is to locate the antenna as high up as possible.

A 6 dB antenna (nine-foot whip) mounted on the side of a pilothouse. The objective is to locate the antenna as high up as possible.

immersion, vibration, and repeated flexes, the domestic brass tubing model seemed to hold up better.

The granddaddy of them all is the 21-foot, 9 dB gain VHF antenna that gives us an effective eightfold power gain on incoming and outgoing signals. Using a 9 dB gain antenna is the equivalent of transmitting off a quarter-wave ground plane with 200 watts of power. On receive, the 9 dB gain antenna will pull in signals that the 6 and 3 can barely discern above the static.

Most 9 dB gain antennas separate in the center for shipping. Inside their 1½-inch diameter bodies are eight halfwave antennas stacked vertically in colinear array with matching and decoupling sections at the base. I have not found any imitations or inferior models, so one may assume that 9 dB antennas are all of top-quality construction. I have torn apart both a Shakespeare and a Celwave 9 dB gain antenna and found quality constructed brass tubing on the inside along with coax cable matching harnesses.

Some marine dealers pooh-pooh the 9 dB gain antenna, saying it fades in and out in heavy seas because of its extremely low angle of radiation to the horizon. While in theory this is true, in actual operation the 9 dB gain antenna will lay down a stronger signal than any 3 or 6 dB gain antenna, even in the heaviest seas or on the hardest roll. Quite simply, nothing out-talks or out-listens a 9 dB gain antenna.

When buying a VHF system, a sailboat owner should normally use a halfwave or ⅝-wave antenna on the mast. I would suggest an emergency 18-inch piece of wire in case of dismasting, to be mounted directly on the back of the VHF set. A 10-foot, 6 dB, transom-mounted antenna is a viable alternative, but in actual tests the zero dB gain masthead antenna will usually outperform the 6 dB antenna at water level.

The small-boat operator will be well served by a 10-foot, 6 dB gain antenna, which affixes easily with a single ratchet mount that allows the antenna to be laid down for trailering. This gives better range than a 3 dB gain, 54-inch, white fiberglass whip, which mounts identically.

For large yachts and commercial boats, the 9 dB gain, 21-foot whip makes sense for maximum range. This whip requires both an upper and a lower support mounting bracket. If you also have loran or marine single sideband, the 21-foot whip will provide a perfect match.

Coaxial Cable

A marine VHF antenna is connected to the transceiver using coaxial cable. Some antennas have the coax cable built in, this cable being adequate for most short hookups. If a longer cable is needed, however (such as when an antenna is intended for masthead use), no cable is built in. For moderately long runs, use RG-8/X (or RG-8X) coaxial cable, which offers considerably less signal loss than the smaller RG-58AU (or RG-58A/U) cable. If your VHF antenna run is long and you want the ultimate in performance, select RG-213/U cable for minimum losses at 156 MHz. The commercial boat operator may go one step further and put in the semirigid Belden 9913 coaxial cable, which offers almost no loss at all over a 100-foot run at 156 MHz.

A coaxial cable is a shielded transmission line in which one conductor is mounted coaxially inside the other. Think of it as a rod-within-a-sleeve configuration. Due to skin effect, radio frequency current is carried on the outside surface of the inner conductor and the inside surface of the outer conductor. This keeps the energy within the cable from escaping except at the ends, where you want it. Generally, the larger (and more expensive) coaxial cable will offer radio energy less resistance with less loss than will smaller cable. This is simply because there is more cross-sectional area of conductor material to carry the current. Conductor losses are a direct function of the conductivity of the conductors, too, with most coaxial cables consisting of copper or copper and aluminum.

Coaxial cable impedance (usually 50 ohms) is a function of the ratio of the diameters of the inner and outer conductors. Most marine radio transceivers have an output of 50 ohms and are compatible with 50-to-52-ohms-

Cut-away view of coaxial cable.

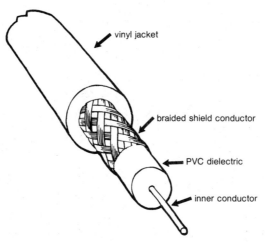

vinyl jacket

braided shield conductor

PVC dielectric

inner conductor

impedance coax cable. This immediately rules out using discarded cable TV coax (72 ohms), including that huge CATV coax cable that a friend snipped from a coil left outside by the local cable TV company.

Another important consideration for coax cable in a marine environment is its moistureproof capabilities. Coaxial cable jackets made of plastic alone will eventually leak moisture, but "noncontaminating" jackets made of polyvinyl chloride will resist the threats of moisture provided the cable ends have been properly terminated and sealed.

The inner dielectric (nonconducting element) can also provide a nice home for moisture, and both foam-core and air-core coaxial cables will allow moisture, through capillary action, to travel up and down the inner core and the outside copper braid. Noncontaminating coaxial cable with a solid PVC dielectric will keep moisture from getting to the center conductor and will help decrease the capillary action of moisture along the outside braid. There are some coaxial cables that not only have a solid dielectric but are also backfilled with a sticky "goo" that completely covers the outside braid within the PVC jacket to repel moisture. While this may be the ultimate coax, it's messy to work with and pretty hard to find these days.

Purchase coaxial cable only from reputable ham radio dealers—CB-type coax is out of the question. Although CB radio coaxial cable may carry the "RG" (Radio Government) specification, the CB cable manufacturers produce a cheapened version of this coax that doesn't actually meet the original government specs. They skimp on the number of individual center conductors as well as the number of individual conductors in the braid of the copper shield. Most CB coax is quite leaky because of the huge gaps in the braid, and it distorts signals and causes impedance mismatches when the cable is flexed to any extent.

RG-8/X cable is a good size for interconnecting cables, jumpers, and short mobile runs between a handheld transceiver and a small, solid-state, linear amplifier. Good-quality RG-8/X (sometimes called miniature RG-8/U) takes the regular PL-259 antenna connector, but the slightly larger diameter UG-176/U reducer. This reducer is as common as apple pie, and you can purchase it anywhere. For a run over 20 feet, a better choice, as mentioned, is the larger coaxial cable called RG-213/U. This is exactly the same size as RG-8/U, but the designation RG-213/U signifies a type IIA noncontaminating, plasticized, synthetic-resin, protective black jacket that will resist abrasion and will not be damaged by ultraviolet sunlight rays. You can run this cable in the bilge or submerge it in water without a chance of contamination or leakage, and it should last a minimum of twenty years. Coaxial cable without this special jacket and PVC interior may only last two years—another point against CB-type feedlines. The larger RG-213/U is almost twice as expensive as RG-8/X (59 cents versus 29 cents per foot), but it's worth the price. At 156.8 MHz, a 100-foot run of RG-213/U causes only about 2.3 dB loss.

Transceivers

The pleasureboat operator may use fewer than 30 marine VHF channels for transmitting, but there's no real reason not to purchase a 55-channel synthesized VHF set that will tune in every U.S. channel plus a few Canadian channels at a flick of the switch. You don't pay much more for this capability. If you buy a set with 78 channels, on the other hand, you aren't getting any more U.S. channels—just a few European telephone channel capabilities. Shop accordingly. When a set boasts "101 channels," the manufacturer is using an advertising ploy; give one black mark for hyperbole.

All marine VHF sets offer 25 watts output, the maximum allowed by the FCC. In fact, thanks to imported power transistors, 25 watts is just loafing for most sets. In addition, all nationally advertised marine VHF transmitters must be accepted under Part 80 of the FCC rules and regulations. These requirements are stringent, so there is not much difference between one transmitter and another. If the set is designed for permanent installation, it will put out a clean 25 watts with good transmit audio.

Unlike the transmitter section, the receiver section of marine 25-watt VHF sets varies from extremely poor to extremely good. Manufacturers can cut costs in a VHF set by giving you an inefficient receiver. Try out the set at the electronics display of a dealer, and listen for adequate audio. Crank the volume all the way up and see whether or not it's really ear-splitting. It will need to be if you are in an open cockpit and you need to hear the set over the din of your engine at full throttle. The unit may be advertised as having four watts audio power, but these specs mean little. Hearing is believing. Check the channel readout—can you see the digits in the daylight? Dull

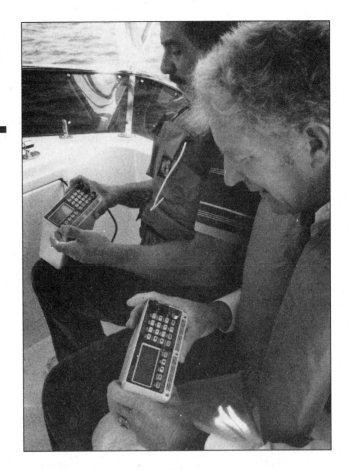

Digital selective calling (DSC) VHF transceivers undergo sea trials along the Atlantic Coast. Author West, in foreground, looks over DSC incoming message.

light-emitting diodes (LEDs) are fast being replaced by the new bold liquid crystal displays (LCDs) that can be seen day or night.

It's pretty hard to determine receiver sensitivity as well as channel selectivity, and again, the specifications that accompany each VHF set are usually nothing more than copies of specs from their competitors. Sensitivity is the measure of the receiver's ability to hear weak signals, and you may read, for example, that a particular receiver is sensitive to a 0.35 microvolt signal at 20 dB quieting, or a 0.25 microvolt signal at 12 dB signal noise and distortion (SINAD). The greater the number of microvolts, the less the sensitivity of the receiver. Much more to the point, remember that sensitivity is easy to achieve, and most sets are sensitive regardless of price. Selectivity (the ability to reject adjacent channel frequencies) and intermodulation rejection (the ability to reject "invading" signals formed from the mixing of out-of-band frequencies) are the critical factors in receiver quality, and, unfortunately, a good way to judge these is by the transceiver's price tag. Inexpensive VHF sets may allow out-of-band signals to come through on Channel 16, so

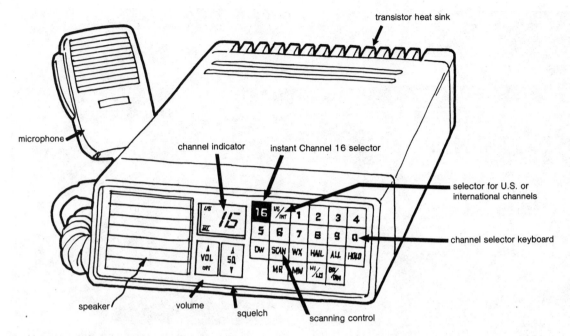

transistor heat sink

microphone

channel indicator

instant Channel 16 selector

selector for U.S. or international channels

channel selector keyboard

speaker

volume

squelch

scanning control

There is little standardization of display and keypad labels among VHF sets. This unit includes an automatic channel-scanning capability, connection to a loud hailer, weather frequencies, and a dimmer control for night illumination. All VHF radios must also have a switch or keypad for low and high power output. The price range for a synthesized keyboard unit is $300 to $900 plus another $30 to $40 for the antenna. A typical size is 6 inches wide, 10 inches deep, and 3 inches high.

instead of hearing the Coast Guard when you're in Boston Harbor, you hear the local towing company. Quite common with cheap sets. The meaningless, copied specifications may state that both selectivity and intermodulation rejection are higher than 60 dB, but it is better to turn on the radio at the showroom and have it hooked up to the biggest VHF antenna they have on the roof. Listen to Channel 16, and if you hear strange beeps, moans, groans, and tones that come and go, chances are the receiver is experiencing intermodulation and poor out-of-band signal rejection.

The squelch circuit is another indication of quality. Try this simple test—turn the squelch off so that background noise comes through the loudspeaker at a reasonable level. Now slowly advance the squelch until the background noise disappears. Did the noise stop abruptly or did it slowly fade away as the squelch was advanced? Abrupt squelch circuits cause a DC voltage gate to switch the receiver on and off—each time with an accompanying "pop"—as signals come and go in the squelch. You can hear this "pop" even when the volume is turned all the way down by listening carefully to the loudspeaker. It is not an indication of a good, sensitive VHF

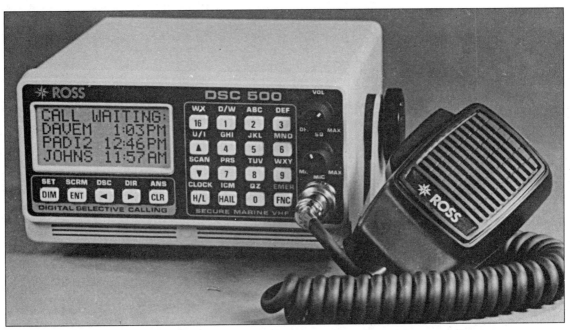

VHF DSC transceiver indicating incoming calls waiting. This unit contains built-in scrambling, too.

set. The better receiver and squelch circuit will gradually filter the background noise as the squelch goes into its silent mode. Extremely weak signals won't pop in and out of the squelch, but will appear gracefully as smooth audio coming through your loudspeaker. Instead of a crackling noise on a weak signal, you will hear the distant voices quietly emerge.

Except in crystal sets, the transceiver is frequency selected by the synthesizer within your VHF set. You have a choice of keyboard channel entry or the more traditional rotating knob. The keyboard-entry VHF sets have more features, such as memorization of channels (just keyboard-enter the channels you select), channel scanning (the set monitors by turn each preselected channel, stopping on an incoming signal), channel searching (the set searches *all* the factory-installed channels), and priority channel operation (the set remains on the working channel but scans the priority channel at brief intervals, locking there if it receives a transmission). You can preprogram some units to operate at high power on certain channels and low power on others; a few units offer a hailer-speaker accessory, which substitutes for a foghorn and can be used as an intercom.

Rotating-knob units sit on one channel unless manually adjusted. Manufacturers are producing fewer of these because of this limitation and because the mechanical contacts may become fouled or corroded in time.

The simplest of VHF radios uses a rotary channel selector, but some such units have no more than 12 to 24 channels. That number is adequate for most boat-owners unless they are cruising in international waters, where channels are used that are not authorized by the FCC for U.S. waters. Above the rotary channel selector on the unit here is the channel indicator, and to the right is the button for low/high power output. Farther right are the on/off/volume and squelch controls. The price range is $150 to $300 (without antenna), and a typical size is 6 inches wide, 10 inches deep, and 3 inches high.

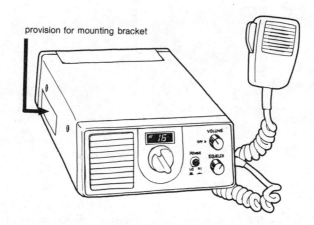

provision for mounting bracket

The keyboard units substitute miniature microswitches or pressure-sensitive membranes for mechanical contacts. Rotating-knob sets are still preferred by some mariners, however. Fishermen find the knobs easier to manipulate with gloved fingers than the small pads of a keyboard set, and a channel change can be accomplished without looking by rotating the knob through the requisite number of clicks from the previous, known channel. There are some excellent rotating-knob sets on the market.

If you plan to expose a keyboard unit to the weather, make sure the keyboard is covered by a weatherproof membrane. Some rotating-knob VHF sets are fully waterproof and can be completely hosed down without adverse effects. Behind each knob is a neoprene gasket that seals moisture out. If a radio is weatherproof or waterproof, you can be sure that the advertising literature will make a point of this. If the feature isn't mentioned in the literature, keep the set bone dry.

Installation

Mount the antenna as high as possible and at least three feet away from metal spars and standing rigging except when mounted atop these. Never clamp it to stainless steel stanchions or canopy frames, since these metal objects will absorb some of the signal.

It will do no harm to run the coaxial cable with other wiring. Since the signal is kept inside the coax by the outer braid, there should be no pickup of unwanted noise. If you have excess cable, chop it off. An unnecessarily long coil of coax behind the set will only rob you of power output and weaken signal receive capabilities. If you have never soldered a coaxial cable connector (PL-259, with or without the UG-255 adapter or reducer), let someone qualified do it for you. The coaxial cable connector improperly soldered, whether at the back of the radio or the base of the antenna, is a very

Two VHF transceivers that incorporate a big rotating knob for channel changing and sealed membrane keypads for built-in loud hailer options. Both units boast big, bold LCD channel readouts for easy viewing in the daylight.

common failure in most new installations. As an alternative, use a crimped, no-solder connector. These are available anywhere antennas are sold, and more and more manufacturers are starting to include them with their VHF radios and loran and satnav receivers, knowing that owner installation of this gear is on the increase. These connectors, which are simple to install, work very well but do not provide the longevity of a soldered connection. Still, they typically last about three years before the signal becomes intermittent and the connector must be replaced.

Once the cable connector is in place, you will want to test the continuity of the connection. This test cannot be done with regular ohmmeter equipment. Since most VHF antennas look to a DC meter like a direct short, it will take a specialized antenna test meter to doublecheck the operation of your antenna as well as the connection to the PL259. While some inexpensive CB-type meters for antenna checks may work, you really need an antenna test meter calibrated for VHF frequencies. A simple way to test your antenna connection without a meter is to insert the center pin of your plug in the VHF set socket. Listen for the weak weather station signal. Now push the remaining shell of the connector assembly onto your antenna receptacle, and the weather station should increase slightly in signal strength. If it does, your connection is proper. If you slide the shell onto the connector and the weather station disappears completely, you've got a problem with your connection or with the VHF antenna itself.

In a powerboat, mount the radio where it's easy to see and operate from the helm. Mount it handy to the companionway in a sailboat. Unless it's a waterproof or weatherproof radio, keep it out of any area that might get wet. Keep any external speaker at least three feet from the compass. Place the microphone hanger at a convenient location, but one where the mike is not likely to be left switched on.

Right: Proper method of installing a coaxial connector on RG-213/U cable. This cable connector is used with VHF, SSB, loran-C, and satnav antenna cables. Proper soldering requires experience. The alternative is to use crimped, no-solder connectors, which can be installed with pliers.

Below: Proper method of installing a coaxial connector on RG-8/X cable. This cable is used for medium-length runs with VHF, SSB, loran-C, and satnav antennas. Attempt this soldering only if you have done it before. Again, crimped connectors are the alternative.

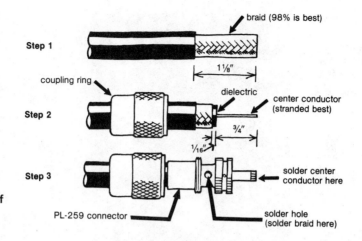

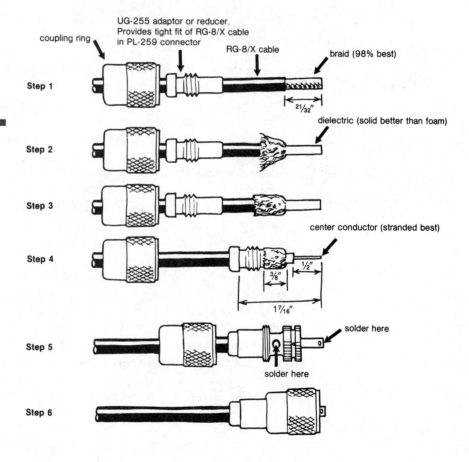

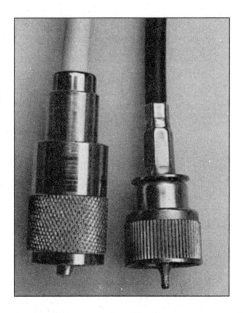

The crimp-type coaxial connector (right) is serviceable but not as rugged and durable as a soldered connector (left).

Run the red and black 12-volt wires supplied with your VHF set to your switch panel. Rather than tacking them onto any red and black wire you might find at your navigation station, go directly to a healthy 12-volt source that feeds voltage selector switches. Use a voltmeter to doublecheck that there is no more than a half-volt drop when you transmit on high power into a dummy load (nonradiating) test antenna network. If the dial lights dim dramatically when you transmit, the voltage input to the set is inadequate.

If you purchased your set with a remote control unit for a flying bridge, run the wires as recommended by the manufacturer. Manufacturers' instruction books are usually excellent, and you should follow their suggestions precisely.

After you have doublechecked all connections, start tuning around the channels and listening for distant stations. Engine noise and fluorescent lights do not affect VHF radio as they do SSB and AM radios, but hot or noisy ignition circuits can produce signals that, although not apparent as background noise, will "piggyback" on weak incoming broadcast signals, confusing them. If weather channel signals transmitted 100 miles away come in loud and clear, everything is fine with your set. Don't transmit until you obtain proper FCC licensing (see below).

Handheld Units

VHF handhelds are terrific performers. A handheld is not recommended as the only marine VHF set aboard a large boat, but one of these little sets

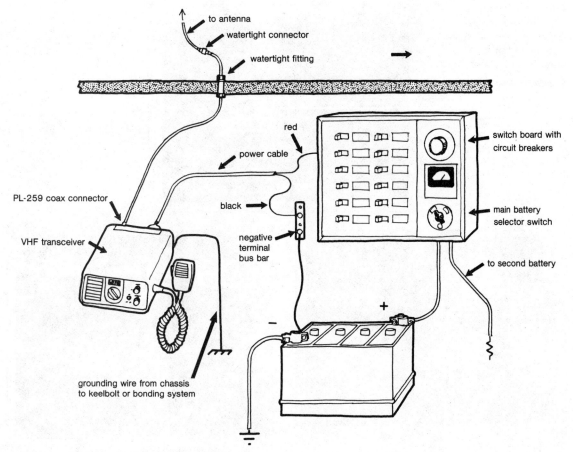

to antenna

watertight connector

watertight fitting

red

power cable

switch board with
circuit breakers

PL-259 coax connector

black

main battery
selector switch

VHF transceiver

negative
terminal
bus bar

to second battery

−

+

grounding wire from chassis
to keelbolt or bonding system

Typical hookup of a VHF radio through a switch panel. An alternative to wiring though an electrical panel is to connect the radio's power cable directly to the battery, making sure fuses are in line with the radio.

could make a great single radio installation aboard a very small boat. The handhelds are usually all-frequency synthesized. Although some manufacturers still try to peddle crystal-type VHF radios, both stationary and handheld, your better buy is a synthesized set that is just as reliable and picks up every channel.

VHF handhelds may use either keyboard-entry synthesis or thumbwheel channel selection. The thumbwheel channel selection method usually leads to a lower price tag, but the thumbwheels are very leaky and must never get wet. Keyboard entry usually leads to a more weathertight handheld that can survive a little bit of spray. No handheld will take a complete underwater dive.

Some units offer a choice of battery packs. A high-power pack may give you 5 watts, but it will wear down after an hour or two of broadcast time. Medium-power (1 to 3 watts) and low-power packs will last progressively longer. Most can be recharged.

You can hook up your handheld to an external antenna, improving its range dramatically over what is possible with the little rubber antennas the units come with. Always use an external antenna on a VHF handheld if it is the only radio aboard.

There are a plethora of accessories for any handheld, but choose only those that match your style of operation. As mentioned, you can even get an external power amplifier that takes the 3 watts output and amplifies it to 25 watts, but it's cheaper to buy a complete VHF 25-watt system in the first place.

The licensing for VHF handhelds is identical to that for a regular 25-watt marine VHF set. Operating the handheld on shore is disallowed by the FCC.

Licensing

All radio stations aboard a vessel must be licensed by the FCC. You cannot transfer this license from one boat to another or from person to person. Application for a marine VHF license is on Form 506, which is normally packed by the manufacturer with every VHF transceiver. There is a thirty-five dollar fee. The completed and signed application is sent to the Federal Communications Commission, 1270 Fairfield, Gettysburg, PA 17325. It takes about six weeks to receive your call letters. On Form 506-A there is a special provision that allows you to use a temporary identifier as a call sign the second you put Form 506 in the mail to the FCC. Your call sign will consist of numbers and/or letters that comprise your vessel registration number or documentation number.

A personal operator's permit is no longer required for pleasureboat radio communications. The FCC recently deleted the necessity of filing FCC Form 753; but you *do* need to fill out this form for any marine single sideband installation.

A marine radio operator's permit is, however, required for persons who

A typical handheld VHF radio with self-contained batteries. Some units are all-channel in their capabilities while other have a limited number of channels. Range is shorter than it is with radios using a conventional antenna, although some models will take an external antenna for extended range. The price range is $150 to $600, and a typical size is 8½ inches high, 3½ inches wide, and 1½ inches thick.

VHF handheld marine transceivers may work farther range by switching to a telescopic antenna. Author West communicating on an airboat in the Everglades.

operate a voice radiotelephone aboard cargo ships of 300 or more tons; aboard a vessel sailing the Great Lakes that is more than 65 feet long or carrying more than six passengers for hire; aboard a vessel carrying more than six passengers for hire, regardless of size, that is navigated in the open seas or more than 1,000 feet from shore; or from certain shore locations. If you do operate a commercial vessel and need a marine radio operator's permit (formerly known as the Third Class operator's permit), contact the Federal Communications Commission for more information.

Form 506 is also used in applying for a handheld license if you plan to use your handheld on many different vessels, but not one in particular, or if you plan to use it in an unregistered small boat.

Operating Procedures

Most instruction manuals include a radio logbook. This is a handy place to keep call sign information of stations you may communicate with, or to write down phone numbers in case you need to make a marine radiotelephone call to shore. Try to keep your log updated, and certainly note any distress messages you hear.

Most manufacturers and some marine electronics sellers include a transmitter certification card indicating that your set has been properly tuned and certified for operation. This important information must be kept with your logbook. If you find that your transmitter has not been certified by a technician, you are required by law to obtain this certification. Don't have a tech come all the way down to the boat and charge you an arm and a leg for doublechecking your transmitter frequencies, but do try to obtain a certificate from the original seller or directly from the manufacturer. The days of the FCC walking the docks and checking logs are over, but keep it legal.

You don't need to own a boat to obtain a permit for a VHF radio. Perhaps you cruise with your friends on their small boats that might not have a permanently installed radiotelephone aboard. It makes good sense that someone on board have a handheld VHF set, in case of an emergency. But someone needs a VHF license in order to carry that handheld out on the boat.

FCC Form 506 specifically permits the licensing of a handheld for "portable" operation. You would indicate, in the explanation box on Form 506, that you regularly cruise aboard boats that don't have a marine VHF on board. The license will cover your portable VHF handheld, regardless of what boat you may travel on.

The rules do not permit you to operate a VHF handheld or 25-watt set from shore without a very special permit. The private coast station permit is a tough license to obtain, and is usually reserved only for businesses that regularly communicate on the marine radio bands. You cannot obtain a shore station license just to stay in touch with your friends at sea. However, if your yacht club or marine business regularly uses the airwaves, they would need to obtain a private coast station, and this requires FCC Form 503.

The Federal Communications Commission strictly enforces VHF radio and SSB radio, plus radar licensing requirements. You must have a valid ship station license for this equipment—and that's right, radar, too. The way the FCC enforces this rule is through the U.S. Coast Guard or the local harbor patrols. If they board your vessel, and find that you don't have a valid station license, you could receive a fine in the mail a few days later. Your ship station license should be current and should cover VHF, marine SSB, any EPIRBs, and radar. You do not need a license for weather facsimile reception equipment, nor do you need a license for cellular telephone. CB radio is also excluded from licensing requirements. Just make sure you have a current license, hanging on your bulkhead, next time someone inspects your vessel. It's the law!

Good operating procedures are necessary to keep communications flowing smoothly on the crowded marine VHF channels. Over the last few years, the VHF marine radio channels have become even more overcrowded and even more undisciplined. The only time you are permitted to talk about anything other than relevant ship business is when you are tied into the marine operator. CB jargon is inappropriate and illegal. Random channel-hopping is also illegal. By law you must stick with channels that agree with your type of operation.

It is also illegal to call the Coast Guard for a radio check. They have such sophisticated monitoring equipment that any type of signal will sound loud and clear to them. Call another boat instead.

The U.S. Coast Guard and the Radio Technical Commission for Marine Services (in cooperation with the FCC) recommend standard procedures for establishing communications on marine VHF and high-frequency channels. These procedures are detailed in piloting books and in VHF instruction manuals as well as government literature. Contact your local Coast Guard detachment if you can't locate the procedures elsewhere. These operating procedures should be followed.

Maintenance

Little maintenance is required to keep your marine VHF system perking along. Check all outside antenna connections now and then to make sure you have no bare wires or corroded cable plugs. Many VHF antennas bring the coax directly into their interior, so there is nothing to worry about. Baseloaded whip antennas, however, may require an outside PL-259 connector, and it's best to unscrew this connector periodically and check out what's happening inside. If the cable and connector have turned green, replace the feedline and plug.

Any sort of plug located on the exterior of your vessel should be sealed with a flexible silicone sealant. This stuff will make more of a job of removing the connector for periodic inspection, but it will seal out the weather and corrosive elements that might otherwise attack an outside antenna connection.

Check periodically to ensure that all plugs in the back of the VHF set are snug. With the radio tuned to a transmitting weather station, wiggle each wire by turn and listen for a breakup of reception. If the weather station should begin to break up when you wiggle a wire, chances are that wire needs to be replaced or its connection repaired. To check the mike cord, establish communications with another vessel and then wiggle the mike cord as you're talking. If your signal breaks up, you may need a complete new microphone setup. Most mike connections go bad where the cord disappears in the plastic mike or where the cord has worked loose from the chrome chassis connector.

On the water, use your VHF set in the receive mode on Channel 16 often. Not only could this very well save a life, it also helps dry up any moisture that might be inside the VHF cabinet. Transistors don't wear out, so keep your set on whenever you're underway.

Additional Buying Tips

Buy a VHF set wherever the terms are good. You can do the installation easily, following manufacturer's instructions, without help from a trained technician. FCC rules allow you to do this and specifically indicate that no FCC sign-off is required.

Wherever you buy the radio, shop for the best price, using catalogs as a good indicator. Most catalog houses pride themselves on being able to offer the most competitive prices.

Don't be misled by claims that you are receiving "a $50 tune-up value" when you buy the equipment from a company that thoroughly checks it out and peaks it for maximum transmit and receive capabilities. The factory has already squeezed every last watt out of a VHF radiotelephone and peaked it for maximum reception, and there is little that can be done by any technician to get any more performance out of the set.

You should investigate who's going to fix the radio in case it should arrive dead. Will the organization from whom you purchased it exchange it for a new one? Will they tell you to send it back to the factory for a three-week wait for repair? Will they fix it while you wait? An even exchange is the best option; some companies do this, and others don't. Buy from those that do.

CHAPTER 4

Cellular Telephones

by Gordon West

Most of us, when we go cruising, are happy to get away from the phone, but there may be times when taking or making a phone call on a day off is vital to business. If you carry a beeper and have had it go off on the boat, only to struggle for hours to reach the office through the marine operator on your radio, you're a possible candidate for a cellular telephone.

How They Work

The cellular telephone system is a precise clone of a home or office phone, minus the wires. Direct dialing to any shore-based phone worldwide or another cellular phone in a boat or car, direct call receiving, call forwarding, conference calling, and an answering machine are available. You can tie your vessel's security system or fire or flooding alarm into the phone to alert the local harbor master automatically. Often, the per-minute cost of a cellular phone call to or from a boat will be three times less than a comparable call on a marine VHF radio.

The cellular telephone service operates on 800 MHz, near Channel 88 on a television's UHF dial. A 50-MHz band embracing hundreds of channels has been allocated for vehicular, portable, and marine cellular telephone

Close-up of control head for a marine cellular telephone system.

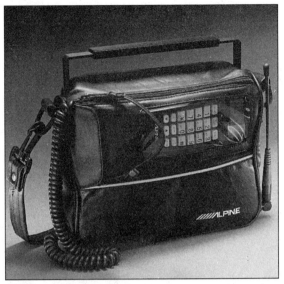

Transportable cellular telephone, well protected from salt spray, with its built-in all-day battery system.

calls. Major metropolitan areas are divided into tiny radio cells that may be reassigned to another user as soon as the mobile or portable unit travels from one cell site to another. A computer-controlled main switching office (MSO) automatically hands off your conversation to a new cell as necessary, and this handover is so quick that it's barely noticeable during the conversation. All you might hear is a quick click and a slight change in voice levels. Up to sixty channels are available within each cell site, so waiting for an open channel is unusual in most places. Still, the system can get overloaded on a Los Angeles freeway during rush hour. The 800 MHz FM cellular signal is generally clear until you reach the usable end of a particular cell.

Most coastal cellular telephone cell networks have been designed to serve freeway travelers and downtown commuters with the best primary coverage available. Marine coverage is secondary, and although coverage does exist outside metropolitan areas, you will have to investigate whether your cruising waters are covered. There are literally scores of local cellular telephone providers. Call your local telephone operator and ask for information on mobile access or cellular phone services.

Since the ultrahigh frequency signals travel line-of-sight and won't bend around objects, it's quite possible to lose cellular telephone coverage in waters that are "shadowed" by land. One would expect no coverage on the back side of an island, for example, although it is sometimes possible to stay outside the shadowed area by giving at least a five-mile berth to tall island hills. Similarly, one can expect marginal reception below bold headlands and coastal cliffs. Once you get out to sea a few miles, coverage improves.

What's Available

Several equipment options, ranging from permanent installations to little handheld sets, are available. If you presently operate or intend to operate a cellular phone in your vehicle, you might investigate the possibility of having the trunk-mounted transmitter and receiver unit available for quick removal to be placed aboard your boat. A separate control head would then be permanently installed aboard the boat, enabling you to transfer your trunk transceiver equipment (which weighs about 10 pounds) to and from the boat.

For permanent marine installations, a 12-foot white fiberglass cellular telephone antenna, which looks exactly like a marine VHF antenna, is recommended. It's placed as high as possible on the vessel's superstructure for maximum range. Manufacturers of these antennas include Celwave, Shakespeare, Hy-Gain, Antenna Specialists, and Ora.

For mariners desiring permanent installation of the entire system aboard their boats, several manufacturers offer complete systems specifically designed for the marine environment. Having looked over these sets, I can't see that they differ much from a vehicular setup, except that a white control head is used and most such phones give you the ability to plug in remote heads, which would be desirable on large boats wanting more than one phone station.

Prices for permanently installed cellular telephone sets have dropped dramatically over the last four years. Top-of-the-line equipment that might have cost $3,000 originally is now available for around $1,000. Budget cellular telephone sets that were introduced at $1,000 are now as low as $500. The differences between high- and low-end permanently mounted sets are in their memory capabilities, the "hands-free" option, availability of add-on devices, and, in summary, the bells and whistles. All sets offer about the same power output, range, dialing capability, and transmission quality.

Fifteen manufacturers offer transportable, carry-aboard sets that can be tied into an external antenna system for increased range. A transportable set looks something like a large lunch pail, and it can operate up to eight hours on the hefty battery pack built into its chassis. While its little telescopic or "rubber duckie" antenna does a nice job in close, a much bigger antenna would add needed range when you're out beyond five miles or so. An antenna like the Metz antenna in the accompanying photo is frequently used in place of the 12-foot whip of the permanent installation.

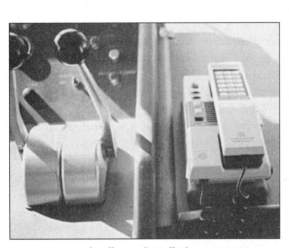

A permanent wheelhouse installation.

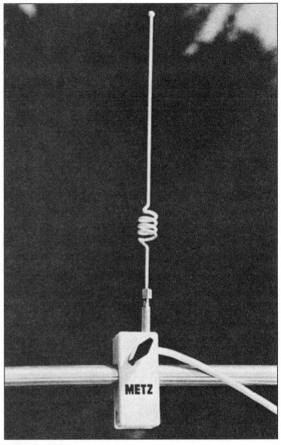

The Metz cellular antenna may be clamped onto a rail.

Portable cellular phone gives you palm-of-the-hand telecommunications, but don't expect to talk for more than 40 minutes between battery charges. The beauty of these handheld sets is their extremely small size—smaller than a cordless home phone. They work well for short intervals, but you must have a way of recharging the batteries.

Call your local cellular telephone provider for more details about specific coverage areas and the best equipment recommended for your particular type of cruising.

Confidentiality

Don't expect cellular telephone calls at sea to be confidential. Anyone with a programmable handheld, mobile, or base scanner that tunes up to

800 MHz can eavesdrop on your conversation. Marine calls are particularly susceptible to eavesdropping, because a single cell will carry the majority of the phone call. The Electronic Communications Privacy bill imposes stiff fines on individuals caught eavesdropping on cellular calls; while it's not illegal to own a scanner that tunes in these calls, it's a crime to monitor them. Unfortunately, the new bill has done nothing more than call attention to 800 MHz phone calls and has created an instant market for 800 MHz scanners. One manufacturer of scanners, Radio Shack, claims they will discontinue the cellular telephone band on a new handheld model. For the foreseeable future, however, cellular phone calls are far from confidential. Try tuning your TV set on UHF Channel 88, and hear for yourself.

You can't beat the practicality of a cellular phone aboard your boat if you must stay in touch with the outside world at all times. Providing you stay inside a cellular telephone coverage area, the channels are usually wide open, with no waiting for a dial tone or retrieving a call. All you do is pick up the handset, listen for the dial tone, and start talking.

Monthly phone bills are between $100 and $150, depending on how much you talk and how many long-distance phone calls you make. If you use your equipment only now and then, your bill will be below $100 per month, but unlike the marine VHF service, you are charged about $35 for monthly service whether you use the equipment or not.

Now that cellular telephone systems are so inexpensive and service is so great, it makes perfect sense to take along your cellular telephone on your next trip out on the water. If you are on an extremely small boat, the little transportable, or even the handheld portable sets, work well. Try to operate them as high as possible above the water for best range.

On bigger boats, the transportable or fixed units, hooked into a quality marine cellular phone antenna, will give you some outstanding results. And how far can you talk on cellular telephone at sea, on an outside antenna? Would you believe over 300 miles?

That's right, cellular telephone "super range" may occur on those hot, windless days due to a condition called "tropospheric ducting." Your cellular telephone radio waves are bent well beyond the visible horizon by a warm air mass (an inversion) hanging over the coast line. The inversion layer is usually associated with sinking air (subsidence) from a high pressure system, and the high-pressure cell could extend for over 300 miles up and down the coastline—or out to sea. This gives you 300 miles of crystal-clear cellular telephone, as well as VHF, range. As long as the local weather conditions don't change much, this range will continue through the night, and maybe into the next day. As long as you can see that band of smog hanging over the water, chances are your cellular phone will go a lot farther than what the local carrier may guarantee.

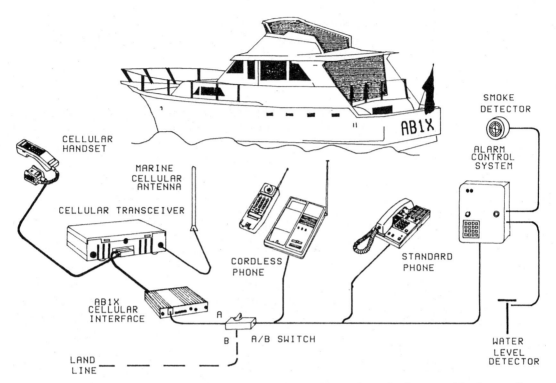

Installation of a simple two-position switch and an interface module gives a shipboard cellular telephone operator the option of receiving phone calls over a cellular telephone via the land lines **when docked, or of using a standard or cordless telephone. Alarm sensors may also be interfaced with the system.**

Many cellular telephone companies are extending the range to sea by putting some of their antenna installations on buildings and bluffs right beside the ocean or lake. These shoreside antenna systems dramatically increase cellular coverage over most major popular cruising areas. After all, the cellular telephone carriers don't want to miss out on the lucrative business that normally drops off on the weekends. If they can extend, to sea, their marine coverage, they can cash in on all of those mariners who just can't leave the dock without their cellular telephone equipment. So don't believe it when someone says that cellular telephones don't work out at sea—they do. Try to get your equipment up as high as possible, and use a marine-rated cellular telephone antenna, and get set for some long-distance cellular phone calls.

CHAPTER 5

Satellite Communications

by Gordon West

The last five years have brought mariners wanting to call home significant changes. For cruisers out on the lakes, over in the harbors, or within 30 miles of the coast line, the marine VHF service was one of the best ways to go . . . until cellular phones came to town.

Now cellular telephones have found their way aboard boats, and most mariners have abandoned their marine VHF public correspondence channels and make all of their local phone calls from portable and transportable cellular telephone sets.

Out on the high seas, small boats and medium-sized yachts would communicate over long distances using age-old techniques that ham radio operators love to do—bouncing signals off of the ionosphere. The emission mode is called single sideband, and single sideband transmissions from ship to shore have for more than two decades provided mariners with relatively inexpensive phone call capabilities. I mean, when you are down in the South Seas, and you want to call the office and tell them that you're going to be another couple of weeks out of the office, it's well worth the $5 per minute to bounce your signals off of the airwaves and make that phone call home.

But you'll read about it here first—the high seas single sideband marine telephone service is soon to have some stiff competition as an alternative way

The white dome in the foreground, and the white dome on the container vessel's superstructure are both communications satellite antenna systems, INMARSAT-A.

for global, on-the-water, phone-home service. Welcome to outer space, and welcome to satellite communications for small boats.

Unlike the single sideband frequencies, satellite communications don't rely on the ionosphere for a bounce back to earth. Satellite signals will travel up to 22,000 miles away, and get a rebroadcast back to earth that gives you crystal clear communications without the Donald Duck effect on marine SSB. With satellite phone calls, your voice is clear as a bell . . . a bell . . . a bell. . . . Once you get used to a slight echo sometimes heard on the lines, and once you get used to a very unnatural one-second delay in you-talk/they-talk, you'll be able to communicate via satellite with the same clarity as making an overseas phone call to Europe. It's the delay that gets me, but as long as you don't have a fast-paced conversation, talking through the geostationary satellites is a great way to go when you're beyond touch of cellular or marine VHF.

Satellite communications have been available to the maritime community since 1976. COMSAT Corporation inaugurated the service for the marine industry, and for you. But only very large ships could really take advantage of INMARSAT standard A equipment. This is that big white dome you see on super-tankers. The INMARSAT standard A gear would use a big dish antenna that would automatically lock onto the distant satellite suspended in space, and stay locked on even though the vessel was pitching, rolling, and turning. Much like a gyroscope, the big dish inside the radom did a nice job of getting your calls through, loud and clear. The rate of a standard A phone call is about $12 a minute.

But marine electronics manufacturers figured out ways to make the standard A dish antenna smaller, yet just as capable of working through the suspended-in-space satellite. They now have the disk antennas down to less than 100 pounds, but we are still talking about a sizeable $20,000 investment (minimum), and a big white dome on the back of your small boat.

INMARSAT standard C now scales down your communications with shore to a suitcase-sized package. But standard C does not give you voice capabilities. Rather, standard C (think of "C" for computer) is a highly compact and affordable store-and-forward messaging system that would allow you to interconnect with international Telex, Teletext, and packet-switched data networks for ship-to-shore and shore-to-ship communications, as well as for safety purposes.

If you are really into laptop computers and take your laptop everywhere you go out to sea, standard C is just for you. Think of all the work you can

INMARSAT-M and A compared. INMARSAT-M is for smaller vessels.

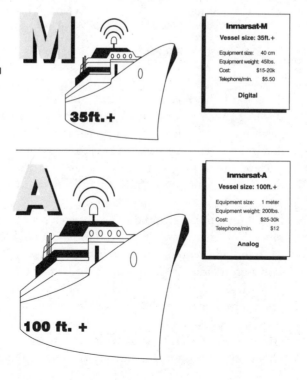

Inmarsat-M

Vessel size: 35ft.+

Equipment size:	40 cm
Equipment weight:	45lbs.
Cost:	$15-20k
Telephone/min.	$5.50

Digital

35ft.+

Inmarsat-A

Vessel size: 100ft.+

Equipment size:	1 meter
Equipment weight:	200lbs.
Cost:	$25-30k
Telephone/min.	$12

Analog

100 ft. +

INMARSAT SHIP EARTH STATIONS

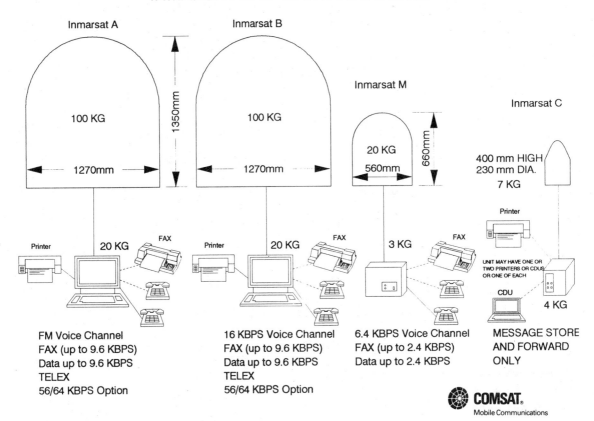

Inmarsat A

100 KG

1350mm

1270mm

Printer   20 KG   FAX

FM Voice Channel
FAX (up to 9.6 KBPS)
Data up to 9.6 KBPS
TELEX
56/64 KBPS Option

Inmarsat B

100 KG

1270mm

Printer   20 KG   FAX

16 KBPS Voice Channel
FAX (up to 9.6 KBPS)
Data up to 9.6 KBPS
TELEX
56/64 KBPS Option

Inmarsat M

20 KG

660mm

560mm

3 KG   FAX

6.4 KBPS Voice Channel
FAX (up to 2.4 KBPS)
Data up to 2.4 KBPS

Inmarsat C

400 mm HIGH
230 mm DIA.
7 KG

Printer

UNIT MAY HAVE ONE OR
TWO PRINTERS OR CDUS
OR ONE OF EACH

CDU

4 KG

MESSAGE STORE
AND FORWARD
ONLY

COMSAT®
Mobile Communications

do aboard the boat, and then send your files back to the office via INMARSAT. Your antenna system opens up out of a suitcase and fans out, beaming your signals straight up into the sky. The powerful data stream doesn't even require a dish antenna to focus your bytes to the geostationary satellite. Just as long as the antenna is out in the open, you are on the air to that distant computer. Once you upload your file, it takes approximately 10 to 15 minutes for a reply from the other end. But what you get is error-free communicating, and the cost for each page of information is not much more than what it would cost you to send a FAX from a downtown hotel.

Standard C equipment is available for under $10,000, and if you already own a great laptop PC, you may already have everything you need.

Now for the latest—INMARSAT standard M. Think of "M" as in miniature. Now we're back to talking about real live telephone calls, not computer calls. Standard M is specifically designed for those boats that cruise beyond VHF radiotelephone range but demand instant dial-up phone service to shore for emergency signals to the Coast Guard.

INMARSAT standard M is a new digital voice communications service being offered through the global INMARSAT network of satellites and land/earth stations. It supplements the existing services already offered by INMARSAT: INMARSAT A for voice, high speed data, FAX, and Telex—and INMARSAT C, store-and-forward Telex and message. Standard M provides instant, reliable, real-time voice communications with boats on the high seas virtually anywhere in the world.

Calls to and from vessels at sea are relayed via one of four geostationary satellites, depending on your earth region, to an earth station. Your call is interconnected into the international switched telephone system. From there the call is routed through the normal long-distance telephone carriers to its ultimate destination. Four satellites are parked in orbit, and are always in view wherever you cruise. One earth station is located on the East Coast and another on the West Coast. You don't need to worry about the earth stations—your call gets to shore automatically.

Your INMARSAT M small-boat system will consist of a radom-enclosed, stabilized, dish-type antenna, plus a compact electronic box and telephone handset. Don't panic—the radom is only two feet high and about two feet in diameter. It weighs under 50 pounds, and is nowhere near as large as the big standard A terminals. Yes, there is a dish antenna on the

Typical Transmission Path For COMSAT's Mobile Link℠ Service

Typical transmission path for COMSAT's mobile link service.

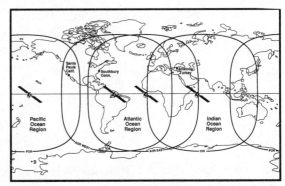

COMSAT's earth stations for INMARSAT 4 ocean coverage.

inside, but it, too, is gyro-stabilized, and it locks onto the distant satellite with incredible accuracy. Even on a small boat in heavy seas, a little wobble off-target won't upset your phone call quality.

Now the reason the quality stays so good is that your voice is chopped up into millions of digital bits, all accomplished inside of your ship station unit. The real-time data stream then streaks up to the geostationary satellite, and the satellite retransmits it back to earth. Because it's digital information, it can't get noisy or misinterpreted. When you say, "I'm not ever coming back to work," it will sound exactly like that back at the office, even though conditions were marginal for the communications path.

And what does your voice sound like at the other end of the circuit, and what does their voice sound like at your end of the circuit, after going through a scramble-unscramble digitizing process? I was surprised at the clarity—while listening to real live phone calls, it was hard to tell what was analog (regular) and what was digitized and then converted back to analog. Except for a slight loss of bassoprofundo lows, the voice sounded absolutely natural. It certainly sounded a lot better than trying to listen for the Donald Duck and Mickey Mouse sounds of single sideband!

Using the INMARSAT A or new INMARSAT M system is just like using your home phone. Pick up your ship's satellite handset and wait a second for a dial tone. Then direct-dial the number you want to reach. Wait a couple of seconds, and you'll hear the telephone ringing at the other end. When you're finished, hang up the phone.

Likewise, someone calling you from shore simply dials an access code to get into your satellite system, then dials your boat's telephone number. The phone on your boat will ring, just like at home. You'll be charged by the minute for any satellite calls you place, just like a long-distance call from home. COMSAT sets the rates for satellite calls, and the charges for INMARSAT M are expected to be considerably lower than those for INMARSAT A. Right now, INMARSAT M will cost under $9,000 for the equipment, and as little as $5 a minute for phoning home. Magnavox (Torrance, California), a longtime manufacturer of all types of INMARSAT systems, claims that the new INMARSAT M terminal is going to be ideal for sportsfishermen, charter yachts, cruising sailors, and other small-boat operators who cruise beyond the range of VHF coast stations or cellular telephone coverage.

And will the geostationary satellites become the only way to phone home using outerspace "repeaters"? Maybe not—the future of phoning home from sea might go through a constellation of polar-orbiting satellites. Some already in space now allow scaled-down equipment and omnidirectional antennas to stay in touch easily from these electronic whirling birds up a mere 200 miles. Since the orbiting satellites are so close to earth, there is

no annoying echo or delay in the phone circuit.

Motorola (Schamburg, Illinois) proposes to launch seventy-seven satellites in a low earth orbit that would allow mariners to make or receive telephone calls anywhere on the earth. The best part of the envisioned "iridium" system is that your phone calls would be made from a handheld cellular-type portable setup rather than a big satellite dish antenna. In fact, if these seventy-seven satellites really become the rage, your signal might also be merged into the cellular phone system when you are close to shore. Either way, close in or far away, you would dial phone calls at sea just like you would on your regular cellular telephone.

What all this means is to keep your eye on space vehicles and orbiting satellites for the future of shipboard telephone service. Marine single sideband may shortly be relegated only to those amateur radio operators that enjoy bouncing signals off the ionosphere, and having everyone come out of their speakers sounding like Daffy Duck. I am a ham, and I enjoy it, but when I really want to make a phone call, I don't want to rely on the ionospheric F-layer.

With satellites in the sky, making phone calls at sea is as simple as picking up the handset and dialing the number. Communications from space are available right now.

CHAPTER 6

Marine Single Sideband Radio

by Gordon West

Marine single sideband (SSB) radio enables mariners to communicate ship-to-ship or ship-to-shore over much greater distances than VHF transmissions can cover. The maximum possible communications distance is determined by the interplay of many factors, of which the time of day, the choice of marine SSB frequencies, and the quality of the shipboard installation are generally the most important. In favorable circumstances, communications around the world are possible.

If this sounds interesting, you'll also be interested to know that SSB radiotelephones are now available at substantially lower costs and with more features than in the past. Marine SSB equipment is more expensive than VHF radiotelephone gear, however, and it is not a replacement for VHF. The FCC requires you to have a permanently installed VHF set aboard before you can add any other marine radio, and your SSB set should never be used when the VHF radio would suffice. To do so would only cause needless crowding on the marine SSB frequencies.

A complete marine single sideband station consists of a transceiver, an antenna, and—where channels on more than one of the seven designated marine SSB bands are to be used—an antenna coupler (also known as a tuner) between the transceiver and the antenna. Both the transceiver and the coupler must be electrically bonded to a proper ground, "proper" in this context implying elaborate but not too difficult to install. Without a good ground, the SSB station simply will not function adequately. When it works well, however, a marine SSB radio is a provider of entertainment, information, and communications for fishermen, commercial vessels, offshore sailors, and bluewater voyagers; most important, it could be a lifeline in an emergency situation.

How It Works

The term "single sideband" designates a type of radio transmission that the military and ham radio operators have been using for years to transmit messages throughout the world. In 1971 the FCC phased in single sideband transmissions for the long-distance marine radio service. At the same time they introduced the expanded marine VHF service for local communications and phased out the amplitude modulated (AM) double sideband sets. A single sideband signal concentrates your voice into a tightly compacted radio wave capable of traveling hundreds or even thousands of miles. This very efficient radio signal is a faithful reproduction of your actual voice pattern. Unlike a commercial AM broadcast station that sends out duplicate voice waveforms plus an energy-robbing "carrier," marine single sideband eliminates the unneeded mirrorlike lower sideband and the power-robbing carrier, which has no function except to hush background noise when nothing is on the air. All the radio energy from your voice is concentrated in an upper sideband waveform that gives you worldwide talk power. Only when you speak will radio energy jump out into the airwaves, and between each word your transmitter and battery system relax. This system imposes a very low current demand on your storage battery system.

Because the transmitted signal is compacted into a very narrow band width, distant receivers are able to reject almost half the normal noise level from the air waves. FCC-required frequency tolerances keep single sideband

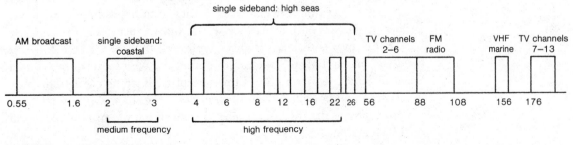

Frequency allocations at a glance.

sets precisely on frequency to minimize that "Mickey Mouse" effect on receive. Simply by adjusting a clarifier knob on your transceiver, you can produce a normal-sounding voice from a transmission by a distant ship or shore station.

A marine single sideband transceiver broadcasts on one of eight allocated frequency bands: 2 MHz, 4 MHz, 6 MHz (used mostly by stations on the Mississippi River), 8 MHz, 12 MHz, 16 MHz, 22 MHz, and the new 25-MHz band. The 2-MHz band is known as the medium-frequency or "coastal communications" band, because frequencies in this band (between 2 and 3 MHz) are typically used for coastwise contacts just beyond VHF range. These frequencies are referred to by their actual values in kilohertz, but frequencies within the high-frequency 4-MHz through 25-MHz bands—referred to collectively as the "high seas" frequencies—are given channel designations. All high seas channels were allocated new clear frequencies on July 1, 1991.

When a transmission is made on any of the bands, one component of the radio signal hugs the surface of the ocean. This is called the groundwave, and it will travel approximately 100 to 200 miles. The groundwave usually does the work in single sideband communications between a boat and a nearby shore station or another boat less than 100 miles away; it is the functional component of transmissions in the 2 MHz band. Groundwave propagation is consistent day or night, depending for the most part only on a good, strong transmitted signal, though it can be interrupted by thunderstorms or other atmospheric disturbances.

The "skywave" component of the transmitted radio signal enables the long-distance communications for which single sideband radio is noted. Skywaves travel upward, bounce off the ionosphere (a multilayered envelope of ionized gas surrounding the earth), and are refracted back to earth hundreds and sometimes thousands of miles away. The height, ion density, and refraction capabilities of the ionosphere are dependent on radiation from the sun and thus change with day and night, with the seasons, and with the 11-year solar cycle; the distance covered by skywaves of a given frequency when they refract from the ionosphere varies accordingly. In general, lower frequencies bounce back to earth close in, while frequencies in the 12-MHz band refract over fairly long distances, typically 3,000 miles. In the 22-MHz band you may be able to communicate from the West Coast of the United States into the Mediterranean. If the ionosphere is strong enough, the skywave often will bounce a second time, doubling the maximum possible communications distance. You can easily talk all the way around the world on 22 MHz at such times.

During daylight hours the ionosphere rises and its ion density increases; the range available on the higher frequencies increases accordingly. The

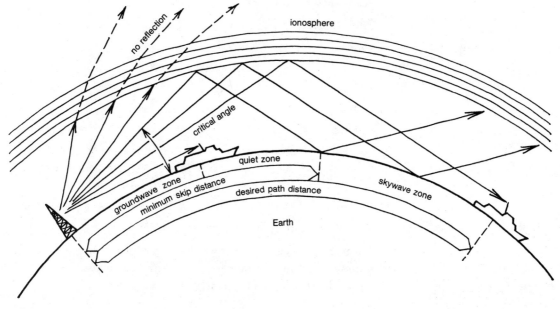

Single sideband skywave and groundwave paths.

skywave components of lower-frequency transmissions are absorbed by the ionosphere, however, while their groundwave components are inhibited by the higher daytime noise level near the earth's surface. Maximum ranges of 2-MHz, 4-MHz, and 8-MHz transmissions tend to decrease during the day.

During the night, the ionosphere gradually lowers and its ion density decreases. Skywaves in the 16-, 22-, and 25-MHz bands may not be refracted at all after the evening hours. Nonetheless, you still may be able to enjoy a communications range of several thousand miles using one of the lower-frequency bands.

Skywaves are unaffected by local weather conditions.

After a few weeks of playing around with a single sideband radiotelephone, a user will begin to get a feel for the expected range on any one particular band of frequencies. As a rough guide, here is what to expect for ship-to-ship communications in the groundwave range: 2 MHz—150 miles (perhaps more at night); 4 MHz—100 miles; 6 MHz—75 miles; 8 MHz—70 miles; 12 MHz—50 miles; and 16 MHz—50 miles. For comparison, a VHF radio (156 MHz) might give you about 40 miles ship-to-ship. The following table will give you an idea of what to expect from the skywave component of your SSB transmission.

To increase your maximum communication range, you should go to a higher frequency. If your signal is literally skipping over the desired station,

Frequency Band	Daytime Range	Nighttime Range
2 MHz	Skywaves absorbed	1,000 miles
4 MHz	Skywaves absorbed	1,500 miles
6 MHz	500 miles	2,000 miles
8 MHz	700 miles	3,000 miles
12 MHz	1,500 miles	Worldwide in the direction of the sun.
16 MHz	3,000 miles	Worldwide in the direction of the sun until 8 P.M. local time, becoming inoperative after that.
22 MHz	Worldwide	Little skywave reflection after sunset.

however, you should switch to a lower frequency. In general, the greater the maximum communication range afforded by a particular band at a particular time of day, the broader the intervening skip zone.

SSB Services and Broadcasts

For any mariner outside VHF range, the marine single sideband service can be a lifeline in an emergency. The U.S. Coast Guard and other distress agencies throughout the world monitor 2,182 kHz (in the 2-MHz band) as the international distress frequency, allowing you to contact shoreside and marine rescue agencies immediately when outside VHF Channel 16 range. There are literally thousands of stations guarding this channel for a distress call 24 hours a day. The U.S. Coast Guard includes five additional working channels—424, 601, 816, 1205, and 1625—in their Automated Mutual-Assistance Vessel Rescue program. Imagine using your marine SSB set to place a call for help when you're thousands of miles away from any shore station. Through their AMVER system, the Coast Guard can pinpoint the position of commercial and military vessels passing through your area and signal them to change course and steam to your location to render assistance.

A marine SSB set gives access to other services besides emergency assistance. Shoreside commercial telephone stations stand by on dozens of frequencies, ready to place a mariner's phone call. These shore-based phone companies operate elaborate transmitting and receiving antenna systems to enable clear communications, and they transmit "traffic lists" to ships at sea that have telephone calls waiting from shoreside parties. They also broadcast weather reports, storm warnings, and other safety-related notices to mariners, and with their massive antenna systems they can patch a

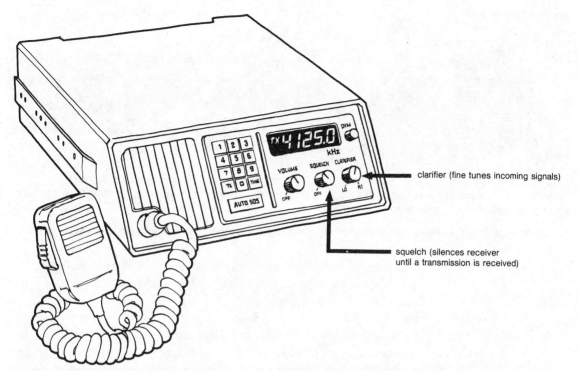

clarifier (fine tunes incoming signals)

squelch (silences receiver
until a transmission is received)

A typical synthesized SSB transceiver has controls very similar to a synthesized VHF radio. The keyboard is used for frequency selection, and to the right of it is a digital display of the chosen frequency with a dimmer control to adjust the brilliance. The price starts at $1,500 without antenna. A typical transceiver size is 12 inches wide, 10 inches deep, and 5 inches high. If you decide on a 23-foot whip antenna, expect to pay $100 to $150.

mariner into rescue coordination centers, hospitals, and emergency-at-sea medical systems, without charge, should an emergency arise.

Incidentally, shoreside marine telephone stations also make it easy to predict the best band to use for rock-solid communications. Every four hours when they read the traffic lists and give the ocean weather conditions, they transmit simultaneously on each one of their authorized bands. By switching bands while they are transmitting, you can determine which band offers the best reception. Where you hear them best is where they will hear you best.

Private coast stations share the ship-to-ship channels, meaning that a mariner can communicate directly, at no charge, with, say, a marine supply company. Other "private coast stations" might include your own marine business, yacht clubs, marine salvage companies, and private air ambulance companies—in short, any marine business that needs to communicate regularly with distant ship stations. You can even establish a base station at your office to stay in touch regarding marine matters when you're far out at sea.

Two complete SSB systems. ICOM SSB offers everything in one compact enclosure. SEA equipment features optional remote controlled second-station system. Both units feature synthesized circuitry for "any channel" transmit and receive.

Depending on the frequency capability of your SSB transceiver, you may be able to receive other services that share frequencies adjacent to the marine band channels. For example, it is possible to tune into worldwide international broadcast stations and find out the latest news here and abroad. You can eavesdrop on the military, State Department, and foreign embassy communications that fill the worldwide high-frequency spectrum. You can tie a weather facsimile receiver into a marine SSB set and receive crystal-clear weather charts of your cruising area. You can tune in amateur radio frequencies and hear local weather reports through one of the many maritime amateur radio "nets." (If you hold a valid ham license, general class or above, you might also use a marine single sideband transceiver with broad frequency capability to transmit on any amateur radio frequency in an emergency.) And you can pick up the international time signals wherever you cruise, using one of many different frequencies. Tick, tick, tick, at the sound of the tone, it is exactly . . . You may also be able to receive transmissions originating from U.S. Air Force flights, the Strategic Air Command, Air Force 1 (the president's plane), Civil Air Patrol, U.S. Intelligence Agency, Antarctic stations, Interpol, U.S. weather ships, the Hurricane Research Center, and Volmet-Aviation weather broadcasts. A single sideband marine transceiver with all-frequency receive capabilities will literally tune in the world.

SSB Equipment

Transceivers

In sharp contrast with most other marine electronics, it's a fifty-fifty split between Japanese and American manufacturing and marketing of single sideband equipment. While a handful of single sideband manufacturers have created some excellent marine single sideband equipment, big leaps in technology and quantum jumps in price reductions have been few and far between. The switch from crystal-type to synthesized, no-crystal single sideband sets has finally taken place among American manufacturers, and the prices of both types have been high. Many sideband stations, complete with tuner, have been selling for well over $3,000.

In the past five years, however, the Japanese have entered the manufacturing picture, and in just one year they completely revolutionized the thinking on marine single sideband among manufacturers as well as purchasers. The very first Japanese-manufactured single sideband set, type-accepted by the FCC, featured 48 programmable channels, 150 watts of peak power output, capabilities for any marine channel between 2 MHz and 29 MHz, and a price tag under $1,500, not including an automatic antenna tuner and some sort of a whip or long wire antenna system. With the latter items included, the complete single sideband station still sells at half the price American manufacturers had been charging for sets with half the features.

Within 60 days after the debut of the 48 channel, completely synthesized, $1,500 marine single sideband set, American manufacturers and their dealer system dropped the price of their keyboard-entry synthesized SSB sets by $1,000. No doubt American manufacturers took a hard look at these new Japanese SSB sets, which were more powerful, had more channels, were priced more competitively, and were equal performers to what was made in the U.S.A.

This SGC SSB transceiver may also double as a sensitive general coverage receiver. All frequencies are controlled via a weatherproof soft-key pad.

The price of a synthesized set with broad frequency capability is unlikely to go much lower than $1,500, but we can expect to see more Japanese-style transceivers hitting the U.S. market. The earliest entry was followed in early 1992 by two other sets with similar capabilities for similar prices. There is absolutely nothing wrong with Japan's marine electronics technology. They simply have a lower-paid labor force that can turn out a ton of product at an extremely low cost to a manufacturer-importer in the States. When production overtakes distribution, prices drop, and we get the benefit of high-technology equipment at low prices.

In light of recent developments, a synthesized SSB set has to be considered a better buy than a crystal set. With the former it's easy to program frequencies and channels. Instead of purchasing expensive additional crystal elements—one for transmit and one for receive, a pair for every channel you want—and paying an FCC-licensed technician to install them, you can let frequency synthesis do all the work with just one reference crystal. The crystal is built into the radio, and you have only to keyboard-enter the frequencies and channels you may wish to tune. Most mariners need about five frequencies in each band, and an overall total of 30 memorized frequencies is usually plenty. The older-style crystal radios offering eleven channels simply don't offer enough frequency capability to satisfy the needs of most cruising mariners.

A synthesized set that will memorize more than 100 "user programmable" channels will allow you to preprogram not only marine frequencies, but also some of those receive-only worldwide general coverage frequencies mentioned earlier. Licensed ham operators can even program transmit-and-receive marine net frequencies. Old channels can be "erased" in favor of new ones at will.

Most single sideband transceivers offer at least 100 watts output, although there are some that put out 20 watts or less. Higher output means a stronger, more solid signal, provided the shipboard installation is a good one.

Antennas

After a good groundplane, the antenna is the second most important requirement for a solid transmitted signal. For powerboats, a fiberglass whip antenna is usually the best choice and easiest to install. Two models are available—a 23-foot "trap" antenna that doesn't need a tuner, or a 23-foot white fiberglass antenna, without traps, that does need a tuner. Either works well when tied into a good ground system, but most mariners choose the 23-foot white fiberglass whip without traps, and mount an antenna tuner below the antenna base. The trap antenna has high efficiency, but it is also fairly expensive—about $1,000—and usually needs to be "matched" after the installation, a job that must be performed by a technician.

Sailboat owners frequently elect to use a backstay or a hoisted wire (No. 14 plastic-covered copper wire is good) for an antenna. Either alternative is inexpensive, avoids the wind resistance and what some would consider the unsightliness of a long whip, and frequently gives better results. Insulators must be placed in the bottom and top of the backstay, but these incur no loss of rigging strength. If a dismasting occurs, however, the antenna will be lost when it is likely to be most in demand. A spare whip antenna should be carried for such a contingency.

An automatic antenna coupler is almost always necessary to tune up an insulated backstay or hoisted wire. With a backstay antenna, the coupler is mounted aft in the lazarette; a foil grounding strip goes to one side of the tuner, and the "hot wire" goes to the backstay on the other side. If you choose the microprocessor-controlled, relay-switching tuner, you will also need a tiny current draw from a 12-volt source to work the relays on the tuner.

There is no magic length of random wire for any particular frequency. The tuner will electrically lengthen or shorten a backstay or hoisted wire. Keeping the antenna in the clear is a big consideration, however. If your backstay or hoisted wire antenna is surrounded by a lot of other stays, you are likely to lose some energy into your rigging. By the same token, when a powerboat whip is mounted too close to a grounded tuna tower, valuable energy is lost.

Antenna Tuners

Unless a pretuned, prematched, 23-foot-whip trap antenna is used, any marine SSB set will need a separate antenna tuner to match the impedance of a whip or backstay antenna system to the set for frequencies between 2 and 25 MHz. The usual antenna tuner or coupler is weatherproof and mounts out of the way beneath the antenna system, and it can range in price from $600 to $1,000. Top-of-the-line couplers have almost unlimited frequency capabilities.

Automatic antenna tuners do not necessarily need to be the same brand-name as the SSB marine or SSB ham transceiver. There are $600 fully automatic marine antenna tuners that will work with anyone's ham set or marine sideband. All they require is 12 volts and the coax cable input to the transceiver. The output is a single wire connection that will work with any 20-foot, non-resonant, white fiberglass powerboat whip, or any length insulated backstay, sidestay, or random wire. And like all automatic antenna tuners, they require a copper foil ground.

These "universal automatic" antenna couplers receive their transmit command from the actual power in your sidebands. Good news—no longer must you run a data line between the equipment and the tuner. As soon as

An automatic antenna tuner hidden in a lazarette, firmly mounted on wooden pads epoxy-bonded to the fiberglass hull. The copper grounding foil makes a solid electrical connection to the tuner's ground terminal. This tuner will work with ham as well as marine single sideband radios and will tune any length backstay or whip within a few seconds.

SGC automatic antenna tuner with the cover off. Notice copper ground foil attached to ground lug. Any SSB transceiver, including hand sets, will work through this unique automatic antenna coupler.

the tuner senses incoming power, it automatically selects the right amount of inductance and capacitance and passes your SSB ham or marine signal on to the whip or backstay. They are over 90 percent efficient, and generally put out a slightly stronger signal than the manufacturer's own SSB tuner that only works with their own SSB radio.

FCC rules specifically permit the use of a common antenna tuner between two different SSB sets. This would allow the universal automatic antenna tuner to work from both a ham radio single sideband transceiver and a marine radio single sideband transceiver. A simple 50-ohm, two-position switch would allow the mariner to select whichever radio for the single tuner and the long wire or whip antenna setup.

On extremely small boats a six-foot, multi-band marine whip might also

Small multi-band, six-foot, SSB whip antennas might be used for ham and marine SSB frequencies.

be used for both ham and marine SSB frequencies. The whip would not require any automatic antenna tuner at all! But the whip must be placed over a horizontal rail to achieve a good groundplane and match. These $300 "all-band" whips would require the operator to select the band of operation before transmitting and receiving. This is as simple as going to the whip, plugging into the right MHz or meter band, and you are on the air. For charter operations or delivery skippers, the whip might break down into two sections, and the whip combined with a small SSB set makes a nice traveling companion for the next coastal journey.

And more good news about SSB antenna systems: no longer must a massive amount of copper foil ground be run into the hull for a good groundplane. Recent tests conducted with the professional groundplates illustrate that even the smallest groundplate will work quite nicely on long-range frequencies. As long as there is copper foil run between the groundplate and the automatic antenna tuner or whip, a terrific signal will be developed. It's that magic connection to the sea water or fresh water that really makes the difference. Do consider the groundplate as a good sound investment for long-range SSB communications.

Grounding (And Buying Tips)

Good grounding is a must for good single sideband range, the kind of range that cruise ships, supertankers, solo sailors, the Navy, and the Coast

Guard depend on. Your antenna is merely the radiating portion of the entire antenna system, and it needs to see a mirror image of itself before it will send out an SSB signal. This mirror image, called a counterpoise, is created by using sea water as a groundplane. The resulting balanced system may be compared electrically with a dipole antenna system—½ wavelength long on the frequency band of operation, with voltage and current loops equally distributed throughout the half wavelength system. In marine applications using a vertical antenna, this system is more precisely referred to as a Marconi antenna setup. The white fiberglass whip is tuned to an electrical ¼ wavelength, and the ground system will make up the other ¼ wavelength. The ground system is the counterpoise, and the antenna is the radiator. The effect is much like that of a diving board or the side of a pool on a diver or swimmer—the sea water gives your signal a solid surface to push off from. This is why ham radio operators would love to have sea water or a lake surface as their antenna ground, and why coastal commercial AM broadcast stations put their giant antenna systems in the mudflats. You can develop your own ground system with about a day's labor aboard your boat. The secrets of success lie in the exclusive use of copper foil and the provision of ample ground system surface area touching the sea water.

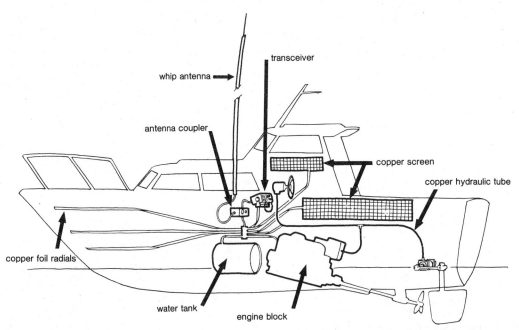

Possible components of a powerboat SSB groundplane system. Good grounding increases transmission and reception range. Copper foil works better than copper strap for radial strips and for bonding of groundplane elements.

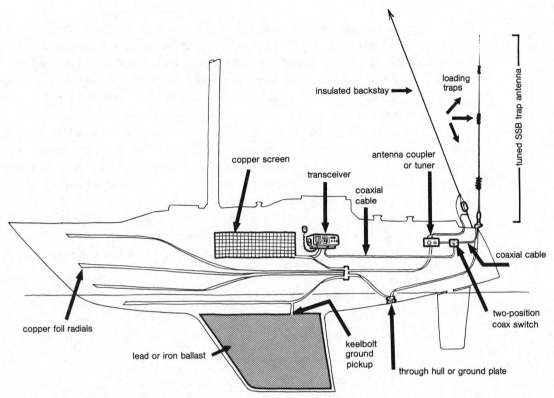

Possible sailboat groundplane system. The best and largest ground component when available is the lead or iron keel, which, even if internal, provides a capacitive ground. Two alternative antenna systems may be required in racing sailboats by the rules governing offshore events. The trap antenna shown here would be installed if a dismasting were to occur.

Consider the consequences of an inadequate ground system. The most powerful antenna will radiate no signal if it has no counterpoise to push off from. Reception and transmission ranges will be severely reduced. In technical terms, the less ground, the lower the radiation resistance of the antenna system. This resistance will lead to power loss, and the SSB equipment will not only talk poorly but will also get quite hot in the transmitter section. An inadequate ground can actually lead to a "hot mike," wherein the operator receives a radio frequency burn each time the mike is held next to his mouth. Poor grounding will also lead to erratic movement of analog dial instruments, bizarre behavior of autopilots while the SSB set is in operation, and possible burnouts in the integrated circuits of other onboard marine electronic gear.

A boat manufacturer can add a terrific ground system when the hull is being laid up. Lightweight copper screen is one of the best ways to provide a good surface area ground, and copper screen could be laminated between the fiberglass layers. Thin sheets of copper foil could also be used. Even the conducting mesh that holds ferrocement hulls together can be used quite nicely as a ground counterpoise system. Since grounding foil and screen are relatively expensive, however, most boatbuilders leave out the grounding systems and expect the customer to provide his own once the boat is finished. This is a shame—it's so easy to build in when the hull is under construction, and far more difficult to add after the vessel is completed.

Some technicians put ground foil and ground screen in the cabin overhead. This is true in expensive powerboats and in a few sailboats. While an overhead ground system is better than nothing, it lacks the capability of coupling with the ocean or lake as the ultimate ground system. For marine radio as well as for loran, a good ground system will make several contacts to the ocean below. A good ground system would include the following, in descending order of effectiveness:

- external ground copper plate
- lead keel
- metal water tanks
- steering system hydraulic lines
- 100 feet of foil below the waterline
- metal oil-catch pans
- interconnected through-hulls
- foil radials
- engine block

Note that the engine block is last on the list, because it does not have a large amount of flat surface area close to the water. The whole idea is surface area, and this is why a keel bolt, underwater tanks, through hulls, and anything flat and touching the water does such a good job.

Another very important consideration is not to use wires for ground. Even if you use welding wire the size of your thumb, you cannot achieve a good ground counterpoise with round wire. Round wires tend to cancel out at radio frequencies, and they look invisible as a ground counterpoise interconnect. This is why copper foil must be used between the chassis of your transceiver and your ship's ground, and between the chassis of the automatic antenna tuner and ship's ground. Good marine electronic stores that sell SSB equipment also sell three-inch-wide, thin (exact thickness is unimportant) copper foil, as well as copper screen, for grounding. In a pinch, you can use a one-inch-wide copper plumber's tape, but three-inch foil is better. It takes about a day to work this foil below decks and below the waterline, picking up everything of ground potential. If you can get at your keel bolt or tap a screw into the keel, your grounding is even better!

In a powerboat with no keel, you need to pick up as many ground potentials as possible. You can use a stainless steel hose clamp to grab each underwater metal source. If your vessel is bonded with a small green wire to each through hull, run your foil in parallel with the green wire and pick up all through hulls. You cannot rely on the green wire itself as an effective ground pickup.

As mentioned, copper foil must be run from the underwater ground system all the way up and attach directly to each piece of low- and high-frequency radio gear. While this may seem an insurmountable problem, foil handles quite nicely even in tight places. It is easily soldered to the underwater ground system and then routed up the side of the hull to the navigation station. It may be glassed into the hull, painted over, glued in, or even left exposed. The foil may be bent to a 90-degree turn, and if it must pass through a small hole, it may be rolled up in a not-so-tight configuration and squeezed through the orifice. Avoid a concentric-type run, which tends to cancel oscillating radio frequencies. Flat is best.

There are several sticky marine compounds that will adhere the foil to the underside of a hatch or the side of a hull. Almost anything will work, and there is little danger of any substantial voltage developing on your ground foil run. Neither will your ground system substantially change your corrosion exposure to sea water. Galvanic corrosion problems occur when dissimilar metals are immersed in sea water. Electrolysis is another form of corrosion, wherein stray currents may begin to eat up underwater metals. Good wiring techniques for your 12-volt system, independent of your ground system, will eliminate electrolysis.

The three-inch copper foil that emanates from the underwater ground system must ultimately be terminated on the instrument, but most manu-

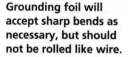

Grounding foil will accept sharp bends as necessary, but should not be rolled like wire.

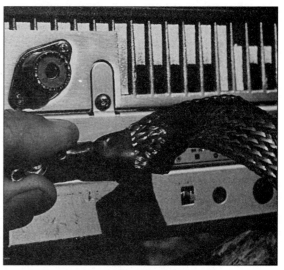

Copper foil is attached directly to the automatic antenna tuner for best grounding. Flexible braid is

attached to the ground lug on the rear of the SSB set.

facturers of marine single sideband sets (as well as loran and weather facsimile receivers) don't provide any easy way of adding ground foil to the stern end of their electronics. The best method is to run the foil up the back of the equipment and use existing sheet-metal screws to make a firm connection. Where a ground post stud with nuts and a washer is provided, all the better—run the foil to the stud, double it back on itself several times for strength, punch a hole in it, and then make the connection. Don't negate all your hard work of running the foil by using a small jumper wire to connect the foil to the radio. You would be putting a weak link in your ground system at radio frequencies.

I usually make an accordion of the excess foil in back of the equipment so that I might remove the radio for servicing with the foil attached. If you put bends in the right spots, the foil will resume its natural collapsed state when the equipment is put back in place. The sharp corners on the ground foil are capable of piercing the plastic protective covering on electrical wires, so make sure that red and black voltage-carrying wires are not allowed to rub against the side of the foil.

My personal preference is to ground everything at the navigation station with foil. This would include the casing of the wind and speed equipment, the autopilot control box, loran, radar, VHF, and just about everything else that lights up. The more grounding you provide for your central electronics, the fewer problems you will have with stray radio frequency noise.

The ground foil must also run to remote antenna tuners, including the tuner on a loran antenna setup as well as the single sideband tuner, which is usually several feet from the equipment. These tuners may be all the way aft, adding another dimension to your ground foil run. It's best to run the foil from the ground source directly to your tuner, rather than stringing everything out in series like Christmas tree lights. Picture one ground foil run from the keel bolt to the electronics, and a second ground foil run from the keel bolt aft to the sideband tuner and a stern-mounted loran whip. These tuner ground circuits are mandatory for reliable operation. If you try to run a sideband set with a remote tuner that is ungrounded, you stand the chance of not only burning up your equipment, but also damaging your other onboard electronics with stray RF. If it's not easy to run ground foil from your central underwater ground source aft, figure out another way to do it. It has to be done.

Again, you can pick up additional ground counterpoise surface area potential by adding substantial metals along your copper foil run. Stainless steel hose clamps make it easy to pick up bronze through-hull fittings, water tanks, copper hydraulic lines, bilge pump valves and copper lines, small underwater grounding plates, and anything else that may give you some additional underwater surface area.

The engine can also constitute a small percentage of the underwater ground system. You will probably require a wiper brush if you plan to use the shaft and prop as additional groundplane counterpoise. Since the gearbox is filled with oil, and oil is not a good conductor, the wiper brush is helpful not only for grounding but also for corrosion control. Some good surface area can be obtained on big powerboat propellers.

Small multi-band, six-foot, SSB whip antennas may use any horizontal stainless steel rail as the groundplane.

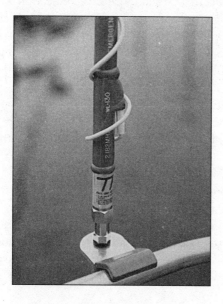

Also recommended is to pick up all through-bolts that anchor your standing rigging. By grounding your rigging you can create a zone of protection inside the rigging in case of a nearby or direct lightning hit. While lightning strikes are totally unpredictable, good grounding techniques may provide some additional safety to those inside the zone of protection. Lightning strikes on ungrounded rigging may result in discharges between stays as well as miniature lightning zaps between metals in close proximity. Good grounding will usually lead the major portion of the lightning bolt into the sea water, satisfying its quest for earth. Installers of ground systems in areas of high lightning activity should consult local lightning experts, who have developed special exit plates that will pass tremendous amounts of energy into the sea water safely, without blowing out a through-hull or popping holes in a lead keel.

Mariners with sailboats having poured, encapsulated lead keels, and those with metal-hulled vessels, have the easiest time obtaining a good ground counterpoise. If the keel is visible, a second nut on the exposed thread will anchor the ground foil. Seal this connection to prevent deterioration from the bilge water. It may also be recommended by local experts to tie in the aluminum mast to this keel bolt for lightning protection. The run from the mast to the keel bolt must be smooth, direct, and without sharp turns in order to pass lightning effectively into the underwater lead. Again, consult local experts and the American Boat and Yacht Council (ABYC) book.

Steel-hulled vessels provide easy attachment for the foil. Merely scrape away any protective coating from the hull and make a low-resistance, good-surface-area contact. Again, seal this connection well.

Installing an adequate grounding system is not simple, and you may wish to have an FCC-licensed technician do the work. If you do, expect to pay your local marine electronics dealer *at least* $700 for the work (more for a more complicated installation) *unless* you buy the transceiver from that dealer and include the installation as part of the sales package. This removes the installation charge from a strict time-and-materials basis, and it's certainly a wiser course than buying the radio from a discounter and then hiring a dealer for the installation. Insist on having the installation agreement in writing, however—along with the servicing warranty terms—and insist on further work at no extra charge if the initial installation is unsatisfactory.

A compromise is to buy from a dealer, do the time-consuming part of the installation yourself (running copper foil and screen throughout the boat, and grounding to keel bolts, etc.), then get the dealer's technician to solder the connectors, install the transceiver, and check out and certify the installation. You'll save some money, but you'll probably also lose the guarantee of any further work at no charge should the installation prove unsatisfactory.

The very compact SSB transceiver occupies little room. Everything is contained within the chassis, which can nestle right alongside the other nav gear in a typical station. The sets are not waterproof, so keep them clear of portholes or hatches that might admit water. You can, however, build the equipment into a wheelhouse instrument panel without worry of lack of ventilation. Since SSB radios are transistorized, the slight amount of heat they develop merely dries out their insides. You may well want to keep the equipment down low for easy channel selection, making it comfortable to operate. Then, some night in a cozy harbor, you can simply flip through the worldwide frequencies to pick up some action. A heavy-duty mounting bracket is shipped with each rig.

Each transceiver is shipped with a red-and-black power cord. This is the 12-volt connection, and it is fused in case you should get turned around on polarity. A 150-watt marine single sideband transceiver will draw approximately 18 amps on voice peaks. Only when you talk is current consumed in these proportions—so don't worry, you're not drawing a continuous 18 amps out of your battery while the mike button is pressed down!

It's recommended that you hook up your 12-volt connections directly to your ship's battery system. This allows you to stay on the air in case of a malfunction of your electrical panel, which is when you may need your set the most. If you have some hefty 12-volt wires leading from your buried battery compartment to your fuse panel, however, you may prefer to go ahead and make your connection at the panel. Clip off any large amount of excess power cable, but leave just enough coiled up behind the radio so it can be pulled from its mount for adjustments or examinations while turned on.

Route your power cable along the same track as your ground foil, taking care that the sharp foil edges don't nick the cable. Don't use the ground foil as the black side of the power cable—these are two separate "ground" systems. Routing them together creates a neat installation, and the foil partially shields the power cable from ignition interference.

Use wire lugs to attach the cable to a terminal strip on an electrical panel or, if the power cable does not already enter the console, on the back of the radio itself. Since the radio power lead is already fused, you do not necessarily need to go through an external circuit breaker. You can if you want to, but that adds one more weak link in your power cable assembly.

If you run the power cable to your battery system, choose a battery that is less apt to fail in an emergency. A battery located above the waterline, for example, is less vulnerable to flooding.

If you need to extend the wires supplied by the factory, use No. 6 insulated two-conductor, and make certain that any splices are well soldered or

These multi-band SSB whips may also work on ham frequencies, and band changes are accomplished by simply plugging into the band of your choice. They no longer need to be twenty to thirty feet long, either.

perfectly crimped and are well protected from the salt environment. Crimped (versus soldered) connectors are discussed in the chapter on VHF radios. Always fuse the battery connection, right beside the battery terminals.

Eliminating Noise

Once your SSB station is installed, turn it on and start listening to the bands. There will be more atmospheric noise on the lower frequencies than on the higher frequencies. With your engines and other motors turned off, this noise is just the usual background static present on every band until a signal appears. Strong signals will usually completely mask the noise, but weak signals on 2 and 4 MHz will only quiet it by about 50 percent. The more sensitive your receiver, the more atmospheric noise you are going to pick up. This is normal; any attempt to filter out atmospheric noise would cause distant radio signals to fade away too.

The type of noise that can be eliminated is that generated by your engine ignition system or by other onboard motors. Fluorescent lights also create noise that is usually heard on the lower frequencies. Onboard noise sources can be filtered at the spot where they are generated. There are filters for alternators and filters for fluorescent lights. You can put resistor spark plugs on your gas engine and tachometer filters on your electronic tachs. Fuel pumps and bait tanks can be silenced with appropriate filters.

Tune in a relatively weak signal on your SSB set, then start the engine. If the signal is still there, your noise problems are few. If the signal disappears—especially if it's a strong signal—you will need to identify noise-makers and get a filter for each. For a complete list of noise-elimination filters, see a marine electronics specialty dealer. Refer also to the chapter on noise suppression in this book.

When noises external to your boat, such as a passing skiff with an outboard, can be heard clearly on your SSB set, simply depress the noise-blanker button on the front of the radio. This will cancel out the repetitious popping sound almost completely. While it may also help dampen repetition-type noise originating on your boat, noise filters at the source are a better way to go. As in plugging leaks, you must methodically get every single one.

Going on the Air

You are required by the FCC to have a licensed marine VHF set aboard your vessel before adding marine single sideband. The same call letters are used for both, but you may need to modify your license. Dig out your marine station license and look at the authorized frequency privileges. In addition to 156–158 MHz, does it include 2,000–4,000 kHz and 4,000–26,000 kHz? If not, you will need to amend your present station license using FCC-applied-for additional frequencies.

Assuming you have a synthesized transceiver, it will have been preprogrammed by the dealer or distributor that sold you the equipment. Very likely the preprogrammed channels will closely follow the recommended channelization for a particular cruising area. Reprogramming different frequencies is easy; simply refer to your owner's manual for programming instructions.

If you followed precisely the installation instructions for transceiver and antenna tuner, you probably won't need a technician to come aboard and test everything out. The instruction manual that came with your SSB lists several ways to verify full power output. However, you do need a technician to "sign off" in your logbook and provide the FCC certificate.

Before transmitting on any frequency, listen! In fact, spend a complete week listening to different frequencies in different bands to get a feel for the protocol of marine single sideband communications.

When listening to ship-to-ship and ship-to-private-shore-station calls, you generally will hear both sides of the conversation. When tuning into the ship-to-shore marine telephone station, however, you will only hear the

An antenna farm in a California harbor. The following antennas can be combined to keep your boat from looking like a porcupine: CB and VHF; VHF and loran; weather facsimile and ham; ham and marine SSB; and AM/FM radio and TV.

shore station side of the conversation. This is because ship stations transmit on a separate (duplex) frequency when speaking to marine operators. When your turn to talk to a shore station telephone company arrives, the very professional marine telephone operators and their service technicians will ask you the necessary questions about where you are, who you are, and what number you want. Follow their instructions and you will have no problems communicating through the telephone service. The same holds true for emergency communications with the U.S. Coast Guard AMVER stations.

Your first call will probably be for a radio check. Since it's illegal to call the United States Coast Guard for this purpose, try the distant high seas marine operator. Wait until they are finished with their local weather reports before giving them a call, choosing the band that sounds the strongest to you. Marine telephone companies, if they're not really busy, are more than happy to accommodate a radio check.

You can also receive radio checks from pleasure boats that you might hear on ship-to-ship frequencies. If a station sounds weak to you, they will probably say that you are weak to them. The same applies to the telephone service—if they're not coming in strong, you won't be either. Most commercial vessels will probably ignore any calls for a radio check.

Weak signals are not necessarily a result of something wrong with your installation. Sometimes ionospheric conditions simply won't favor any band. Try the next band up—and the next band down—to improve signal reports. Try a different time of day, and expect that some days you'll have better signal levels than others. Since SSB radio waves are dependent on ionospheric conditions, it's quite normal for signal levels to change. You may also notice that signals will fade in and out on the higher frequencies—those in the 12-, 16-, and 22- MHz bands. Again, this is completely normal and should result in almost no loss of intelligibility during a call.

Another way to check the high-frequency operation of your equipment is to try and receive as many foreign broadcast stations as possible. These stations should come in loud and clear at the proper times but are subject to brief ionospheric fades. If you are hearing plenty of activity on these frequencies, plus strong signals from other boats and shore stations, your installation is probably fine, and you will enjoy worldwide communications with single sideband equipment.

If you do decide to have an FCC-licensed technician check out as well as certify your equipment, a local marine electronics dealership will likely be happy to send down a tech with the proper field-strength equipment to "sign off" your station (at a time-and-materials cost). If you installed the equipment yourself, the technician will check out your antenna tuner setup, doublecheck all connections to ensure that they are weatherproof, make some field-strength measurements, and exchange signal reports with distant stations. Since an electronic technician is quite familiar with the characteristics of single sideband frequencies, he'll know when your set is on the air and operating perfectly. If there is any way to squeeze a few more watts out of your system, he will do that, too.

There are approved procedures for making both normal and emergency calls on the marine SSB radio, procedures developed by the Radio Technical Commission for Marine Services in cooperation with the FCC. These are set forth in the *Marine Radiotelephone User's Handbook,* copies of which can be purchased from the RTCM, P.O. Box 19087, Washington, D.C. 20036. Your local Coast Guard station and books about piloting and seamanship are other sources of this information.

Before placing telephone calls, you will need to register your station with the appropriate marine telephone operators. If you plan to cruise extensively throughout the world, it's best to register with all four U.S. coast stations providing high-frequency "high seas" service. This enables you to make a phone call and have them automatically bill it. The four stations and their addresses are: Station KMI, American Telephone and Telegraph Co., P.O. Box 8, Inverness, CA 94937; Station WLO, Mobile Marine Radio, Inc., 7700 Rinla Ave., Mobile, AL 36619; Station WOM, American Telephone and Telegraph Co., 1350 N.W. 40th Ave., Fort Lauderdale, FL 33313; and Station WOO, American Telephone and Telegraph Co., P.O. Box 558, Beach Ave., Manahawkin, NJ 08050.

Each station operates on upward of 18 channels. When calling the distant marine telephone operator, remember that much of their equipment is

International Voice Channel Designators (4-16 MHz)

Channel No.	Coast Transmit (kHz)	Ship Transmit (kHz)	Channel No.	Coast Transmit (kHz)	Ship Transmit (kHz)	Channel No.	Coast Transmit (kHz)	Ship Transmit (kHz)
401	4065	4357	812	8228	8752	1230	12317	13164
402	4068	4360	813	8231	8755	1231	12320	13167
403	4071	4363	814	8234	8758	1232	12323	13170
404	4074	4366	815	8237	8761	1250	12290	Safety
405	4077	4369	816	8240	8765	1251	12353	Simplex
406	4080	4372	817	8243	8767	1252	12356	Simplex
407	4083	4375	818	8246	8770	1253	12359	Simplex
408	4086	4378	819	8249	8773	1601	16360	17242
409	4089	4381	820	8252	8776	1602	16363	17245
410	4092	4384	821	8255	8779	1603	16366	17248
411	4095	4387	822	8258	8782	1604	16369	17251
412	4098	4390	823	8261	8785	1605	16372	17254
413	4101	4393	824	8264	8788	1606	16375	17257
414	4104	4396	825	8267	8791	1607	16378	17260
415	4107	4399	826	8270	8794	1608	16381	17263
416	4110	4402	827	8273	8797	1609	16384	17266
417	4113	4405	828	8276	8800	1610	16387	17269
418	4116	4408	829	8279	8803	1611	16390	17272
419	4119	4411	830	8282	8806	1612	16393	17275
420	4122	4414	831	8285	8809	1613	16396	17278
421	4125	4417	832	8288	8812	1614	16399	17281
422	4128	4420	850	8291	Safety	1615	16402	17284
423	4131	4423	851	8294	Simplex	1616	16405	17287
424	4134	4426	852	8297	Simplex	1617	16408	17290
425	4137	4429	1201	12230	13077	1618	16411	17293
426	4140	4432	1202	12233	13080	1619	16414	17296
427	4143	4435	1203	12236	13083	1620	16417	17299
450	4125	Safety	1204	12239	13086	1621	16420	17302
451	4146	Simplex	1205	12242	13089	1622	16423	17305
452	4149	Simplex	1206	12245	13092	1623	16426	17308
453	4417	Simplex	1207	12248	13095	1624	16429	17311
601	6200	6501	1208	12251	13098	1625	16432	17314
602	6203	6504	1209	12254	13101	1626	16435	17317
603	6206	6507	1210	12257	13104	1627	16436	17320
604	6209	6510	1211	12260	13107	1628	16441	17323
605	6212	6513	1212	12263	13110	1629	16444	17326
606	6215	6516	1213	12266	13113	1630	16447	17329
650	6215	Safety	1214	12269	13116	1631	16450	17332
651	6224	Simplex	1215	12272	13119	1632	16453	17335
652	6227	Simplex	1216	12275	13122	1633	16456	17338
653	6230	Simplex	1217	12278	13125	1634	16459	17341
654	6516	Simplex	1218	12281	13128	1635	16462	17344
801	8195	8719	1219	12284	13131	1636	16465	17347
802	8198	8722	1220	12287	13134	1637	16468	17350
803	8201	8725	1221	12290	13137	1638	16471	17353
804	8204	8728	1222	12293	13140	1639	16474	17356
805	8207	8731	1223	12296	13143	1640	16477	17359
806	8210	8734	1224	12299	13146	1641	16480	17362
807	8213	8737	1225	12302	13149	1650	16520	Safety
808	8216	8740	1226	12305	13152	1651	16528	Simplex
809	8219	8743	1227	12308	13155	1652	16531	Simplex
810	8222	8746	1228	12311	13158			
811	8225	8749	1229	12314	13161			
1801	19755	18780	2209	22024	22720	2232	22093	22789
1802	19758	18783	2210	22027	22723	2233	22096	22792
1803	19761	18786	2211	22030	22726	2234	22099	22795
1804	19764	18789	2212	22033	22729	2235	22102	22798
1805	19767	18792	2213	22036	22732	2236	22105	22801
1806	19770	18795	2214	22039	22735	2237	22108	22804
1807	19773	18798	2215	22042	22738	2238	22111	22807
1808	19776	18801	2216	22045	22741	2239	22114	22810
1809	19779	18804	2217	22048	22744	2240	22117	22813
1810	19782	18807	2218	22051	22747	2251	22159	Simplex
1811	19785	18810	2219	22054	22750	2252	22162	Simplex
1812	19788	18813	2220	22057	22753	2253	22165	Simplex
1813	19791	18816	2221	22060	22756	2254	22168	Simplex
1814	19794	18319	2222	22063	22759	2255	22171	Simplex
1815	19797	18822	2223	22066	22762	2501	26145	25070

Channel No.	Coast Transmit (kHz)	Ship Transmit (kHz)	Channel No.	Coast Transmit (kHz)	Ship Transmit (kHz)	Channel No.	Coast Transmit (kHz)	Ship Transmit (kHz)
2201	22000	22696	2224	22069	22765	2502	26148	25073
2202	22003	22699	2225	22072	22768	2503	26151	25076
2203	22006	22702	2226	22075	22771	2504	26154	25079
2204	22009	22705	2227	22078	22774	2505	26157	25082
2205	22012	22708	2228	22081	22777	2506	26160	25085
2206	22015	22711	2229	22084	22780	2507	26163	25088
2207	22018	22714	2230	22087	22783	2508	26166	25091
2208	22021	22717	2231	22090	22786			

automated, and you'll need to make at least a 30-second call in order to raise their station on the first try. Giving your vessel name and call letters once won't do it. Call the marine telephone service by their call letters over and over again, repeating your vessel name and call letters many times and giving your approximate location. This gives the telephone station technicians time to select the best antenna for your incoming signal.

Ship-to-ship and ship-to-private coast shore station SSB marine channels, along with their channel designators. Safety channels are identified with a designator "S". Regular ship-to-ship channels are designated "A" through "E".

2182	SAFETY ONLY	Marine, international distress & calling Coast Guard short-range
4125		Ship-to-ship, 4S, short-range safety
6215		Ship-to-ship, 6S, short-range safety
8291		Ship-to-ship, 8S, medium-range safety
12,290		Ship-to-ship, 12S, long-range safety
16,420		Ship-to-ship, 16S, very long-range safety
2065	SHORT RANGE	Ship-to-ship, nights, short-range
2079		Ship-to-ship, nights, short-range
2096.5		Ship-to-ship, nights, short-range
3023	POPULAR SHIP TO SHIP CHANNELS	Ship-to-ship, search and rescue
4146		Ship-to-ship, 4A, short-range
4149		Ship-to-ship, 4B, short-range
4417		Ship-to-ship, 4C, daytime short-range
6224		Ship-to-ship, 6A, medium-range
6227		Ship-to-ship, 6B, medium-range
6230		Ship-to-ship, 6C, medium-range
8294		Ship-to-ship, 8A, long-range
8297		Ship-to-ship, 8B, long-range
12,353		Ship-to-ship, 12A, long-range
12,356		Ship-to-ship, 12B, long-range
12,359		Ship-to-ship, 12C, long-range
16,528	VERY LONG RANGE SHIP-TO-SHIP	Ship-to-ship, 16A, very long-range days
16,531		Ship-to-ship, 16B, long-range
16,534		Ship-to-ship, 16C, very long-range
18,840		Ship-to-ship, 18A, quiet channel, long-range
18,843		Ship-to-ship, 18B, quiet channel, very long-range
22,159		Ship-to-ship, 22B, extremely long-range
22,162		Ship-to-ship, 22C, extremely long-range
22,165		Ship-to-ship, 22D, extremely long-range
22,168		Ship-to-ship, 22E, extremely long-range

CHAPTER 7

Amateur Radio for Mariners

by Gordon West

It is now easy to obtain an amateur radio license for cruising. No longer are mariners required to be electronic engineers or master Morse code operators to pass the theory and code requirements. The FCC has lowered licensing requirements, and obtaining an amateur radio voice-class call sign is no harder than a week with a textbook, two weeks with code cassette tapes, and finding three hams to give you that entry-level Novice class examination. New rules now allow the Novice class operator to begin using voice immediately on one worldwide band and two VHF repeater bands. In years past, the Novice was only allowed code privileges. That's all changed now, as the FCC attempts to generate more interest in ham radio and encourage mariners who have been operating on ham frequencies without a license to become legal operators.

Licensing

The FCC Notice of Proposed Rulemaking Docket 83-27 outlines a volunteer examination program in which local hams have taken over the responsibility of giving tests. Public Law 97-259 amended the Communications Act of 1934, and that allowed the FCC to make this change. No longer will exam questions be kept secret. The questions, as well as the four multiple-choice answers for each, are now public domain. These question-and-answer test guides are similar to the FAA airman's study manuals that have been around for many years. The FCC, as well as the FAA, feels that if the applicant knows all the questions and answers that could be on the examination, they surely are qualified to become a pilot or amateur radio operator. While not all amateur radio operators agree with this new philosophy, the successful passing rate of amateur radio written and code examinations has dramatically increased.

Three classifications of license are most appealing to the cruising mariner. Licenses are additive—in other words, you can't skip over a license to take a higher-grade test. All the license exams can be taken in one sitting, however, if you're good at an all-day exam session.

Novice License. This is the traditional entry-level license. The theory test will consist of 30 questions taken out of a pool of 300 published questions on elemental electronics and basic rules and regulations. The 30-question test is multiple choice and does not require the drawing of any schematics. The theory exam is easily passed with only three or four weeks of study.

A five-words-per-minute (wpm) code sending and receiving test is also required for passing the Novice test. It takes only about 30 days to learn the international Morse code at this rate.

The test is administered by volunteer examiner hams who hold a General class or higher ticket and are at least 18 years of age. The volunteer hams will choose the questions from the 300-question pool in certain categories. The test may be verbal, written, or a combination of both, and the code test is simply a typical transmission of one ham to another with you copying down what was sent. You must send a few words, too, to demonstrate your ability to send code with a hand key. It takes only about eight weeks for call letters to arrive.

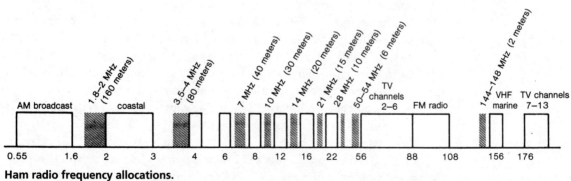

Ham radio frequency allocations.

The Novice class license-holder now has voice and digital computer privileges on the amateur radio worldwide 10-meter band, on the popular 222-MHz repeater band, and on the 1270-MHz repeater band. These new privileges, in addition to the previously existing worldwide code privileges, will certainly entice more mariners into obtaining this license. The Novice class operator is allowed 200 watts of power output.

Technician Class. The Technician class license test requires no code test or no further code as a novice—just the successful passing of 25 questions (multiple-choice answers) from a pool of 250 published questions and answers. I've seen people memorize the test guidebooks over a weekend and pass the Tech test with flying colors. While I don't recommend this type of cramming, it can be done. The questions cover intermediate electronics knowledge and knowledge of the rules and regulations. If you study published question-and-answer test guides, the examination will be identical to the material you have reviewed. The test is taken in front of three licensed ham radio operators appointed by a volunteer exam coordinator (VEC) to administer higher-grade ham radio exams. There are volunteer examination teams all over the country, and the examinations are usually offered almost on a weekly basis. The successful passing of the examination allows immediate use of the new privileges.

No-code and Technician-plus class operators may use voice on the 10-meter band, the very popular two-meter repeater band, and on the 222-MHz, 450-MHz, 902-MHz, and 1250-MHz bands. On these bands are repeaters, automatic telephone patch stations, fellow mariners, and even access to the ham radio orbiting satellites. The Technician class operator may use up to 1,500 watts of power output.

The new no-code amateur radio examination makes it easy to obtain the Technician voice class license. For the first time in amateur radio history, it is no longer necessary to pass a Morse code test for your ham radio call letters. That's right, mariners wishing to stay in touch on those fabulous repeater frequencies no longer need to pass a code test.

The amateur radio no-code license will require the mariner to pass a simple 30-question, multiple-choice, written Novice exam and a simple 25-question, multiple-choice Technician test. Both tests are administered by fellow ham radio operators as volunteer examiners. The team of three volunteer examiners could even test you aboard your boat.

The no-code Technician class license allows you to operate on frequencies from 50 MHz on up. This includes the popular six-meter band, two-meter band, 222-MHz band, 440-MHz band, 900 MHz, 1270 MHz, and more. On these bands you will find long range repeater networks capable of extending the range of your VHF ham equipment by hundreds of miles. Orbiting satellites can also be used by the no-code Technician class operator on these bands. Telephone autopatch privileges, too—all without having to take the dreaded Morse code test!

But the Morse code examination is still required for the higher-grade General class license. It's the General ticket that allows you full use of all of the worldwide bands. But that's something you can do after you get on the airwaves—so start out your ham radio career by obtaining the new no-code license for Technician privileges. My exclusive amateur radio licensing books (there are five) are available from all Radio Shack stores throughout the country. Just look for the Gordon West name on it, and see how easy it is to get your amateur radio no-code set of call letters with two simple multiple-choice written examinations, or an upgrade to General, Advanced, and Extra class.

General Class. This is still the big one for mariners. The General class license permits voice operation on the worldwide frequencies. Worldwide ham radio nets are all centered on these frequencies, so the avid mariner should set his sights on the General class ticket.

A 25-question written test is required, as well as a 13-wpm code test. It takes about 60 days using code tapes to go from five to 13 wpm; you're not required to transmit—only to receive a common text as if one ham were transmitting to another. The tests are administered by three volunteer examiners appointed by a volunteer exam coordinator. These volunteers can be fellow mariners who have an Extra class ticket. While notice of the exams must be published ahead of time, they can be given at yacht clubs, marinas, or even aboard cruising boats.

What happens if you should fail an examination element? Until recently, you were required to wait 30 days before retaking that element, but now the FCC has dropped the 30-day waiting period, and most volunteer examiners will let you retake any failed element the next day. Mariners may take the examination on Monday, fail it, and retake it Tuesday evening. If they fail it again, they can take it again on Wednesday, and again on Thursday if necessary. Since all questions are published, there is little chance that someone would fail it four times in a row.

A ham radio class is the best way to earn your ham radio license. Besides presenting the questions and answers on the exam, classroom study will allow the instructor to give you operating techniques, make equipment recommendations, and show you the fine art of intercommunicating on the ham radio bands. Home-study courses constitute another alternative. Courses specifically for mariners not only cover the questions and answers, but also give recommendations on marine antenna systems, grounding, and equipment best suited for the marine environment. Available from this author is a complete radio licensing course containing code and theory cassettes, theory books, a practice code oscillator setup, FCC paperwork, and a practice and real Novice class examination that you can have a fellow ham administer to you. Write to Gordon West Radio School, 2414 College Dr., Costa Mesa, CA 92626.

What's Available

The "big three" in ham radio are Kenwood, Yaesu, and ICOM. While there are a half dozen other ham radio equipment manufacturers, these three offer the best value in transistorized transceivers that can easily be modified to work on marine single sideband frequencies in an emergency.

Kenwood, Yaesu, and ICOM all offer $850, compact, worldwide, high-frequency ham transceivers that tune everything between your RDF band (200 kHz) and 29.990 MHz (the top of the 10-meter ham band). These sets operate at 100 watts output single sideband, and are almost identical in their performance with the more expensive marine single sideband radios. In fact, in an emergency, as will be seen, a simple modification to your ham band set will allow it to transmit on any marine frequency to signal for help.

These $850 transceivers operate right off 12 volts. A separate power converter (for about $150) is necessary if you plan to use the unit at home on 110 volts AC. Since these 12-volt radios don't contain the big transformer power supply, their size is quite compact. They require almost no ventilation, and as long as you keep them from getting wet, they'll perform well aboard your boat. Incidentally, there is absolutely no difference between the insides of a marine single sideband set and a ham radio set when it comes to moistureproofing.

You may be asking, "Why not buy a ham radio at half the price of a marine single sideband and use one radio for two services?" For one thing, it's not legal. The FCC specifically forbids a ham set to be used on marine

This amateur radio transceiver features 100 memory channels, ideal for storing marine ship-to-ship frequencies for monitoring.

frequencies. Can the FCC tell if you are doing so? Absolutely not, unless they visit your boat. The frequency stability, power output, and modulation characteristics are identical. Nevertheless, the practice is strictly illegal and should be avoided. For mariners without ham radio experience, the ham set is too complicated to consider using on marine frequencies as a substitute for a marine sideband. Marine sideband sets are simple to operate—idiot-proof in fact—with a minimum of knobs. Everything is preprogrammed, and you simply turn one knob for the right frequency, pick up the mike, and start talking. On the face of a ham set, there are usually no fewer than 20 knobs and buttons. Frequencies are dialed in megahertz rather than in channel numbers. Marine telephone and Coast Guard channels are all duplex (separate transmit and receive), so you would have to load two different sets of frequencies into your ham radio variable frequency oscillators in order to work these services in an emergency. Then you must remember to push the split button to have your set transmit on one frequency and receive on another. And you must, of course, be sure to select the right sideband—all marine channels are upper sideband.

The well-seasoned ham can easily dial in marine frequencies on a ham set in an emergency. Otherwise, legally, the ham set should not be used on any marine channel, although in the real world of radio the avid ham routinely misuses his set for this specific purpose.

Another choice when purchasing a ham radio setup is between a built-in or an external automatic antenna tuner. One or the other is necessary for most marine installations. Transceivers with built-in automatic antenna tuners are recommended if you plan to operate mobile whip antennas (one per band) on the stern of your sailboat. Each time you change bands, you must change the mobile whip to correspond with the new frequency you

The fully automatic antenna tuner mounts away from the SSB, in a locker or lazarette. There are no controls to adjust. The automatic tuner is the best way to match an SSB transceiver to any type of antenna and ground system.

plan to use. The most popular ham bands are 15 meters, 20 meters, 40 meters, and 80 meters for maritime mobile operation. You will also need specially tuned whips to cover the marine 4-, 6-, 8-, and 12-MHz Coast Guard channels. Although these whips are "pretuned," the built-in automatic tuner will help trim out any anomalies of your ground system. (Review SSB grounding in the previous chapter.) These built-in tuners allow a perfect match to well-installed mobile whips.

Built-in automatic tuners will *not,* however, work with random wire antennas, insulated backstays, or the nonresonant powerboat 23-foot white fiberglass whip. This type of antenna system requires a "reactance-type" long wire tuner. These boxes are always separate from the transceiver, mounted way aft or directly under a powerboat whip. ICOM offers a $450 fully automatic long wire tuner, Model AH-2. With a good ground system, it will automatically tune any ham or marine frequency with any wire longer than 15 feet but shorter than 150 feet.

Kenwood and Yaesu also offer remote-mounted, fully automatic long wire antenna tuners. You might also choose the Stephens Model 1612 and SGC 230 fully automatic tuners that work with *any* marine or ham SSB set. These $600 boxes do it all!

Installation Tips

The method of installing a ham radio is identical to that for a marine single sideband set. You need a good, hefty 12 volts, a superb ground system (see the single sideband chapter), and an antenna system that is either pretuned using mobile whips or a dipole, or automatically tuned with a long

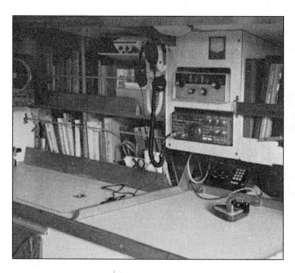

Neat ham radio installations, each coupled to a backup antenna tuner. Manual antenna tuners are normally not recommended for ham installations aboard boats.

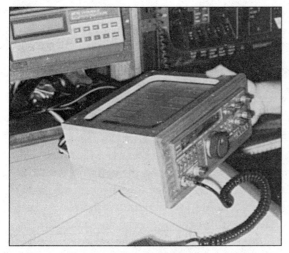

A ham set withdrawn from its console, revealing a glimpse of the grounding foil behind. This is a good installation: the unit is comfortable to operate in its normal position; it is easy to remove for servicing; and the console protects it and the other electronic gear.

A manual antenna tuner can be used with a single sideband transceiver, but SSB operators usually choose a more expensive automatic tuner as a matter of convenience. Many hams, on the other hand, don't mind fiddling with these three dials to match the impedances of antenna and transceiver every time they change bands. This device can be tough to tune, however, so hams, too, often settle on automatic tuners instead.

wire antenna tuner if you plan to use a single, nonresonant whip (for powerboats) or an insulated backstay. Attempting to tune up your standing rigging is hazardous, although it could work in a pinch, and the same applies to trying to tune up your lifelines with a manual tuner. Although it might work, the results would be unpredictable, and there is the likelihood of a nasty burn if anyone were to touch the backstay or lifelines while you were transmitting.

The modern ham radio allows you to tune in any frequency in the shortwave spectrum with ease. You can receive weather facsimile broadcasts, 24-hour English language news, military and Coast Guard weather reports, international "spy" broadcasts, and just about anything else on the radio dial. You can also use a ham set to tune in the AM broadcast band, the Citizens Band, and the marine radio beacon service.

Amateur Radio Considerations

Ham radio is not a replacement for a marine SSB radio. A look at what ham radio can and cannot do for the mariner will clarify this frequent point of confusion and summarize this chapter:

- There are numerous maritime mobile "nets" through which ham radio operators who share similar sailing interests stay in touch.

These informal nets get together at designated times of day and exchange weather reports, traffic lists, and other information, and shoreside ham stations are happy to help their counterparts far out at sea by "patching" a phone call to home through the land telephone lines or by ordering emergency parts. In fact, shoreside ham stations can be of great help in any emergency situation.

- Amateur radio operators engaged in local and coastwise cruising frequently carry 144-to-148-MHz VHF/FM radios (commonly known as "two-meter rigs") aboard. These sets are almost identical in size to the 25-watt marine VHF sets, and the ham VHF set can be tied into the marine VHF antenna system with a coaxial, two-position switch. The ham operator can use his two-meter set to call shoreside stations directly or through "repeaters" and get access to local phone patches. Local telephone calls patched this way are free.

- If you're only looking for a way to avoid the marine operators on VHF or SSB frequencies and make cheap phone calls to your home or business, forget it. No business calls are allowed, and that includes the routine (as opposed to emergency) ordering of parts or supplies. Calls must be of a personal nature. Furthermore, ham radio is a self-regulating hobby, and the primary purpose of obtaining a ham license is to share the enjoyment of communicating with fellow operators worldwide. Shoreside ham radio operators aren't interested in being used strictly as telephone operators.

- The installation of amateur single sideband and VHF equipment is identical to that of marine SSB and VHF equipment. Since both types of systems use frequencies very close to each other, the elements of the installations are precisely the same. A ham single sideband set will use the marine SSB antenna system and frequently the same automatic antenna tuner. Only in an emergency, however, may a VHF or SSB ham set be used on marine frequencies. It is also possible to modify a ham single sideband set to transmit on marine frequencies but only for emergency purposes. The Japanese have recently introduced a two-meter ham radio handheld that will tune in marine VHF frequencies with no modification, too. Either practice is strictly illegal except in an emergency, and a ham could lose his license if caught operating non-type-accepted (under Part 80 of the FCC regulations) equipment on marine frequencies.

- Synthesized SSB sets are now available with sufficient frequency capability to give you access to ham SSB frequencies (at 4, 7, 10, 14, and 21 MHz). When you have the appropriate ham license, and only then, you can transmit on these frequencies using your synthesized marine SSB set. Marine sets with ham radio capabilities are a good investment because the two services are almost identical in frequency, power output, and transmission mode.

Top left. An unusual but practical ham radio antenna system capable of working the world, ar.y time of day or night.

Top right. An insulated backstay connection between the automatic tuner and the insulated stay. GTO-15 wire is used for this.

Bottom left. A ham radio single sideband whip installation. The grounded rail acts as a counterpoise. Be sure to seal the exposed coax connector.

Bottom right. Antenna maintenance includes tightening all connectors once a year. Also inspect for broken or cracked fiberglass shafts; they may be mended or replaced.

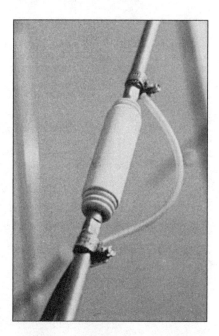

TIME(UTC)	FREQ(MHz)	NET NAME/DESIGNATOR	DAYS	AREAS	INFO:	CONTACT
1400	7.292	Florida Coast Net		FLORIDA	TFC	
1400+	3.968	SONRISA NET	DAILY	BAJA/CAL	R/C, M/M	WA6VZH
1500**	7.193	Alaska Net		ALASKA	TFC	
1445+	7.294	CHBASCO NET	DAILY	BAJA/CAL	M/M TFC	XE2VJD
1600/1500+	7.238.5	BAJA CAL MAR NET	DAILY	BAJA/CAL	(EX KATES NAVY)	N6ADJ
1600>2200+	14.300/313	MAR MOBILE SERV NET	DAILY	ATL/CAR	(ALSO 2400)	KA8O
1630	14.303	SWEDISH MAR NET	DAILY	IND OC	ALSO 0530/2030	
1630	21.350	Pitcairn Net	FRI	SO PAC	TFC	VR6TC
1630+	7.263	RV Service Net	M-F	W/COAST	REC VEH TFC	K6BYP
1700+	14.340	Cal-Hawaii NET	DAILY	CAL/HAW	TFC	K6VDV
1700+	7.240	BEJUKA M/M NET	M-F	C/AMER/PANAMA	M/M	HP3XWB
1700	14.313	INTERNATIONAL M/M NET	DAILY	ATL/MED/CAR	(ALSO 0630)	DK0SS?
1730+	14.292	Alaska-Pacific Net	M-F	ALASKA/PAC	(SOURDOUGH)	KL7IJT?
1730+	14.115	CANADIAN DDD M/M NET	M-F	PAC	(SUMMER, ALSO 0400)	VE7CEM
1800>1900+	14.285	KAFFEE KLATCH UN-NET	MWSa	HAW/TAHITI	"NEWS" M/M	KH6S
1800+	14.303	UK MARITIME NET		ATL/MED	(ALSO 0800)	G4ETO
1800	28.303	GORDON ON THE AIR		M/M Info		WB6NOA
1800	7.076	SO PAC CRUISING NET	DAILY	SO PAC	WX/HARBOR-INFORMAL	
1830+	14.342	MANAMA M/M NET-W/UP	M-Sa	W/C-E/PAC	W/U	KB5HA
1900/1800+	14.305	CONFUSION NET	M-F	PAC/ALASKA	M/M	W7GYR
1900+	14.342	MANANA M/M NET	M-Sa	W/C-E/PACBAJA	WX M/M	KB5HA
1900	7.255	WEST PACIFIC NET		WPAC		
1900**	7.285	HAWAII M/M NET	DAILY	HAWAII	WX,	KH6BF
1900	21.390	Halo Net		N/S AMER	TFC	
1700>1900+	14.280	Int Mission RA Net	M-Sa	C/S AMER/CARR	TFC	WA2KUX
1900+	14.329	BAY OF ISLE NET	DAILY	NZ-S/PAC	(COLIN'S) M/M	ZL1BKD
1900**	3.855	FRIENDLY NET		HAWAII		KH6BF?
1900	3.990	NORTHWEST MAR NET		PAC NW		
2000	3.970	Noontime net	DAILY	WASHINGTON	TFC	W7UU
2000+	7.095	HARRYS NET	DAILY	WEST/SO PAC	M/M	KL7MZ
2000>2200+	21.390	Inter Amer Tfc Net		N/S/C AMER	TFC	
2030	14.303	SWEDISH MAR NET	DAILY	ATL OC	ALSO 0530/1630	
2100+	14.315	TONY'S NET		NZ/SO PAC	WX, M/M	ZL1ATE
2130	14.290	E/C WATERWAY NET		E/C USA	M/M	
2200	3.930	West Indies SSB Net	DAILY	P/R-V/I	TFC	WP4BCV
2200	21.350	Pitcairn Net	TUES	SO PAC	TFC	VR6TC
2200+	21.402	PACMAR M/M NET WARM UP	M-F	PAC-BAJA	ALSO 0200	KB7DHQ
2200+	21.412	PAC MAR NET-15 MTR	M-F	PAC	(ALL) M/M	KA6GWZ
2200	3.940	Sea Gull Net	M-S	Maine	TFC	K1GUP
2230	3.815	Caribbean WX Net		CAR	WX (ALSO 1030)	VP2AYL?
2230	3.958	Mass/Rhode Isl Net	DAILY	Mass-R/I	TFC	N1BGW
2200>2400+	14.300/313	INTERCON NET	DAILY	N/S/C AMER	(ALSO 1100)	K4PT
2310	3.930	Puerto Rico WX Net	DAILY	P/R-V/I	WX (ALSO 1110)	KP4AET?
2330	21.325	So Atl Roundtable		SO ATL	(ALSO 1130)	
2400>0200+	14.300/313	MAR MOBILE SERV NET	DAILY	CAR/BAJA/PAC	ALSO 1600	KA8O
2400	14.320	S E A M/M NET	DAILY	S&W PAC/SEA	(ROWDY'S)	VS6BE
AS NEEDED+	14.325	HURRICANE NET		A/R ATL/CAR/PAC	EMER WX	

List Provided by: W6SOT

LEGEND:

R/C = Roll Call, Passage Maker Positions Taken; WX = Weather Info Available; W/U = Warm Up Session - Check Ins; E/C = East Coast; W/C = West Coast; C/A = Central America; G/C = Gulf Coast; CW = Morse Code Net; Atl = Atlantic; Car = Caribbean; Med = Mediterranean, M/M= Maritime Mobile, "+" = Info checked from several sources. "**" = No current information –probably outdated; ">" = From/To times of net. Dual times listed "/" = Standard to daylight, or winter to summer time changes.

CHAPTER 8

Weather Facsimile Reception

by Gordon West

Weather facsimile equipment enables the mariner to receive satellite images and charts prepared by weather bureaus, a development of immense usefulness to offshore navigators tracking weather systems to find favorable winds and avoid storms. There has been a dramatic recent departure from the tried and proven marine weather facsimile equipment in that you can now print weather fax charts on a shipboard computer or use a television adapter to see and store charts on a shipboard television or video system.

How It Works

"Radiofacsimile" is the descriptive term for sending pictures and maps over radio frequencies. Specific frequency tones translate as white, shades of gray, and black images when scanned electronically twice a second to produce a chart or satellite imagery. There are approximately 40 radiofacsimile weather broadcasting stations throughout the world, and they transmit on shortwave frequencies that may be tuned in with any quality shortwave receiver or general coverage ham set. Although areas of coverage and types of transmitted weather information vary, almost all stations offer the following:

- Satellite imagery
- Surface weather analysis and pressure systems
- Surface weather prognosis for 24 and 36 hours
- Extended surface prognosis for up to five days
- Ocean wave analysis, including height and direction
- Ocean wave prognosis
- Iceberg analysis, or water temperature zones

On the Pacific Coast, weather facsimile stations are more likely to offer water temperature charts than iceberg analyses. On the Atlantic Coast, you can get both.

In the United States, weather charts are prepared (handwritten) by either the Navy or the National Weather Service. The Navy charts are complex and detailed, and it takes a trained weather map reader to receive their full value. The National Weather Service tends to generalize on their charts, making them as readable as possible for mariners who may not have a long background in chart interpretation.

The high-powered transmitting stations are usually government supported—by the Coast Guard, Air Force, or Navy in the United States. A few stations are privately funded in connection with the National Weather Service. Each station broadcasts its weather charts on a specific schedule, but, unfortunately, broadcasts are often late. On manual machines, a lot of paper can be wasted waiting for a weather chart to come on line. The charts are transmitted simultaneously on several different frequency bands, some of which, such as 4 MHz, 6 MHz, and 8 MHz, propagate better at night than during the day, while others, including 12 MHz, 16 MHz, and 22 MHz, propagate better during the day. A mariner has only to tune in the band that offers the best reception for his particular area of cruising. Within 1,000 miles of the transmitting station, 4 or 8 MHz might be the best bet, while 3,000 miles away and in the daytime, the 12 or 16 MHz band is the better choice.

The weather charts are updated every six hours, and satellite images are updated whenever new pictures are available. Due to the loss of several weather satellites during launch, the number of satellite pictures may be limited to only two or three per day.

You can receive a list of weather facsimile transmitting stations by writing S.S.C., 615 S. El Camino Real, San Clemente, CA 92672 or calling (714) 498-5784, and if you are really interested in weather forecasting, you may wish to order their radiofacsimile instruction book for $5. S.S.C., one of approximately 10 manufacturers of weather facsimile equipment, has

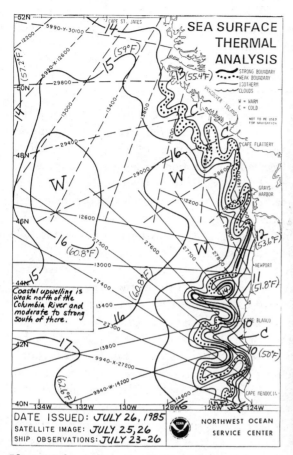

SEA SURFACE THERMAL ANALYSIS

STRONG BOUNDARY
WEAK BOUNDARY
ISOTHERM
CLOUDS

W = WARM
C = COLD

NOT TO BE USED
FOR NAVIGATION

Coastal upwelling is
weak north of the
Columbia River and
moderate to strong
South of there.

DATE ISSUED: JULY 26, 1985
SATELLITE IMAGE: JULY 25, 26
SHIP OBSERVATIONS: JULY 23-26

NORTHWEST OCEAN
SERVICE CENTER

Above. Information on water temperature is
transmitted by weather facsimile stations.

Right. Satellite imagery from a weather fax. The
portion reproduced here is at full size.

been a pioneer in the field, and they have contributed greatly to the advancement of weather facsimile for mariners.

What's Available

The shipboard weather facsimile installation consists of a 3-to-30-MHz shortwave receiver with single sideband capabilities, an antenna and ground system, and a printer. The more advanced setups feature a specialized receiver that scans for the best band of reception, automatically activates and stops the recorder when chart broadcasts are started and stopped, and can be programmed to receive weather broadcasts from stations on different bands at different times of day. Thanks to smart, microprocessor-based receivers, all of this scanning, starting, stopping, and prioritizing is done electronically with little additional cost to the customer.

The traditional weather facsimile system contains the receiver and printer in one housing. As an alternative, for the mariner who already possesses a good single sideband receiver, there are separate rotating drum recorders available. Drum recorders, which are also used in the traditional weather facsimile packages, first used wet paper to "burn" their images, but the paper has a tendency to dry out, and year-old, sealed paper is simply not the same as brand-new wet paper. It also costs at least $25 per roll, and today there are almost no wet-paper machines left. The papers now used in drum rollers won't dry out, and they give high-resolution prints. These papers may be illuminized, electrosensitive, or thermosensitive, each type having its strong points. Illuminized gives the sharpest picture but is the

Conventional weather facsimile receiver and recorder, built into one nice neat unit.

A weather fax converter will link a shortwave receiver to a computer printer, providing charts similar to the sea surface thermal analysis shown earlier.

most expensive. Thermo and electrosensitive papers give good readouts and cost less per roll. A single weather chart requires approximately eight inches of paper and 10 minutes, with the unit scanning at 120 times per minute. The process is similar to the stylus depthsounder, in which the rotating stylus will eventually print out a picture that is recognizable.

You may not need a complete weather facsimile setup if you presently own a small PC-type laptop or fixed computer system. Just a little shortwave receiver capable of tuning in upper sideband, and a hunk of wire, and you are ready to use your computer for 17 shades of gray weather facsimile reception.

Older weather FAX receivers may recover only about 10 out of 17 shades of gray in their presentation. While 10 shades of gray is not bad, 17 shades of gray will give you sparkling satellite imagery. Your computer has enough built-in memory to store all of the information being received. Since the transmission of weather FAX signals are on common shortwave bands, any type of shortwave receiver with upper sideband capabilities might work well. Important—not all cheap shortwave portable receivers have upper sideband, so check it out carefully. Radio Shack has a couple of models with USB/LSB shortwave capabilities, and these sets are excellent.

Everything for weather facsimile reception is on a small disk program and the supplied interconnect cable. One end of the cable plugs into your PC's COMM port, and the other end of the cable is fitted with a miniature phone plug that plugs into your shortwave receiver. The supplied disk goes into the disk drive. It contains full instructions on how to turn your laptop or home computer into a modern weather facsimile monitor and chart printer. The FSK demodulator is built inside the dB 25-pin plug.

The minimum system requirements to run the weather facsimile programs are:

- IBM PC compatible with 320K memory
- CGA, EGA, VGA, LCD or monochrome graphics

- 1 serial port
- MS-DOS Version 2.1 or higher
- Optional printer

Laptop computers make great weather facsimile receivers. The higher the resolution of the laptop LCD screen, the better the resolution of your incoming pictures. Laptop screens are good, but they don't give half the detail you would get with a color CRT, run in black and white, with VGA or CGA graphics.

One of your most important considerations for weather facsimile equipment is what you may already have on board. Do you already have a shortwave receiver or ham set or SSB? If so, you don't need a weather FAX system with a built-in receiver—you already have one.

Do you have a computer at your navigation station or chart table? If you do have a computer, I think it makes good sense to tie it in as a weather facsimile system. Why not use what you might already have on board, rather than buy a piece of equipment that only serves the one purpose of decoding the weather. Get more use out of the computers already on board!

But there is also something to say for the dedicated weather facsimile equipment—it may be preprogrammed to turn on and off at specific times, and this allows for the unattended reception of weather FAX charts. It might also scan between several different weather FAX channels. This is a lot more than what you would get by marrying your PC computer and the small shortwave receiver or SSB set.

And just think . . . if you already have a PC on board, and a marine SSB on board, you are only $99 away from having a complete weather facsimile station. And that's pretty cheap for seeing all the weather around you, electronically!

A shortwave receiver is another, receive-only alternative to a ham radio or SSB transceiver for weather fax reception. It will receive weather facsimile broadcasts if, as in the shortwave receiver sections of the dedicated weather facsimile sets manufactured by S.S.C. and others, it has single sideband capabilities. As mentioned, the shortwave receiver may be built into the weather facsimile housing or housed as a separate module. Ham radio manufacturers such as ICOM, Kenwood, and Yaesu offer high-quality nonportable shortwave receivers that will tune in and lock onto weather facsimile signals in the single sideband mode. The Sony 2010 portable shortwave receiver can also be used with good results, but Sony and Radio Shack are the only manufacturers of portable shortwave sets that offer single sideband reception. Like a ham or SSB transceiver, a shortwave set needs to be wired to a recorder or computer printer to produce a chart.

The antenna system need be nothing more than a fiberglass whip or even a long piece of wire run up in the rigging. Wire with a plastic insulating

Weather facsimile chart reception from home or laptop PC–compatible computer. Most computers will do the job nicely with the $99 software available from several sources.

sleeve should pick up lower as well as higher bands. Weather facsimile antennas that are tuned broadband are also available from many manufacturers; Metz leads the pack with their stainless steel antenna, which can be stowed out of sight. All antenna installations require a good RF ground for maximum reception on SSB frequencies. The principles of grounding are discussed in the single sideband chapter.

Another form of digital weather information is from a NAVTEX receiver. Mariners may now have up-to-date weather information—and a wide range of important navigation and safety data—presented in a convenient report, with a range of 200 miles or more from shore. The NAVTEX receiver is about the same size as a loran set, and it has a keyboard control, an LCD readout that indicates the types of incoming messages, and selected operating modes. A built-in dot matrix printer uses three-inch thermal paper for reading out the NAVTEX messages. NAVTEX, the abbreviation for navigational telex, is the international marine radio telex system implemented as part of the global maritime distress and safety system, sponsored by International Maritime Organization and International Hydrographic Organization. IMO plans to require NAVTEX receivers on ships over 300 gross tons after August 1, 1993. This rulemaking will assure continued expansion of NAVTEX transmitting coverage.

Currently there are 43 NAVTEX transmitting stations in 19 countries worldwide. Six NAVTEX stations are operating today off the East Coast of North America, and six new NAVTEX stations are scheduled to be operating off the West Coast shortly.

NAVTEX stations transmit messages 24 hours a day to NAVTEX receivers within a range of 200 or more miles from shore. These messages include maritime safety information, such as navigation and meteorologic warnings, search and rescue alerts, weather forecasts, ice reports, pilot service data, local mariner notices, plus loran-C and GPS system messages. NAVTEX units receive and check continuously transmitted messages to determine if messages have been received before and if they are of preprogrammed interest.

The NAVTEX receiver operates with a commercial long wire antenna or a small active antenna. Messages are transmitted over the NAVTEX 518 kHz receiver frequency, using SITOR signal processing. Although NAVTEX is truly designed for the big commercial boat, it doesn't mean that small boat mariners can't take advantage of the incoming information by also tuning in.

There are even some weather facsimile systems that allow for NAVTEX reception, too. This is handy—your computer doubles as a NAVTEX receiver along with its extra capabilities of weather facsimile reception. Now have I sparked your interest in purchasing a small PC laptop computer for your navigation station? Digital transmissions are the latest thing in staying in touch about weather and other important information bulletins.

Another source of weather information is from a NAVTEX low-frequency receiver and NAVTEX recorder system. This is normally found on larger yachts.

CHAPTER 9

Radio Direction Finders

by Gordon West and Freeman Pittman

Just below the AM broadcast radio band are the frequencies allocated for radio beacon navigation. The U.S. Coast Guard operates about 200 marine radio beacon stations that dot the coastline and islands in all U.S. cruising areas, and every major boating area and seaport worldwide maintains similar stations. To use them for position-finding or course-holding you need a fairly simple electronic device—a radio direction finder, or RDF.

With all the publicity loran and GPS navigation systems have received in recent years, RDF has been all but forgotten. Yet it's an excellent choice as a backup in case one of the newer, more precise systems fails. And RDF is an easy system to use. Furthermore, there are many areas of the world outside the continental United States where loran signals are inaccurate or nonexistent (such as Hawaii, most of the Caribbean, and the waters between Baja California and Panama). And a GPS receiver can still be higher-priced than an RDF designed for the recreational market (though GPS prices are continuing to trend downward).

The federal plan for RDF is for the station count to fall to around 150 by the year 2003, as projected users—mainly commercial—dwindle from the current estimated 500,000 to around 300,000. But there are no plans to terminate the system. They are presently carrying differential GPS signals on their sub-carriers, too.

The Radio Beacon Network

The "point source" radio beacons in the Coast Guard's RDF network transmit on frequencies between 275 and 335 kHz. All marine radio beacon locations are indicated on marine charts, and frequencies and broadcast schedules are given in the Defense Mapping Agency's publications No. 117A and No. 117B, *Radio Navigational Aids*. Some local marine electronics dealers give away frequency lists that include local radio beacons. Aeronautical radio beacons (190 to 415 kHz and 510 to 535 kHz) operated by the FAA can also be used for direction finding; these are sometimes located on marine charts, or you can pencil in their precise locations if you know them. Aeronautical charts will show the locations of these beacons. Finally, commercial AM broadcast stations (550 kHz to 990 kHz) may be used for direction-finding purposes if the transmitters are advantageously located and precisely known.

Radiobeacon System Characteristics

Predictable Accuracy	Availability	Coverage	Reliability	Fix Rate	Fix Dimension	Capacity	Ambiguity Potential
Marine ± 3°	99%	Out to 50nm or 100 fathom curve	99%	Function of the type of beacon: continuous or sequenced	One LOP per beacon	Unlimited	Potential is high for reciprocal bearing without sense antenna

Radio beacon system characteristics, from the Federal Radionavigation Plan.

Direction-finding Receivers

Unfortunately, as RDF has been forsaken by many navigators who opt for a loran or GPS receiver, choices in RDF hardware have been severely limited. You must search manufacturers' product lists and mail-order catalogs carefully to find affordable models.

There are two basic types of radio direction finders for tuning in "point source" stations on radio beacon and AM broadcast band frequencies. One category includes the portable "desktop" and the handheld radio direction finder (RDF), either of which can cost as little as $200 or as much as $400

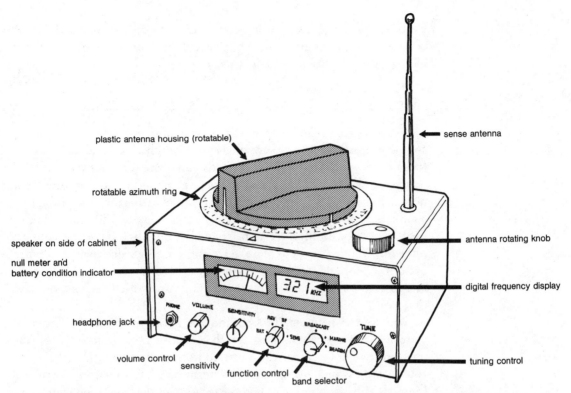

plastic antenna housing (rotatable)

sense antenna

rotatable azimuth ring

speaker on side of cabinet

antenna rotating knob

null meter and
battery condition indicator

digital frequency display

headphone jack

PHONE VOLUME SENSITIVITY REV BF BROADCAST TUNE
BAT SENS MARINE BEACON

321 KHZ

volume control

sensitivity

function control

band selector

tuning control

This portable RDF is typical of the tabletop models that were once the mainstay of electronic navigation. Now it's very hard to find this kind of RDF for sale. It receives the radio beacon and AM broadcast bands. Some models also have a beat frequency oscillator control which helps in tuning a weak station by providing a squeal when the BFO is on. Other models may include the 2-to-3 MHz marine band, but it is of little value for navigation purposes. The function control knob's four positions enable the user to check the voltage of the batteries, to choose beacon or AM stations for direction finding or straight reception of AM broadcast stations (without the direction finding function), or to energize the sense antenna. Dimensions are 10 inches wide, 12 inches long, and 6 inches high. Price: $200 to $500.

or more. The other category is the automatic direction finder (ADF), which is permanently mounted in the nav station, and which will cost between $1,000 and $1,500. Both types tune the same frequencies, but the ADF "fixes" on the point source station automatically, while the RDF requires you to do this manually.

With portable and handheld radio direction finders priced around $200, it makes sense to have one of the small units aboard even if you depend primarily on loran and GPS. The latter have complex microprocessor circuitry and external antennas mounted in the weather, and on both counts they are vulnerable in ways that an inexpensive RDF set is not. And with its own batteries, a portable RDF will function even when the ship's power has been lost. Loran signals can become less predictable inside harbors and close to jetties, situations in which (provided the harbor or jetty is provided with a radio beacon) an RDF is at its best.

How They Work

The U.S. Coast Guard operates two types of radio beacons: marker beacons that broadcast low-power signals from local harbors, and more powerful radio beacons that mark headlands (these are often located in lighthouses), major harbor entrances, drilling rigs, and other such features. The normal range for low-power beacons is 10 miles, while the high-power beacons can transmit their signals over distances of up to 150 miles, making them useful for position fixing by triangulation. High-power beacons are sometimes found in groups of up to six, transmitting sequentially in a timed pattern on a single frequency. Both types transmit very slow Morse code identifiers, making it easy for you to determine which beacon you have tuned in.

Radio waves between 200 kHz and 900 kHz (which includes the commercial AM broadcast stations as well as marine radio beacons) normally travel in straight lines radiating outward from the transmitter. In theory, all you need do is pick up the signal, determine what direction it's coming from, identify its source, and find the location of that source on your chart, and you'll have a line of position (LOP) along which you must be located.

The heart of a radio direction finder is its specialized antenna, which is highly directional to incoming radio waves. Let's use a portable desktop RDF as an example. In this model, the antenna windings are housed in a plastic bar that turns freely atop the receiver. Reception is strongest when the bar is broadside to the incoming signal path, but when you swing the antenna end-on toward the signal source, the signal will disappear (a phenomenon known as the "null"). Because it can be located with much more precision than can the position of strongest signal reception, the null is used for direction finding. The receiver is usually equipped with a meter to help locate the null visually. When it is located, you read the bearing on the 360-degree compass rose under the antenna.

Either end of the antenna will elicit a null, resulting in what is known as an ambiguity. You must make an independent determination as to which of the two possible directions (180 degrees apart) the signal is coming from. This ambiguity should rarely be difficult to resolve. If you are navigating on the West Coast, for example, a shore station signal is bound to be toward your east.

With a handheld model the principle is the same, but you aim the entire receiver at the null.

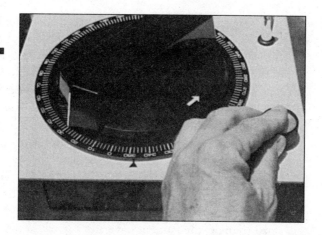

In the automatic direction finder (ADF) the antenna is a fixed double loop mounted outside the pilothouse, and signals are electronically "nulled out" while the twin loop assembly remains stationary. A pointer on a screen or a digital readout will display the bearing of a signal. The ADF antenna also frequently incorporates an external sense antenna to resolve that 180-degree bearing ambiguity.

The procedures for using a portable RDF are simple. Let's say you want to home in on a low-power radio beacon transmitting from a harbor entrance, as noted on a chart. Swing your vessel into the approximate direction of that harbor, then tune in your RDF to the frequency listed on the chart. Doublecheck that the identifier signal you hear is indeed the marker beacon on the harbor entrance. Now swing the antenna and look for the null. If the signal disappears precisely over the bow, you are heading toward the harbor, but if the signal disappears on the starboard bow, you need to alter course to starboard in order to home directly on the harbor entrance. If after a half hour of cruising on a steady course the radio beacon signal again appears a few degrees on the starboard bow, you are probably being set by wind or current. In this way an RDF can tell you how wind and current are affecting the accuracy of your dead reckoning.

You of course want to establish the bearing to the beacon first and plot the direction on the chart. You want to be sure there are no obstacles between you and your destination as you follow the beam.

Obviously, these procedures will work just as well when you want to run a course directly *away from* a radio beacon, adjusting course to bring the null directly over the stern.

One of the most important uses for an RDF or ADF is for obtaining position fixes. Coast Guard or commercial broadcast transmitters will often enable you to get the two or more bearings needed for a fix, even in low-visibility conditions, when you need it the most.

Using a portable desktop RDF, set the rotatable azimuth ring to 000 to read the bearings in degrees relative to the ship's bow, or rotate the ring to your current magnetic heading and read the absolute magnetic bearings. Try to find at least three stations, which should be in different compass quadrants; the closer the crossing angles of any two bearings are to 90 degrees (60 degrees if three bearings are available), the more accurate your fix. The stations might include a high-power beacon transmitting from a distant harbor on your port bow, a strong AM radio station with a shoreside transmitter on your starboard beam, and a small jetty marker directly astern of you. If the bearings are measured relative to the vessel's heading, convert them to absolute bearings in degrees magnetic. Plot the three lines of position (LOPs) from the charted transmitter locations. The LOPs should form a small triangle, the familiar navigator's "cocked hat." Your probable position is within this triangle.

There is also a simple radio direction-finding technique for checking speed over the ground. Find two shoreside radio beacons and on your chart draw a line from each to intersect your course heading at 90 degrees. Now measure the distance along your course between the two intersecting lines. Suppose that distance is 11 nautical miles. Start the clock when the RDF null shows you are exactly abeam of the first beacon, and stop it when you are abeam of the second. If two hours has elapsed, your speed is about 5½ knots.

The accuracy of RDF bearings is seldom better than 3 degrees one side or the other, and sometimes it can be worse. When stations transmit signals that must bend around land masses or travel over hills or through valleys, the radio waves are likely to be redirected before they reach the ocean. For this reason it is important to know when the signals you are receiving from a radio beacon or AM broadcast station have traveled significant distances over an intervening land mass. These signals may have been redirected by as much as 20 degrees. This is one reason why marine charts don't list inland aeronautical radio beacons or AM broadcast stations for direction-finding purposes.

A second effect, known as coastal refraction, occurs when the land signal reaches the water's edge. Passing over a new surface of different composition, the radio waves are bent. If the signal crosses the shore at a 90-degree angle, nothing happens, but any angle either side of that will cause some refraction, the amount depending on temperature, humidity, and the season. Again, the answer, wherever possible, is to choose radio beacons close to the shoreline, with no intervening islands or land masses between them and you. Any other radio bearings should be treated with skepticism.

Yet another characteristic of radio waves just below the AM broadcast band is that they may bounce off the ionosphere (an envelope of ionized gases above the earth) at night, sometimes giving you highly erratic bearings to the point source beacon. These "skywaves" may approach from a direction as much as 35 degrees away from where the station is transmitting. Be extremely cautious of nighttime bearings on distant high-power radio beacons and AM broadcast transmitters. Within 40 miles of the transmitting station you are not likely to have any problem, but beyond that distance groundwave signals may be overridden by skywaves, and this will give you a false bearing.

Other, sometimes major, inaccuracies can be introduced after the incoming signals reach your boat, but these you can control with the proper precautions. Metal surfaces and objects, for example, will deflect and distort radio waves. With this in mind, operate a handheld RDF in the stern of a sailboat and hold it out (making sure you have it strapped around your neck or wrist) over the lifelines. Keep a portable desktop RDF or ADF at least two feet above metal structures when direction finding, or better (since you can't very well operate your receiver two feet above the metal mast and rigging), develop a deviation card for the receiver in its normal position aboard the boat. The procedure is this: On a clear day, take a series of visual bearings on a local radio beacon (one on a jetty would be good) using a pelorus or a hand-bearing compass, and compare each such bearing with the corresponding RDF or ADF bearing. Three people—one on helm to swing the vessel, one to call off visual bearings, and one to take the RDF or ADF bearings—make the operation smooth. If there are major deviations, you may need to find a new location for the receiver. Metal stanchions can cause deviations of up to 10 degrees, and even the aluminum frame of a pilothouse window can redirect incoming radio waves. When you find a suitable and convenient spot, develop the deviation card for that spot. The operation is analogous to "swinging a compass."

When you use a portable RDF, which should be sitting on a table top or other convenient horizontal surface, make sure the set's lubber line is parallel to the vessel's fore-and-aft centerline. Naturally this applies equally to the four-bay antenna of a permanently installed ADF. Just as important, make sure the helmsman holds a steady course while you take the bearings. Both these precautions are critical to the accuracy of the bearings.

You may need to shut down your engine to pick up weaker signals. The most common sources of electrical interference include fluorescent lights, engine ignition systems, alternator whine, and electric motors.

What's Available (And Buying Tips)

As noted earlier, due to the popularity of loran and GPS there have been few advances in the technology of radio direction-finding equipment over

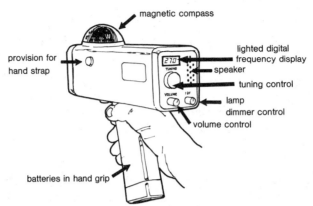

magnetic compass

lighted digital frequency display

provision for hand strap

speaker

tuning control

lamp dimmer control

volume control

batteries in hand grip

Handheld RDFs come in a variety of packages, but essentially they have a pistol-type grip, with the antenna and receiver controls above the grip and a small compass mounted above the antenna section. Some have a locking button that can be pressed when the null is audibly observed, which locks the compass card at that position. This is a useful feature when the boat is rolling or pitching heavily, or at night when the compass card may be hard to read due to its small size. The price of a handheld RDF ranges from $200 to $500.

the last few years. An RDF is really nothing more than a very sensitive radio receiver with a specialized antenna system. (With a desktop model, when you're not taking bearings you can use the set as an entertainment radio.)

About the biggest thing we have seen in the portable RDF is the switch from a slide rule–type frequency readout to a liquid crystal digital readout. This is a bigger improvement than it sounds, enabling you to tune in precisely the frequency of a very weak-sounding transmitter. There are times when the Morse code identifier of a radio beacon is garbled, but the signal is nevertheless strong enough for accurate detection of the null. With a precise digital frequency readout, you can be assured that you are indeed tuned into the right station. The old frequency scales could be a few kilohertz off, sometimes causing mariners to tune in the wrong station accidentally.

Most portable and handheld RDFs operate off flashlight batteries, and none is weatherproof. Keep RDFs and ADFs out of the moisture.

Some desktop RDFs have an auxiliary "sense" antenna, the function of which is to resolve that 180-degree ambiguity. Given an accurate frequency tuner, an audible Morse code signal, and a local chart, however, you should have no problem deciding which of the two possible directions is the actual one. If the sense antenna comes on the unit you want, fine, but its presence or absence need not be a criterion of selection.

Handheld RDFs differ from the portable desktop sets in that the antenna is housed in a pistol grip and the entire unit is rotated for null determination. A magnetic compass is substituted for the azimuth ring, which makes the unit easy to use but also introduces a new source of inaccuracy: The compass is of course subject to magnetic deviation, and the small size of the compass card limits the precision of the reading. A handheld could be made with a fluxgate compass for higher accuracy, but none is on the market.

Some handhelds come with earphones to make listening for weak signals easier while you're standing in the wind. It's a good feature.

Most of the characteristics to look for in an RDF are similar to those that apply to VHF radios, as discussed in the chapter on VHF. An inexpensive RDF offering CB and FM bands (useless for direction finding) as well as the radio beacon and AM broadcast bands should be viewed with suspicion. Its sensitivity may be low, its selectivity poor, and its null may not be sharp enough for accurate bearings.

Sensitivity, the ability to pick up weak signals, is expressed as microvolts per meter, a smaller value meaning a greater sensitivity. The value should probably be 50μV/m or less on the radio beacon band, 40μV/m or less on the AM broadcast band.

Selectivity is the ability to receive the desired station while filtering out interference from other stations, perhaps with stronger signals, on adjacent

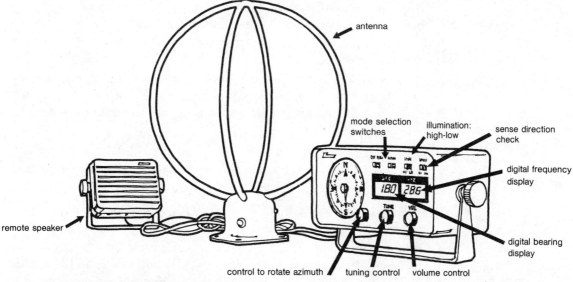

The two elements of an automatic radio direction finder are the topside double-loop antenna and the control and display console. The speaker may or may not be built into the console, depending upon make. The circular azimuth at the left side of the console can be rotated to the course being steered to provide magnetic bearings from the pointer over its face, or it can be aligned "north up" to display relative bearings. There are also digital displays of bearing and frequency. Most ADFs include both marine radio beacon and AM broadcast bands; some also include the 2-to-3 MHz band, which is, however, of little use for navigational purposes. The price range of a unit like this is $1,000 and up with antenna, and a typical console size is 12 inches wide, 10 inches from to back, and 12 inches high. The antenna is typically 3 feet high. This equipment is normally found on most commercial boats.

frequencies. Selectivity is rated in decibels—the higher the value, the better the selectivity. The value should probably be 30 dB or higher.

As with VHF radio, actually trying out the sets side by side outside a marine electronics showroom is preferable to depending on quoted specs.

Automatic direction finders *can* be portable: The antenna is housed in a bar atop the set, as in the portable RDF, but a motor rotates the antenna automatically. Performance of these units is compromised by the motor, whose noise can drown out the signal.

A permanently installed ADF with its large mast- or tower-mounted double-loop antenna can give you greater direction-finding range, many times greater than that afforded by a portable RDF. A permanently mounted ADF should be installed by a technician, since proper installation of the loop antenna's eight- to 10-strand wire is difficult, and because the unit needs to be calibrated when it is installed. Proper calibration increases the accuracy of the unit, but again, a deviation card is necessary. Such an ADF operates off the ship's batteries, so if you lose the ship's power, you lose the ADF. For this reason, and because a good ADF will cost considerably more than a portable RDF, an RDF is the more appropriate choice for an inexpensive alternative or a backup to loran.

A couple of additional things to consider when you shop for a radio direction finder:

- Look for liquid crystal displays on RDFs and ADFs. The more traditional mechanical pointers tend not to be as precise or as trouble-free. LCD readouts for both frequency and direction can give remarkable precision.
- Look for an auxiliary connection on a portable RDF to take an external 12-volt supply. This conserves the unit's internal batteries.
- Look for a light on the RDF for night viewing.

You're lucky if you can find an RDF offered through a mail-order catalog. Almost all units these days are imported, the portables and handhelds from Britain, where there's a larger market for them, and the permanent-mount ADFs from Japan. If you buy an ADF and have it dealer-installed as part of the sales package, insist that it work properly and is properly calibrated, even if that means calling the technician back for one or more additional visits.

Maintenance and Troubleshooting

Always remove the batteries from a handheld or portable RDF before storing it. Old or dead batteries could begin to leak, damaging the battery compartment.

The biggest problem with portable RDFs is intermittent contact in the antenna assembly. The antenna windings housed within the plastic bar spin freely on tiny contacts that transfer the signals from the antenna to the receiver section. These contacts usually develop small amounts of corrosion after a year or so of little use. The usual rotatable loop may be pulled off the RDF set and the contacts cleaned using television tuner cleaner. After the contacts have been sprayed with tuner cleaner, the antenna is reassembled and spun many times.

VHF ADF

VHF automatic direction finders are popular among some fishermen because they can determine the direction of any incoming marine VHF transmission. If a commercial or sportfisherman locates fish, and that information is disseminated over VHF channels, he may soon have company. VHF automatic direction finders are easily spotted by their unique four-pole "Adcock" antenna system, which is comprised of four halfwave vertical elements electronically phased for making bearing determinations. Incoming signals are received by the four-bay antenna system and electronically mixed and matched, and the resulting bearing is displayed by a pointer needle, flashing light-emitting diodes, or a combination arrow and digital readout. If the antenna system is properly mounted high above all other antennas, bearing accuracy on VHF frequencies is usually better than 5 degrees.

The units are obviously useful for search-and-rescue operations, as well. The Coast Guard has similar equipment aboard its cutters. This is an essential reason to keep a handheld VHF—preferably a waterproof one—in a life raft or, if it's one of the pocket-sized ones, in your pocket, should you go overboard.

VHF signals from other ship stations cannot usually be received much more than 15 miles away. This is because VHF radio waves don't bend over the horizon, so that ships must be nearly within line of sight before VHF signals from one can be received by the other. This is why height of the VHF ADF antenna setup is very important.

Since some shoreside VHF stations operated by the Coast Guard or telephone companies have lofty perches, you can often tune in land stations over much greater distances, but few shore stations tell us where their transmitting antennas are actually located. A U.S. Coast Guard station in a particular harbor may use five or six transmitting antennas covering as much as 100 miles of coastline, and the local marine operator for your port might be transmitting from an antenna 75 miles outside the harbor limits.

These remote antenna sites can complicate the use of VHF ADF for navigational direction finding. These sets do *not* have the frequency capability

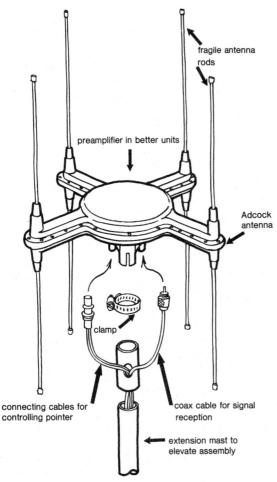

fragile antenna rods

preamplifier in better units

Adcock antenna

clamp

connecting cables for controlling pointer

coax cable for signal reception

extension mast to elevate assembly

The antenna assembly used with VHF ADFs must be mounted above the boat's superstructure and way from other antennas. Alignment of the four antenna elements is critical, but easily done before securing the assembly to the plastic supporting mast.

A VHF ADF antenna, slightly askew, mounted as high as possible for good range. Below it are a radar antenna housing and a radar reflector.

to receive signals from radio beacons or AM broadcast stations. They are highly specialized for homing on other vessels.

Since VHF radio waves reflect quite nicely off buildings, billboards, metal masts, rigging, and even nearby VHF antennas, it may be impossible to home accurately on a distant ship station if you are in a harbor. You might "see" a ship station signal coming from shore rather than from sea. Once at sea, bearings will begin to settle down.

You can estimate the distance to a ship station by its signal strength on your VHF ADF set. If the signal is weak and plagued by static, the station is probably more than 10 miles away. If it's loud and clear, the station is within five miles.

The selection of VHF ADFs is not large. However, you can choose between one that is a stand-alone model and one that is built into a 78 channel synthesized 25-watt marine VHF set. The set operates like a normal VHF radio until you turn on the ADF portion, at which point it switches from the big transmit-and-receive antenna to the four-bay ADF antenna. The ADF antenna doesn't have the gain of a big white fiberglass whip, so reception will decrease slightly. The unit is priced around $1,000. Stand-alone VHF units are the *ultimate*—available from five manufacturers for under $3,000.

The alternative is adding a separate VHF ADF assembly to your present VHF set. Regardless of what type or brand of VHF set you may already own, it's very easy to add VHF automatic direction-finding capabilities to it. These "add-on" devices normally cost around $500 at discount prices, and they are just as accurate as the built-in units. Audio from your present VHF set is taken out of the rear speaker jack and fed into your new ADF companion unit. The unit processes the audio through a phase comparison system while electronically "swinging" the four-bay antenna. It's a sensible way to go if you already have a good, synthesized, 25-watt marine VHF set installed.

These VHF ADF add-on units can also be tied into marine VHF handheld sets. The audio out of the handheld external speaker jack is fed into the ADF unit.

It's critical that the four-bay antenna be mounted well above all other antennas on your boat. Putting it down low will only cause incoming signals to distort, reflect, and refract. Some mariners might consider that weird antenna mounted high above all others on their boat a visual drawback.

When shopping for a VHF ADF inspect the antenna assembly. Are the rods hollow or solid? The hollow antenna elements will break easily, rendering your unit temporarily useless. The solid rods, such as those found on some of the newer units, will take more abuse and will bend rather than break. Be sure, too, that an extension mast is included with the antenna.

CHAPTER 10

Loran

by Gordon West and Freeman Pittman

Imagine yourself groping through the fog without benefit of radar, trying to get back to port with only a few gallons of fuel remaining. For the last four hours there has been no indication of land, no break in the weather—then suddenly you pass a signpost firmly planted in the water that tells you where you are, which way to head for port, the precise distance remaining, and an estimated time of arrival. Sound impossible? The signpost stuck in the bottom is a little farfetched, but a very sophisticated (and not so expensive) loran radionavigation receiver will give you the same "waypoint" information. This type of capability is available in a small box that draws no more current than a running light.

"Loran" stands for LOng RAnge aid to Navigation. One version of it, loran-A, originated during World War II, but not until the late 1970s did loran enjoy much popularity among pleasure-craft users. Loran manufacturers have outdone themselves in producing smart loran receivers—and prices have fallen to a point where any boat 20 feet or longer is a candidate for loran.

In 1974, the U.S. Coast Guard inaugurated loran-C as the successor to loran-A, and as the primary civil navigation system for the U.S. Coastal Confluence Zone (CCZ), covering navigable waters from the shoreline out to 50 miles offshore (or to the 100-fathom contour where this is beyond the 50-mile limit). The Great Lakes were also covered. In recent years, the entire continental United States has been covered. Most loran signals travel well beyond the coastal confluence zone and can, in theory, be used at distances up to 1,200 miles from the loran transmitting chain under ideal conditions.

Concurrent with the expansion and fine tuning of loran stations in the United States, Canada began improving loran-C coverage on its east and west coasts. There is, as well, loran coverage in the North Atlantic, parts of Europe, the Mediterranean, Japan, and Alaska.

Loran makes possible precise and reliable position fixes. The Coast Guard, which operates all U.S. and most overseas stations, guarantees absolute loran position fixes within one-quarter mile in the CCZ 95 percent of the time. A typical fix in a strong signal area is accurate well within one-quarter mile, while on the fringes of loran coverage the average accuracy is within two to five miles. The repeatable accuracy of a fix is much better; you can return to within 50 feet of the exact spot where you lost an expensive anchor (or a person) overboard. It is this repeatability characteristic that enables bottom trawlers to avoid snags that have torn their nets in the past, lobstermen to find their buoys in the fog, and mariners to find in foul weather the navigation buoy whose loran coordinates they recorded when the weather was fair.

Text continues on page 137

Right and following 4 pages. Current North American and international loran-C transmitter chains and their areas of coverage. In the United States new chains include the mid-continent North Central and South Central networks, installed primarily for aircraft navigation. Other chains not shown include one in Saudi Arabia and another in China, although the government there does not admit its existence. Unfortunately for mariners the Central Pacific chain, which covered the Hawaiian islands, has been shut down. The Northwest Pacific chain will be taken over by Japan, except for the Guam transmitter, which will be turned off. There has been much discussion among governments in Western Europe about installing stations on the Atlantic coast to link the Mediterranean and North Sea chains; as yet no agreement has been reached.

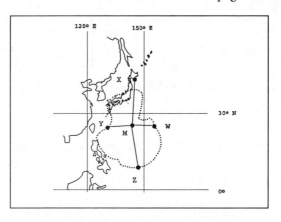

```
SNR                              1:3
Fix Accuracy                     1/4 NM (95% 2dRMS)
Atmospheric Noise                58.1 dB above 1 uV/m
```

Transmitter		Coordinates		CD (uS)	Power (kW)
M	Iwo Jima, Japan	24 48 03.73 N	141 19 30.86 E		1815
W	Marcus Island, Japan	24 17 08.03 N	153 58 53.79 E	11000	1000
X	Hokkaido, Japan	42 44 37.22 N	143 43 09.80 E	30000	600
Y	Gesashi, Japan	26 36 25.11 N	128 08 57.00 E	55000	600
Z	Barrigada, Guam	13 27 50.09 N	144 49 32.99 E	81000	600

NOTE: Estimated Groundwave coverage, actual coverage will vary.

Northwest Pacific—GRI 9970

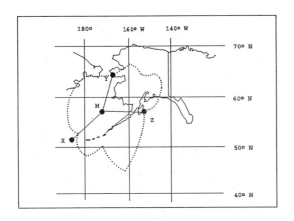

```
SNR                      1:3
Fix Accuracy             1/4 NM (95% 2dRMS)
Atmospheric Noise        48.2 dB above 1 uV/m
```

Transmitter		Coordinates		CD (uS)	Power (kW)
M St. Paul, AK	57 09 12.35 N	170 15 06.25 W			275
X Attu, AK	52 49 44.13 N	173 10 49.53 E		11000	275
Y Port Clarence, AK	65 14 40.37 N	166 53 12.00 W		29000	1000
Z Kodiak, AK	57 26 20.30 N	152 22 10.71 W		43000	400

NOTE: <u>Estimated</u> Groundwave coverage, actual coverage will vary.

North Pacific—GRI 9990

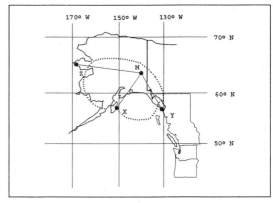

```
SNR                      1:3
Fix Accuracy             1/4 NM (95% 2dRMS)
Atmospheric Noise        49.0 dB above 1 uV/m
```

Transmitter		Coordinates		CD (uS)	Power (kW)
M Tok, AK	63 19 42.88 N	142 48 31.35 W			560
X Kodiak, AK	57 26 20.30 N	152 22 10.71 W		11000	400
Y Shoal Cove, AK	55 26 20.94 N	131 15 19.09 W		26000	560
Z Port Clarence, AK	65 14 40.37 N	166 53 12.00 W		45000	1000

NOTE: <u>Estimated</u> Groundwave coverage, actual coverage will vary.

Gulf of Alaska—GRI 7960

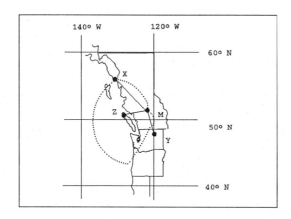

```
SNR                      1:3
Fix Accuracy             1/4 NM (95% 2dRMS)
Atmospheric Noise        46.4 dB above 1 uV/m
```

Transmitter		Coordinates		CD (uS)	Power (kW)
M Williams Lake, Canada	51 57 58.88 N	122 22 01.69 W			400
X Shoal Cove, AK	55 26 20.94 N	131 15 19.09 W		11000	560
Y George, WA	47 03 48.10 N	119 44 38.98 W		27000	1400
Z Port Hardy, Canada	50 36 29.83 N	127 21 28.49 W		41000	350

NOTE: <u>Estimated</u> Groundwave coverage, actual coverage will vary.

Canadian West Coast—GRI 5990

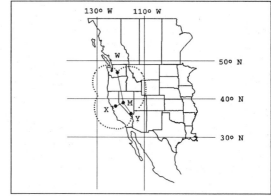

```
SNR                      1:3
Fix Accuracy             1/4 NM (95% 2dRMS)
Atmospheric Noise        52.4 dB above 1 uV/m
```

Transmitter		Coordinates		CD (uS)	Power (kW)
M Fallon, NV	39 33 06.74 N	118 49 55.82 W			400
W George, WA	47 03 48.10 N	119 44 38.98 W		11000	1400
X Middletown, CA	38 46 57.11 N	122 29 43.98 W		27000	400
Y Searchlight, NV	35 19 18.30 N	114 48 16.88 W		40000	560

NOTE: <u>Estimated</u> Groundwave coverage, actual coverage will vary.

U.S. West Coast—GRI 9940

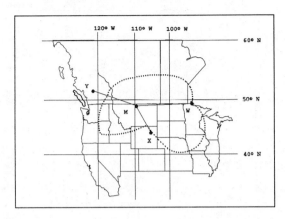

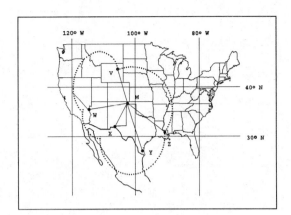

SNR	1:3
Fix Accuracy	1/4 NM (95% 2dRMS)
Atmospheric Noise	57.8 dB above 1 uV/m

Transmitter	Coordinates	CD (uS)	Power (kW)
M Havre, MT	48 44 38.59 N 109 58 53.61 W		400
W Baudette, MN	48 36 49.95 N 94 33 17.92 W	11000	800
X Gillette, WY	44 00 11.31 N 105 37 23.90 W	27000	400
Y Williams Lake, Canada	51 57 58.88 N 122 22 01.69 W	42000	400

NOTE: Estimated Groundwave coverage, actual coverage will vary.

North Central U.S.—GRI 8290

SNR	1:3
Fix Accuracy	1/4 NM (95% 2dRMS)
Atmospheric Noise	57.8 dB above 1 uV/m

Transmitter	Coordinates	CD (uS)	Power (kW)
M Boise City, OK	36 30 20.78 N 102 53 59.49 W		800
V Gillette, WY	44 00 11.31 N 105 37 23.90 W	11000	540
W Searchlight, NV	35 19 18.31 N 114 48 16.88 W	25000	560
X Las Cruces, NM	32 04 18.13 N 106 52 04.39 W	40000	540
Y Raymondville, TX	26 31 55.14 N 97 49 59.54 W	52000	540
Z Grangeville, LA	30 43 33.15 N 90 49 43.05 W	65000	800

NOTE: Estimated Groundwave coverage, actual coverage will vary.

South Central U.S.—GRI 9610

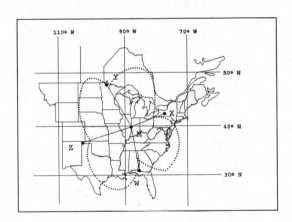

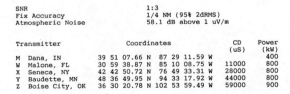

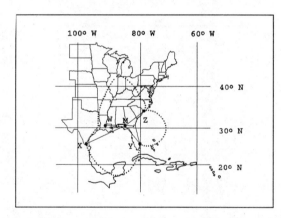

SNR	1:3
Fix Accuracy	1/4 NM (95% 2dRMS)
Atmospheric Noise	58.1 dB above 1 uV/m

Transmitter	Coordinates	CD (uS)	Power (kW)
M Dana, IN	39 51 07.66 N 87 29 11.59 W		400
W Malone, FL	30 59 38.87 N 85 10 08.75 W	11000	800
X Seneca, NY	42 42 50.72 N 76 49 33.31 W	28000	800
Y Baudette, MN	48 36 49.95 N 94 33 17.92 W	44000	800
Z Boise City, OK	36 30 20.78 N 102 53 59.49 W	59000	900

Note: Estimated Groundwave coverage, actual coverage will vary.

Great Lakes—GRI 8970

SNR	1:3
Fix Accuracy	1/4 NM (95% 2dRMS)
Atmospheric Noise	60.5 dB above 1 uV/m

Transmitter	Coordinates	CD (uS)	Power (kW)
M Malone, FL	30 59 38.87 N 85 10 08.75 W		800
W Grangeville, LA	30 43 33.15 N 90 49 43.05 W	11000	800
X Raymondville, TX	26 31 55.14 N 97 49 59.54 W	23000	540
Y Jupiter, FL	27 01 58.53 N 80 06 52.88 W	43000	350
Z Carolina Beach, NC	34 03 46.21 N 77 54 46.10 W	59000	600

NOTE: Estimated Groundwave coverage, actual coverage will vary.

Southeast U.S.—GRI 7980

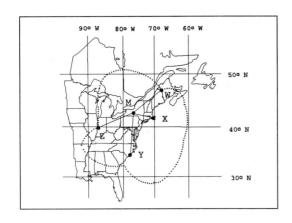

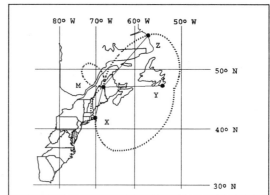
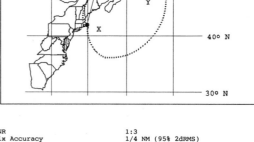

SNR	1:3
Fix Accuracy	1/4 NM (95% 2dRMS)
Atmospheric Noise	55.1 dB above 1 uV/m

Transmitter	Coordinates	CD (uS)	Power (kW)
M Seneca, NY	42 42 50.71 N 76 49 33.31 W		800
W Caribou, ME	46 48 27.31 N 67 55 37.16 W	11000	800
X Nantucket, MA	41 15 12.05 N 69 58 38.54 W	25000	350
Y Carolina Beach, NC	34 03 46.21 N 77 54 46.10 W	39000	600
Z Dana, IN	39 51 07.66 N 87 29 11.59 W	54000	400

NOTE: Estimated Groundwave Coverage, actual coverage will vary.

Northeast U.S.—9960

SNR	1:3
Fix Accuracy	1/4 NM (95% 2dRMS)
Atmospheric Noise	47.6 dB above 1 uV/m

Transmitter	Coordinates	CD (uS)	Power (kW)
M Caribou, ME	46 48 27.31 N 67 55 37.16 W		800
X Nantucket, MA	41 15 12.05 N 69 58 38.54 W	11000	350
Y Cape Race, Canada	46 46 32.29 N 53 10 27.61 W	25000	1000
Z Fox Harbor, Canada	52 22 35.25 N 55 42 27.86 W	38000	900

NOTE: Estimated Groundwave coverage, actual coverage will vary.

Canadian East Coast—GRI 5930

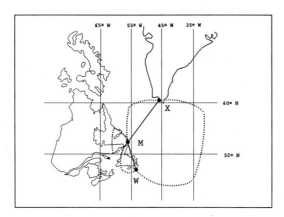

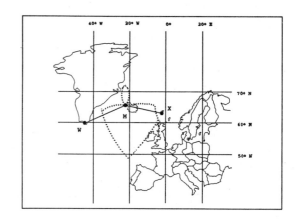

SNR	1:3
Fix Accuracy	1/4 NM (95% 2dRMS)
Atmospheric Noise	43.1 dB above 1 uV/m

Transmitter	Coordinates	CD (uS)	Power (kW)
M Fox Harbor, Canada	52 22 35.25 N 55 42 27.86 W		900
W Cape Race, Canada	46 46 32.29 N 53 10 27.61 W	11000	1000
X Angissoq, Greenland	59 59 17.35 N 45 10 26.92 W	26000	760

NOTE: Estimated Groundwave Coverage, actual coverage will vary.

Labrador Sea—GRI 7930

SNR	1:3
Fix Accuracy	1/4 NM (95% 2dRMS)
Atmospheric Noise	50.0 dB above 1 uV/m

Transmitter	Coordinates	CD (uS)	Power (kW)
M Sandur, Iceland	64 54 26.65 N 23 55 21.20 W		1500
W Angissoq, Greenland	59 59 17.35 N 45 10 26.92 W	11000	760
X Ejde, Denmark	62 17 59.71 N 07 04 25.98 W	30000	325

NOTE: Estimated Groundwave coverage, actual coverage will vary.

Icelandic Sea—GRI 9980

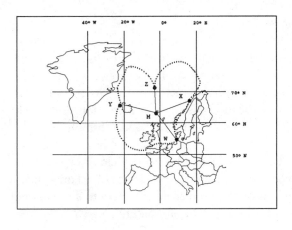

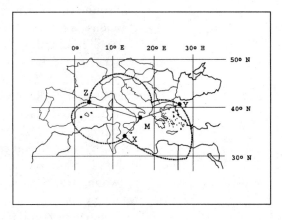

```
SNR                          1:3
Fix Accuracy                 1/4 NM (95% 2dRMS)
Atmospheric Noise            43.1 dB above 1 uV/m
```

Transmitter		Coordinates	CD (uS)	Power (kW)
M	Ejde, Denmark	62 17 59.71 N 07 04 25.98 W		325
X	Bo, Norway	68 38 06.21 N 14 27 47.55 E	11000	165
W	Sylt, Germany	54 48 29.96 N 08 17 36.31 E	26000	325
Y	Sandur, Iceland	64 54 26.65 N 23 55 21.20 W	46000	1500
Z	Jan Mayen, Norway	70 54 52.66 N 08 43 58.14 E	60000	165

NOTE: Estimated Groundwave coverage, actual coverage will vary.

Norwegian Sea—GRI 7970

```
SNR                          1:3
Fix Accuracy                 1/4 NM (95% 2dRMS)
Atmospheric Noise            51.2 dB above 1 uV/m
```

Transmitter		Coordinates	CD (uS)	Power (kW)
M	Sellia Marina, Italy	38 52 20.71 N 16 43 06.71 E		165
X	Lampedusa, Italy	35 31 20.91 N 12 31 30.80 E	11000	325
Y	Kargabarun, Turkey	40 58 21.07 N 27 52 02.07 E	29000	165
Z	Estartit, Spain	42 03 36.63 N 03 12 16.07 E	47000	165

NOTE: Estimated Groundwave coverage, actual coverage will vary.

Mediterranean Sea—GRI 7990

Loran-C System Characteristics

Accuracy			Availability	Coverage	Reliability	Fix Rate	Fix Dimension	Capacity	Ambiguity Potential
Predictable	Repeatable	Relative							
0.25nm (460m) 1:3 SNR	60-300 ft. (18-90m)	60-300 ft. (18-90m)	99+%	U.S. coastal areas, some continental U.S., selected overseas areas	99.7%	10-20 fixes/min.	2D	Unlimited	Yes, easily resolved

Loran-C system characteristics. Loran-C is a low-frequency (100 kHz) hyperbolic radionavigation system. It offers continuous position updating, with signals availability virtually always within the Coastal Confluence Zone for which it was designed. A long-running system, its reliability is proven, and almost all signal reception problems are due to interference or receiver installation problems, rarely to transmitter downtime.

Text continued from page 133

How It Works

We'll start with an oversimplified analogy: a man rowing his boat in the middle of a large harbor. At opposite ends of the harbor are two lighthouses that sound their horns every 30 seconds. Their short horn blasts are synchronous. When the rowboat is exactly halfway between the lighthouses, the man will hear both horn blasts simultaneously. If, however, his boat moves nearer to one lighthouse than the other, he will hear the closer horn first, because it takes the sound from the more distant horn a little longer to reach the man's ear. If the man knows the speed of sound and is nimble at math, he should be able to convert the time lag of the second horn to a corresponding distance. Then, having calculated how much closer he is to one lighthouse than the other, he can plot his line of position (LOP) on a chart. A third lighthouse sounding its horn would enable the man to develop one or two more lines of position, and the point of their crossing with the first would give him a position fix.

Loran works on the same principle; the receiver measures the time difference (TD) between radio signals sent from a master station M and secondary (or "slave") stations W, X, Y, and/or Z. In this case, however, the time differences are computed in millionths of a second (microseconds). Since radio waves travel near the speed of light, a microsecond of time difference is very meaningful to a loran readout. The TD between the master signal and the signal from secondary station X gives one line of position. The TD between the signals from master station M and secondary station Y gives one more. (Loran receivers do not measure the TDs between two secondary station signals.) The crossing point of the two LOPs is the resultant position fix. Additional secondary stations providing additional lines of position can further increase the reliability of the fix, and most master stations are associated with three or four secondaries. The stations thus associated constitute a chain, each chain blanketing its designated geographic area of coverage with short, timed pulses. These radio waves have a frequency near 100 kHz, giving them stable propagation characteristics.

A straight line drawn through a master station and one of its secondaries represents the "baseline" for the two stations. If your course were perpendicular to a baseline and crossed it midway between stations, the time difference for transmissions from the master station and that secondary would be zero at all points along your course, provided our foghorn analogy were strictly true. Actually it isn't, quite: There would be signal interference if the master and all secondary stations transmitted at precisely the same times; therefore the pulse patterns transmitted from the stations in a chain are offset very slightly one from another. The principle is the same, however.

The master station in a chain transmits first, followed immediately by each of the secondary stations in the chain. The time from one master transmission to the next is the "group repetition interval," or GRI for short. Every loran chain has its own GRI "radioprint" (like a fingerprint), and

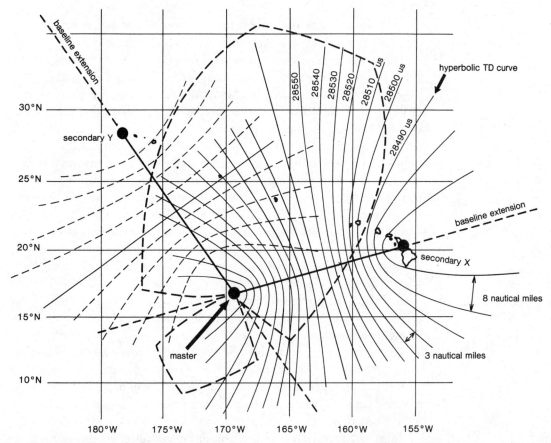

This chart shows how a loran chain is configured and how time difference lines (TDs) between transmitting stations take the form of hyperbolic curves. The nominal coverage area is outlined by the heavy dashed lines. All loran chains have areas of greater or lesser accuracy with regard to crossing angles of the signals from the master and secondary stations. The gradient, or distance between charted TDs, also varies from one location to another, and it has an effect on accuracy. For most navigators, plotting loran positions on a chart using TD lines and an interpolator is a backup technique to be used should the loran receiver's lat/lon readout somehow fail.

this lets a loran receiver identify the chain to which it is tuned. The desired GRI is either entered on the receiver's keypad or (on most receivers) called from memory by the set and automatically tuned in. In areas where chains overlap, the receiver will choose the chain offering the best signal.

Position fixing by means of loran is known as "hyperbolic navigation" because the plotted lines representing given time differences between a master and one of its secondary stations are hyperbolic rather than straight (except for that line of points equidistant between the two stations). Unless you are within 20 nautical miles of one of the transmitting stations you are using, however, segments of these hyperbolas can be treated as straight lines for plotting purposes without introducing appreciable error.

Based on the fairly constant velocity of loran signals over water and the application of theoretical or measured correction factors where the signals must pass over land, loran time difference lines have been printed on nautical charts. These charted TDs are a very good approximation in most cases, except where local anomalies were unmeasured at the time a chart was prepared. Although the accuracy of charted TDs can be expected to continue to improve as time goes by (always be sure you're buying the most up-to-date charts available), you should be prepared for occasional discrepancies between what your loran receiver reads out and what your chart indicates for the TD coordinates of a particular position—discrepancies of one-quarter to as much as two nautical miles. Use the charted time differences only as an initial reference, revising the coordinates for your frequently used locations as you get to know and trust your own loran readouts for local waters. You'll want to double check and verify them from time to time when the weather is fair (using the positions of charted buoys, for example), but the loran coordinates your receiver gives for particular locations in local waters should be highly repeatable.

On harbor charts or charts of other restricted waters, loran TD lines are not printed. But loran is accurate enough when used in the repeatable mode to navigate in many of these places. To do this, you must first collect and record loran positions for all the navigation aids you use, as well as for areas to be avoided. More on this later.

Most loran receivers now available automatically select the most appropriate secondaries. You can override the selected stations manually, but you'll have to have a good reason for doing so. Here is what the receiver is programmed to take into account.

Secondary stations are chosen to provide TD lines with good crossing angles, the nearer to 90 degrees the better. Fixes from such TDs will certainly be more accurate and reliable than those from TDs that intersect at less than 30 degrees. The U.S. government has positioned loran stations to maximize crossing angles in the Coastal Confluence Zone, but the angles may be too small for accurate position fixes in some popular cruising areas, such as parts of the Bahamas, the southeastern United States, and the waters off Baja California. Nevertheless, the repeatability of TD fixes made in these areas should still be quite good.

Another factor in the selection of secondary stations is the "gradient" of the TD lines from that station in your locale. The tighter the gradient (the charted spacing) between lines, the more accurate a position fix. A TD interval of 10 microseconds, for example, might be equivalent to one nautical mile or nine depending on location within the master-secondary coverage area.

A typical dash- or bulkhead-mount loran. It is compact, 6 inches by 6 inches by 2¼ inches, but very powerful, offering position in lat/lon or TD coordinates and memorizing up to 250 waypoints, which can be ordered into up to nine routes. The screen on this receiver shows lat/lon and TDs for a waypoint labeled as "home." Separate alphanumeric (right) and dedicated function keys (left) make data entry and commands easy to understand and quick to perform. In fact, the commonly used functions in most lorans today can be done without reading the instruction manual. Adequate computing power and memory and large screens that prompt the user add to the simplicity of operation. Unlike older lorans, no filter tuning is needed; most sets have automatic tuning or enough fixed filters (six is enough) to tune out known interference sources around North American coasts. The list price, with antenna and cables, for this level of sophistication is around $500.

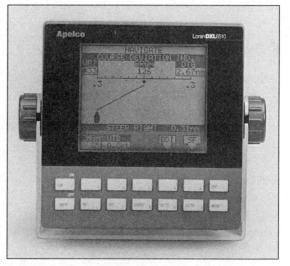

Screen graphics are playing a larger role in loran receivers, with off-course indicators and plotting displays common. Multiple lines of information allow some receivers to show a variety of data. Some show position at all times, others let the user tailor the information shown to the kind of boating he or she does.

Finally, if you are in line geographically with a master and one of its secondaries, even if you are not between them, you are still on those two transmitters' baseline extension. Position finding using that secondary will be inadvisable or even impossible. Your loran receiver should be programmed to avoid using a secondary whose baseline extension you're near.

Many factors can influence the accuracy of loran position fixes. For one thing, the 100-kHz signals may propagate skyward, bounce off the ionosphere, and return as skywaves. The horizontally propagated groundwaves yield much better accuracy, and most loran receivers will precisely time the incoming groundwave pulses, automatically ruling out interference from a slightly delayed (though possibly stronger) skywave.

The groundwave is susceptible to delays, too. Friction of the water and land it passes over slow it. Signals that travel over land are delayed more than those that travel exclusively across water; to complicate things further, different types of topography, ground cover, and even the time of year (is there snow on the ground?) affect the signal. The effect over water is known as the "secondary factor," while over land it's called the "additional secondary factor" (ASF).

Since ASF is relatively constant for a given area, it's possible to compensate for the error. An "ASF correction" can be applied to loran position solutions. Most loran sets have factory-programmed ASF corrections; a few old models may require you to enter on the keypad the appropriate correction for the locale. This is easily done by bringing the boat to a pier-end navigation aid or other precisely charted landmark and simply entering the correct coordinates as present position. The loran will measure the discrepancy in its own position solution and apply the resulting "offset" to every other position on the voyage. This works well, as the error is constant within a 20-mile-diameter circle, but there are local exceptions. Experience is the best guide.

ASF corrections to be entered manually also can be taken from charts or from the *Loran-C Correction Tables*, published by the U.S. Defense Mapping Agency and available from chart houses.

Weather conditions may also affect loran signals. An active storm front between you and a loran station can cause anomalies you can't account for. For this reason some loran chains feature computer-coordinated checking receivers that monitor the signals from the master and secondary stations. These reference monitors are located near important harbors where vessel traffic will be heaviest. Loran chains will not only self-adjust their timing sequence, but will also notify your receiver when a secondary station may be experiencing a technical difficulty, such as a loran transmitter getting out of tolerance by as little as 0.2 microsecond. This may register on the receiver as a blinking digit or a flashing light that flags the problem secondary. This "blink alarm" warns you to double check current readings versus readings taken previously.

Probably the biggest culprit in occluding weak loran signals is interfering noise sources, either from the boat or from one of the several powerful military stations that transmit on either side of the loran frequency band. Luckily, in the latter instance, instead of getting a slightly incorrect reading the navigator gets no reading at all. Manufacturers have identified the major interference sources and all receivers have built-in notch filters to help eliminate the noise.

Loran signals are easily masked by onboard noise sources, and indeed can actually be "wiped out" by ignition interference, electrical interference, and sometimes by noise generated on boats as far as 50 feet away. Fluorescent lights almost always interfere with loran reception. You can actually hear the noise generated by a fluorescent light with a handheld AM radio: Tune the radio between local stations, turn on the fluorescent lights, and listen for the noise. There is very little filtering that can be added to fluorescent lights to attenuate this interference from their electronic chopper circuits. It has been such a big problem that some fluorescent light manufacturers, such as the Guest Corporation, now produce assemblies with interference rejection properties to keep them "quiet" for loran reception.

Another source of loran interference is television and video monitor displays, including rasterscan radar and video fishfinders. In these units, the horizontal oscillator sweep frequency multiplies harmonically into loran receiver range, and the resultant signal can be strong enough to wipe out even the strongest loran signals. You can test for this interference by turning video equipment on and off while watching the loran's signal-to-noise ratio readout. If a loran set goes crazy when you turn on a specific piece of video equipment, corrective action is needed. Good grounding of both the loran receiver and the video equipment will help eliminate this problem. Shielding of the interfering electronics can also help.

Virtually all loran receivers convert the TDs to corresponding latitude and longitude readouts, which many mariners find much easier and more familiar to use. You press a button to choose which type of coordinates you want to read. The lat/lon readout is essential in areas, such as at the fringes of loran coverage, where the TD curves may not be printed on charts or, as is more often the case, where the charted TD lines intersect at impossibly oblique angles and it is very tough to interpolate and transfer the already imprecise TD positions. Baja California and the Bahamas are good examples. In areas such as these, the lat/lon readout, while not, perhaps, highly accurate, is much easier to use. Unlike the absolute accuracy, however, the repeatability of position fixes will usually still be high in fringe areas.

What's Available (And Buying Tips)

More than 50 different loran sets are available today, the majority being imported, and all are good performers. Midrange list prices are $500 to $1,000. The most expensive sets are under $3,000, while the least expensive ones, many of which offer excellent performance in most conditions, are priced below $200.

Mail-order houses are doing a great job of providing the most product for the least amount of money, but buying from a catalog gives you no chance to get the feel of the unit before you purchase it.

As mentioned earlier, many loran sets apply ASF corrections automatically. This is done by means of a preprogrammed algorithm that assumes a given error in a given area. The algorithm is developed based on actual readings taken in waters around the country, but not all these ASF correction programs are created equal. You may still need to do a manual ASF correction for the most accuracy. But don't assume an auto-ASF loran allows manual correction; look for the words "auto and manual" on the spec sheet under the heading of ASF correction. And of course, a few lorans don't have auto-ASF. They require you to punch in the necessary corrections.

ASF correction is not an exotic and expensive option, and should be part of the loran receiver you choose.

All loran units are equipped with notch filters to screen out unwanted noise from frequencies near the loran 100-kHz band. A good set will have four or more, and in most receivers at least two of these are adjustable. Though they initially are factory-set, they also can be calibrated by the dealer to screen out known noise sources in your local waters. Be forewarned that a discounter selling by mail order, if it is not a factory-authorized dealer, may lack the facilities to "tune" a receiver for your locale.

The better receivers have, in addition to preset notch filters, other internal filters that automatically self-adjust to weed out unwanted signals on surrounding frequencies. Alternatively, there may be manually adjustable filters—either external or internal—that can be retuned for new cruising areas and new environmental or onboard noise sources. These may be desirable near large metropolitan areas or to combat high shipboard noise levels from engine ignition systems, fluorescent lights, bilge pumps, tachometers, etc.

Most, if not all, loran receivers are sensitive enough to receive the needed signals and obtain a position fix anywhere in the Coastal Confluence Zone, and the repeatability of fixes is universally good. Bluewater voyagers and those intending to cruise extensively in the fringe areas of loran coverage should be aware, however, that there are differences among receivers in the ability to pick up a weak signal, separate it from unwanted noise, and use it as the basis for a fix. For those comparing manufacturers' specs, a "dynamic range" of 120 decibels (the norm is 110) and an "acquisition signal-to-noise ratio" of -18 to -20 (the usual is -10 to -15) might indicate a heightened ability in this regard (and a higher price tag).

A few older units require you to select and enter the GRI of the chain you wish to use, while most models either use the last chain entered or automatically choose the best one for the locale. In the latter case the choice is made on the basis of signal strength levels, signal-to-noise ratios, crossing angles of the TDs, TD gradients, and the proximities of baseline extensions. These units will apply the same criteria in selecting the most advantageously placed secondaries within the chain. In essence, your thinking is done by the loran's microprocessor, a feature that is best appreciated in unfamiliar waters.

Once the unit is turned on, it may require five minutes to settle down and start giving consistent readouts. Some sets need less than two minutes, but it's usually best to allow at least five. In the interim, the unit goes through a self-testing mode.

When the unit is ready, it will let you know with a beep, or else the display will stop flashing. On displays that are large enough, the present position will show at all times, regardless of what other data is chosen. On any unit you can always recall the position just by pushing the position key.

A loran receiver does much more than fix a position. One of its most important functions is to memorize destinations and the courses needed to reach them. Each destination or point along the way is called a "waypoint." You can load a set of waypoints into the loran before departure. You press the waypoint button and enter each waypoint by its TD or latitude/longitude coordinates. The loran gives distance to the waypoint, course to steer, and, once you are underway, time to go and estimated time of arrival at the waypoint. If you have been to the location once before, it's possible to use the loran's repeatable accuracy to return to the waypoint with a precision of 50 feet or better.

Loran sets typically can store 100 to 300 waypoints or more. Commercial crabbers and loberstermen may use the full capacity for memorizing dropping points for their traps. But while it may be handy to store a number of selected waypoints representing buoys or landfalls in your local waters, few recreational users will use more than 5 or 6 waypoints in a single passage. You can then store the entire set of waypoints as a route you can follow again precisely, day or night, fair weather or foul. The route needn't even be entered digit-by-digit; you can record a route as you travel it. As you reach each turning point, you press a button to enter that position as a waypoint. Each waypoint gets a number in sequence; with some receivers you can also identify it with a name, such as the name of the buoy or light you are passing. Then you enter the set of waypoints in the loran's route library.

Having a waypoint to steer to means the loran must now direct the helmsman. The loran automatically and continuously adjusts the course to steer, to counteract leeway and cross current as well as sloppy helming. Apart from the visual display showing which way to steer, there's a cross-track alarm you can set to go off when you stray too far off the desired course. Remember that lorans usually report off-track error in distance from course rather than in degrees, as for a compass.

Loran liquid crystal displays (LCDs) have become bigger, with better contrast and a wider range of information to view than, say, five years ago.

At night they are backlit for easy viewing, and they consume almost no power at all. However, LCD quality and the way data is laid out on it can make or break the loran as a practical navigation tool. Sheer size allows larger digits, which are easier to see across a bridge or cockpit. Some of the larger displays, though, are laid out for up to seven lines of information—each line is fairly small, and the whole screen looks cluttered. We prefer fewer, larger screen characters.

With more and more lorans being mounted in the open, LCD contrast and viewing angle can be critical. Powerboat helmsmen usually will put the receiver right in front of them, so brightness and contrast are more important than viewing angle. Sailing helmsmen spend more time operating from one side of the cockpit or the other; thus a display that doesn't go blank when you move to one side is a must, as is good contrast. It's easy to compare displays at an electronics dealer before buying; with a unit bought through the mail you're on your own.

The degree of resolution of the readout also varies, with many receivers displaying TDs to the nearest tenth of a microsecond, and a few displaying them to the nearest hundredth of a microsecond. The latter might be considered overkill, implying more precision than even loran can habitually offer, since 0.01 microsecond is equivalent to less than 10 feet on most TD gradients. However, if you're using the receiver in the repeatable accuracy mode to find a favorite fishing spot, dive site, or sailboat racing mark after dark, hundredth microsecond readouts may be very important in your buying decision.

Steering graphics are a popular aspect of loran displays. A series of markers to one side or the other of center show how far off course you are. A hundredth of a nautical mile is a good increment for each segment of the off-course display. Additionally, arrows or plain English instructions tell you which way to steer. Steering graphics can be helpful in poor visibility, and when there's current or leeway, steering by the loran may be more accurate than by the ship's compass. Then again, it may not if there's persistent interference. You want to be confident of the loran's position-fixing in the area to be traveled before you trust it over your main compass.

For most mariners, preference for one loran set is decided by the front-panel controls—how easy is it to make the unit do its thing properly? Contrary to some manufacturers' claims, fewer buttons on the keypad don't make for simpler operation. With as complex and multifunctional an instrument as a loran, the fewer buttons there are, the more keystrokes are needed for each operation. Remembering the right sequence of keystrokes is always harder than finding the button with the right label on it. Turning on the loran and getting a position fix should be no harder than pushing the "on/off" button and then pressing "position."

Some receivers do a better job of prompting you with instructions on the screen to take the next step in entering waypoint information or requests through the keyboard. Manufacturers are sensitive to the fact that they have created something so sophisticated it may be scaring mariners off, and they are trying to humanize the equipment. One unit will flash "Baloney" if you try to enter a waypoint that's in the middle of a land mass, or "Aye aye" in response to a keyboard-entered request.

For open-cockpit use, water-resistant receiver housings are necessary. Most lorans have a gasketed faceplate and a keypad made of a single piece of silicone to keep out spray. Some keypads are a flexible part of the faceplate itself. Plugs are either screw-in with O-rings or are BNC bayonet fittings. There's no need to worry about a loran overheating during operation, so a good seal can be made. Many units may be immersed temporarily without danger, and may even survive a sinking in shallow water. Be sure to rinse the receiver in a gentle flow of fresh water at the end of the trip. Most loran sets are easily removable from their mounts for safekeeping when you're away from the boat.

Handheld lorans don't have the performance of permanently installed ones, but they do have their own advantages. This one contains the same internal components and functions as a dash-mount version by the same manufacturer; it runs on AA batteries, though, and has a telescoping antenna. Signal acquisition in a handheld is usually inferior unless you hold it high and clear of metal objects on the boat. For the vast majority of navigation functions a handheld does the job, and it can do it on your boat when the main power is down, or on anyone else's boat. Handheld prices are about the same as for comparable dash-mount models.

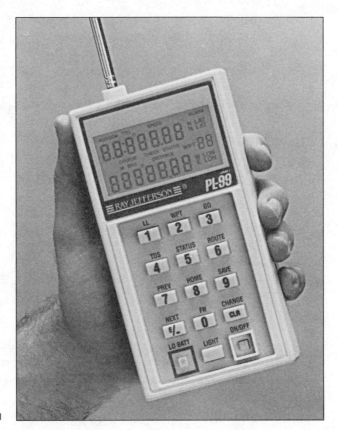

It is also possible to purchase a receiver with a waterproof remote-control head, enabling operation of the receiver from the cockpit while the main unit stays dry below.

A few compact dash-mount lorans may still be available with a battery pack to make them portable. These somewhat bulky units have a more recent successor in the handheld loran. Handhelds are not much bigger than a handheld VHF, and run on six AA batteries. A handheld can work well as the boat's only loran, but it's also excellent as a backup unit in case the ship's power fails, and it's perfect for taking on explorations in the ship's tender.

A typical handheld has the same internals and features as its dash-mount counterpart, but its display will be a small two-line type to save space and battery power. It may also not have quite the waypoint and route memory of the dash-mount version. It may not have the data port allowing interfacing with an autopilot or plotter, either.

A handheld loran's telescoping antenna is more vulnerable to interference and signal blockage than permanent sets' antennas. You have to hold it clear above lifelines and rails and away from tuna towers, rigging, and other electronics. Find the best place on the boat for good reception and use that spot consistently. The receiver will perform with adequate accuracy.

Handhelds shouldn't cost any more their hard-wired brethren. What you pay extra for in charging accessories you save in not having a separate antenna and cable to install.

On the other hand, handhelds usually come with a pocket-type mounting bracket that lets them operate directly off ship's power. In this mode of operation, it makes sense to have a handheld loran with a data port, to drive an autopilot and other electronics.

Telling you which way to steer to offset current and leeway is an invaluable capability. Equally important is that most lorans, even the least expensive, output these same highly accurate steering instructions to an autopilot. On a voyage of almost any length, the loran-autopilot combination is worth at least two extra crewmembers

Through the 1980s, the problem of interfacing compatibility among various marine electronics was gradually overcome by manufacturers through the National Marine Electronics Association. The first standard generally agreed on was the NMEA 0180 output, specifically for loran-autopilot communication. It's a one-way conversation; the loran sends a byte (8 bits) of digital information containing 5 bits of cross-track data, 1 bit of left-right steering command, and 2 bits for signal validity and code identification. The data is sent to the autopilot at 1,200 bits per second, thus many bytes are averaged by the autopilot before it makes a steering correction.

Today, almost every autopilot can be driven by every loran with an NMEA output. Still, it is best to consult a marine electronics specialist or the manufacturers involved to ensure the two products have proven compatible.

Since the NMEA 0180 standard, much more sophisticated interfaces have been developed, some by individual manufacturers for use among their own products, and two more by the NMEA. NMEA 0182 expanded on the information output by the loran and delivered it in a different language, as the standard ASCII characters used in computer programming. But NMEA 0182 was only a stepping stone to a much more comprehensive code, NMEA 0183. NMEA 0182 is available on only a few lorans and autopilots, so read the manufacturers' specs carefully to be sure which code you're getting.

NMEA 0183 is the standard interface for the foreseeable future. And with good cause: it allows two-way, not one-way, data exchange; and it's not just for lorans and autopilots, but any instrument: chart plotter, sounder, speedo, electronic compass, GPS, etc. Being ASCII-based, it allows data to be sent to a computer, or even transmitted over radio to shore stations or other boats. Because there is more data in each message, the bit rate is 4,800.

Being more complex, it took the better part of a decade for all manufacturers to interpret 0183 in a way all their products could understand. By now the majority of marine electronics are basically compatible, and a loran can direct an autopilot, provide position and speed data for a chart plotter or radar, and give a sailboat racing instrument system time and distance to laylines or marks.

This is not to say that the interfacing problem is a thing of the past for any two devices. Always ask the manufacturers of the electronics you want to link up whether their products have been successfully interfaced. Be specific about make, model, and software version. Also find out whether any hidden costs are involved for things like interface or junction boxes, extra cable, or dealer installation and testing.

Lorans offer many secondary functions—some useful, some less so. These include clocks, clock alarms, and interval, countup, and countdown timers. Some sets, having backup batteries or "nonvolatile" memories (which are not erased when the juice is turned off), can be taken home for waypoint programming. Many units have a panic button that, when pushed, will store the precise current position in memory, enabling you to return to the spot where someone or something has been lost overboard.

Here is a list of other features you may wish to consider when shopping for a loran receiver:

- Ability to reject skywaves in favor of groundwaves, if present
- Skywave warning indicator

- Loran chain false indicator
- Loran chain error indicator
- "Off the air" secondary station identifier
- Signal-to-noise ratio readout
- Low signal alert
- Nonvolatile memory that is erasable only on special command
- Automatic sequencing of several displays
- Cross-chain interference rejection
- Convenient mounting brackets
- Low power consumption
- Numerous service stations wherever you plan to voyage
- And of course, competitive pricing

Installation

A loran set is a very sensitive radio receiver without a loudspeaker; you can install it yourself provided proper care is taken. The necessary small current draw from a 12-volt source is easily tapped from the electrical panel. It is best to use an independent 12-volt line that goes directly to a circuit breaker, the breaker, in turn, having a direct connection to the battery. The 12-volt wiring doesn't necessarily need to be big—a pair of No. 12 marine duplex wires will work just fine. Wiring directly through a breaker (for safety) to the ship's battery system eliminates noise sources that might travel up a power lead from another connection point. If tapped directly, the ship's battery will act as a giant filter to help "smooth out" random noise pulses found in other parts of the marine electrical system.

Since the loran receiver draws only about ½ to 1 amp, there is little worry that it's going to pull down your starting or auxiliary battery if you happen to leave your set on over the weekend.

Like any radio receiver, a loran set needs a good antenna and a ground system, the latter to enhance weak signal reception and to help the receiver sort out weak groundwave signals from a high noise level. A good ground is also necessary to prevent dry-weather static discharges from erasing any of a set's waypoint memory. To get the most out of a receiver, a groundplane of 60 to 100 square feet is probably necessary. Components of this groundplane might include keel bolts, the engine block, through hulls, etc., as well as copper screen and copper foil when needed. Copper foil should be run from the receiver chassis and the antenna base to the groundplane. Methods of achieving a proper groundplane are discussed in more detail in the chapter on single sideband radio; while the procedures may be

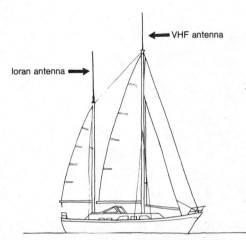

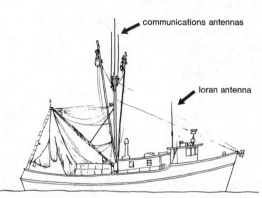

VHF antenna

loran antenna

communications antennas

loran antenna

When power- or sailboats have antennas for VHF or SSB equipment, the loran antenna should be mounted as far from them as is practical. Since any antenna is subject to damage, a spare whip should be aboard.

tedious and time-consuming, the standards of quality need not be as high for the receive-only loran unit as they are for a single sideband transceiver. An owner installation is therefore certainly feasible. (If you do intend to have a professional do the installation, buy the receiver from a marine electronics dealer and include the price of the installation in the purchase package. It will be less expensive than a time-and-materials basis.)

Loran receivers are shipped with a matching antenna system. Most loran antennas, however, are nothing more than nine-foot white fiberglass CB whip aerials. The whip should be mounted out in the open and as far away from noise sources as possible. The heart of the antenna system is an encapsulated pre-amplifier, which the whip screws into. This pre-amp magnifies the incoming signal level and creates a narrow pass band for loran frequencies to enter. You may wonder how this low-noise preamplifier works without a DC voltage cable to provide power to it; current is indeed supplied to it, but that current uses the same coaxial cable that carries the incoming signal from pre-amp to receiver. One coax cable doing two jobs simplifies the antenna installation. If you do not know how to solder coax connectors, use the crimped, no-solder connectors discussed in the chapter on VHF radio. If you should ever break the whip, any CB radio-type whip will do quite nicely on the preamplifier mount. Most loran whips have a 3/8-by-24-inch thread, common among CB antennas.

Height is not important for a loran antenna; anywhere in the clear is fine. You can even rake the antenna back at an angle of up to 45 degrees without significant signal loss. Just keep it away from fluorescent lights,

The transsom-mounted loran antenna on a sailboat. the height of the antenna is not critical, but the angle should be more than 45 degrees above horizontal. Regular CB-type antennas are satisfactory and relatively inexpensive. The coaxial cable from the preamplifier is fed through the extension mast to the receiver at the navigator's station.

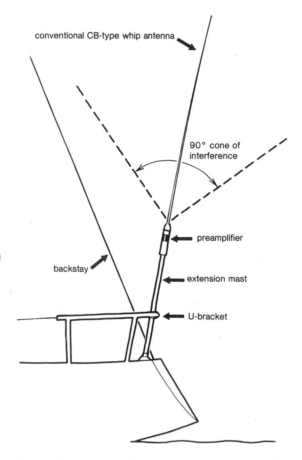

conventional CB-type whip antenna

90° cone of interference

preamplifier

backstay

extension mast

U-bracket

bait tank motors, refrigeration systems—anything that generates electrical noise.

Troubleshooting

If your set does not function properly when the engine is running, noise-suppression steps are probably in order. Filters to eliminate ignition interference are available from marine electronics specialists, as are filters specific to just about any other noise source. Diagnose intermittent reception by having another person watch the display while you turn on and off possible noise sources.

Firm connections to antenna and ground circuit are essential. Any loose or corroded connections should be cleaned, tightened, resoldered, or replaced as necessary.

Nearby military transmitters can mask loran signal reception. If your receiver doesn't work in one locale but does work everywhere else, this is probably the problem. Factory or dealer adjustment of internal notch filters

Approaching a waypoint in current, or with a steering compass with unmeasured deviation, your approach to a loran waypoint may often look like this. There is no error in the loran's steering program. In fact, the cross-track steering graphics available in some lorans can minimize course offset by noting drift and recommending a course that compensates for it.

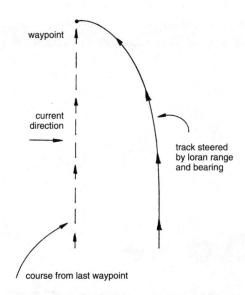

waypoint

current direction

track steered by loran range and bearing

course from last waypoint

may be necessary. You may be able to avoid this by purchasing the unit from a dealer who is familiar with the interference sources in your local waters.

The Future of Loran

Within 10 years, GPS will become the ubiquitous radionavigation system. However, the government will maintain the loran-C system for the foreseeable future as a land-based backup to GPS and as one of the primary means of navigation for air traffic. The Feds' commitment is evidenced by the opening in 1990 and 1991 of two new mid-continent loran chains for air use. That has caused a reconfiguration of coverage for some existing chains. The result has been improved coverage in the Gulf of Mexico.

Unfortunately, at the same time, some other chains are being turned off. The Hawaiian chain went off in July 1992; overseas chains operated by the U.S. Coast Guard will be turned over to the host governments to be operated or shut down.

The last decade has seen increased interest in loran in Europe. The system may expand south of the North Sea and beyond the western Mediterranean. The future of new and existing stations in Europe is uncertain, however.

The GPS receivers may or may not become less expensive than loran sets. Don't expect improved accuracy from loran receivers, though; they won't be able to compete with GPS. Do expect the same interfacing abilities and ancillary features to show up on both types of receivers.

Loran will continue to be an accurate, reliable, low-cost radionavigation system practical for virtually any boat and any navigator.

CHAPTER 11

Noise Suppression

by Gordon West

Electrical interference noise is the nemesis of modern marine electronic gear. Whether noise is generated by a boat's engine or originates from another onboard source or an inadequate installation, any marine electronics dealer that installs gear has an obligation to the boatowner to trace the source of the problem. Common practice when the cost of a major marine electronics package (including installation) is quoted by a dealer is to leave ample room for an extra day on board knocking out problems of electrical noise. When you install your own gear, chronic interference is your problem, not the gear manufacturer's or the dealer's. This chapter should help you locate and eliminate the more common sources of noise.

Electrical noise is not hard to spot on communications receivers, but on specialized pieces of marine navigational equipment, noise can sneak in without your knowing it. To begin this discussion, let's look at the common symptoms that accompany gasoline engine–related noise in marine installations:

- Popping and clatter on VHF set with engine turned on; completely quiet with engine off.
- Single sideband signals disappear into popping and clatter when engine is turned on.

- Your sophisticated audio system "sings" and buzzes, with popping and clatter on weaker AM and FM signals.
- Speckles and rolling bars on the TV set when the engine is turned on.
- Loran signals disappear, and the signal-to-noise ratio indicator on the loran set indicates poor reception when engine is on; with the engine off, loran works fine.
- Low-level satellite passes are not picked up by the satnav receiver with the ignition system on.
- OMNI/VOR reception is impossible just a few miles from the transmitting station.
- Low-frequency Omega, loran, and RDF reception is impossible with the engine running.
- Speckles appear and weak targets disappear on radar scopes.

The recurring theme is that as soon as you turn on the engine the noise comes in, and there is little question that the noise is generated by the engine and its ignition system. The first reaction is to blame the sophisticated electronics for being incapable of filtering out the noise. The fault is not with the electronics, however, but rather with the interfering source. As radio receivers are made ever more sensitive to weak signals, their sensitivity to noise increases in direct proportion. These electronics are not *supposed* to filter out noise, even though some offer noise-blanking and noise-elimination circuits. Such circuits only help the effort; the real steps must be taken at the source. According to Jack Honey, a marine electronics and amateur radio operator noise elimination specialist: "Tracking down and eliminating electrical noise leaks is just like plugging leaks in the bottom of a boat. The job isn't done until every leak has been stopped." Honey's company (Marine Technology Corporation, Signal Hill, California) offers a complete line of EMI noise elimination filters and instructional sheets.

Finding The Leaks

The hardest part of quenching electrical noise is simply locating the point source of the noise being radiated or inductively coupled on the electrical wiring. Once the source is identified, filters and shielding will quickly and effectively cure the problem.

One method of searching is to listen to the characteristic sound of the interference on a communications receiver—or better yet, on an inexpensive pocket AM radio with an earphone. Most noise is broadbanded, with the greatest intensity on frequencies that an AM radio will receive. In order to pinpoint the noise, you may need to wrap the radio in aluminum foil except for a small hole near the built-in loop stick antenna. This shielding will give you highly directional reception, enabling you to move the tiny radio around in the engine compartment to good advantage as you attempt to locate the source.

Another way to find a hotspot of noise is to take apart a defunct cassette player and mount the playback heads on a three-foot wooden or plastic probe. Using shielded wires, connect the heads to a simple audio amplifier with a high-impedance input. Now move the head around until you pick up the noise you are experiencing.

Following are some of the noises most commonly found aboard boats, motorhomes, cars, and airplanes:

Type of Noise	Possible Interference Source
Distinct pops at idle, increasing to roar at high engine speeds	Gas engine ignition system
Popping sound that increases in intensity as engine speed increases	Electronic tachometer
Musical whine, increasing in pitch to a whistle at high engine speeds	Alternator or generator
Intermittent frying noise	Voltage regulator
Whine or buzz from certain accessories, even though the engine is turned off	Accessory motors or power converters
Crackling noise when certain lights are turned on	Fluorescent lights
Constant-pitch low-frequency noise when entertainment electronics are turned on	Television receiver
Persistent noise on a receiver even when its antenna is disconnected	Conducted noise on the power line or from switcher power supply
Grinding noise when in gear	Intermittent electrical grounding of shaft

Finding, Filtering, And Isolating Ignition Interference

"Pigtail" capacitors have traditionally been used for filtering ignition noise, and they work reasonably well at low and medium frequencies. They are completely ineffective at VHF frequencies, however, because of the high inductance of the long lead. Don't expect these capacitors to be an all-out cure for ignition noise.

Let's start with the engine. There are plenty of "switches" in an engine's electrical system that will generate noise. The breaker points in a gasoline engine make and break the circuit from the battery through the coil to ground perhaps 200 times per second. Without good noise filter suppression techniques, the interrupted current and its associated radio frequency impulse noise will flow in the wiring from the coil back up to the ignition key, and from there back to the battery and the ground. This makes a very large and effective loop antenna to radiate noise throughout the vessel. If these wires are cabled in with other wires, RF impulses will be coupled into the companion wires as well.

Another concern is the small arcs in the high-tension part of the distributor and in the spark plugs themselves. These arcs generate radio frequency noise, which can be radiated by the plug wiring and is also coupled through the coil into the primary circuit wiring, where it joins the RF energy produced at the points.

Other problems include alternator diodes, which cause a sudden change in current when they go from forward conduction to cutoff. The older, DC generators and motors have brushes in their moving commutator segments that switch current in both the internal armature winding and associated external circuits. The voltage regulator has a vibrator that chops the field circuit thousands of times per second when it's regulating, with resultant RF noise flowing throughout the wiring harness.

Replace old spark plug wiring with new resistant-type wiring. One such wiring construction features a fiberglass core impregnated with a conductive powder, and it works well in knocking down the popping noise from gas engines. This type of wiring must be changed every two years, however, because of its susceptibility to failure in a moist environment. Belden Corporation markets a spark plug wire under the NAPA label that uses a conductive neoprene tube and seems to stand up better aboard boats. Contrary to persistent rumor, the use of resistance wire to the plugs does not appear to involve any sacrifice whatsoever in engine performance if the balance of the ignition system is in good shape. Jury-rigging plug wires using coax cable with a grounded outside braid will only foul up the ignition system timing.

Use of both resistance wire and *resistor plugs* is more effective than the use of either one alone. Be sure to check your owner's manual for the proper plug type and gap for your engine.

Resistance wire with resistor plugs.

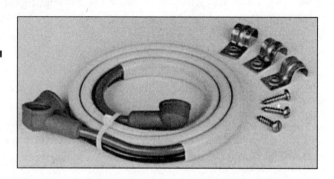

A low-pass or feed-through capacitance filter at the coil in series with the connection to the ignition key and any other connection made to the battery side of the coil is an absolute must. The usual choice is a low-pass, PI-type LC filter rated at 5 amps, with good operative characteristics from 0.1 MHz through 300 MHz. The filter should be mounted solidly to the engine or the coil bracket, as close as is convenient to the battery terminal of the coil. Keep all filter wires as short as possible, and make sure that the bracket securing the filter is well DC-grounded.

Electronic tachometers that pick up 400-volt impulses on the coil will usually radiate noise along the wire to the tach readout unless the entire wiring harness is encapsulated in a ground sheath. Many aren't. If yours isn't, you should shield the tachometer wiring as well as install a tachometer filter at the coil in series with the lead to the tach. Use a low-pass RC filter, which won't load the ignition circuit with additional capacitance yet passes enough signal to operate the tachometer.

Again, you can spot these noise sources by using a transistorized AM radio with an earphone, or a cassette tape pickup head wired into an audio amplifier.

Alternator noise, which is easily identified by the musical whine it generates, comes from the typical three-phase, 14-pole AC alternator with a DC field and a built-in six-diode, full-wave bridge rectifier circuit. The level of whine varies with output current, and thus is controlled by the regulator and the amount of connected load. It may fade to almost nothing as the regulator cuts the charge rate to a fully recharged battery back to just a few hundred milliamps. A 60-amp low-pass filter in series with a heavy alternator output lead is a must; small alternator filters installed at the affected receiver will generally offer only 50 percent relief. The proper filter is a PI section, LC, low-pass filter with low lead inductance, rated to 60 amps continuous from 6 to 115 volts AC or DC. If you're working on a system that uses an old-fashioned generator, the same type of filter is used.

Voltage regulator noise elimination is a bit more tedious. Additional grounding and shielding of the voltage regulator case may help. This done, locate the field wire and possibly a second light-gauge wire running from the alternator to the regulator. If these are cabled in with other wiring, they should be run separately. You might also disconnect the existing wires and substitute shielded wires, making sure the shield of each wire is grounded at both ends. RG-8 coax cable is ideal for this shielding.

You can also filter the regulator wiring with 0.2 mfd, 200-volt capacitors if you keep the leads very short. Never bypass the field lead between the alternator or generator and the regulator with these capacitors, however.

Small motors that radiate noise when turned on can be bypassed with these same 0.2 mfd, 200-volt capacitors between the hot lead and the case of

Power line noise filter.

Transceiver noise filters.

Alternator noise filter.

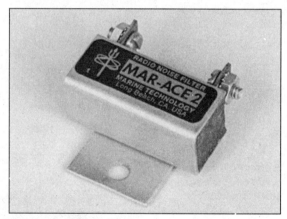

Radio noise filter.

the motor, keeping leads very short. If the capacitors can be mounted inside the case from each brush to ground, all the better. Specific filters available from leading noise filter manufacturers actually contain three capacitors specifically designed for quieting these accessories.

In the case of television or fluorescent light interference with loran, Omega, or RDF systems, you can try relocating the receiving antenna, or, easier yet, simply turn off the TV or fluorescent lights when operating the receiver in weak signal areas. Newer fluorescent lights for motorhomes and boats now have special noise elimination circuits to keep the energy from being radiated down the line.

Conducted interference may sometimes occur if large high-current wiring bundles are located near a sensitive audio tape player or radio frequency receivers. You can sometimes knock down a tremendous amount of conducted interference simply by relocating a wiring bundle just a few inches farther from the receiver. You might also try shielding large wiring bundles with aluminum foil, making sure that the foil does not contact any hot wire. Shielding audio speaker leads is also important, making sure that both ends of the braid are connected to a good ground source.

A relatively new gremlin has snuck into your marine electronics equipment, causing disastrous problems. The culprit is starter spike hash.

When you crank over your engines, your starter motor sends out electrical spikes throughout your 12-volt DC wiring. These spikes, looking quite similar to a data stream of pulses, get into your circuit breaker panel and move up the line to your wheelhouse or flying bridge marine sets. Some marine electronics, when turned off, prevent the spikes from going any further. But not all marine electronics necessarily turn completely off.

Equipment such as loran receivers, your marine VHF transceiver, GPS receivers, and other navigational instrumentation may have an always-on circuit, even though the on/off switch is turned off. These sets require a small voltage to float their internal memory battery, keeping you from losing all of the valuable digitized and channelized information on the tiny internal chip.

Starter motor spikes might scramble marine electronic memory circuits. This device filters out spikes and also provides engine cranking spike isolation.

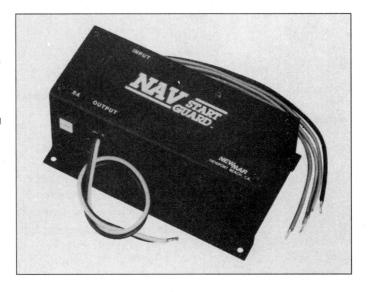

You guessed it—when the starter spikes get all the way through to that sensitive chip, the spikes look like a data stream, and your memory may get instantly erased for good. All of those waypoints—all of those loran and GPS coordinates—all of those presets to your automatic pilot system—all of those default positions to your radar—they all go. When you turn on your equipment, the memories read zero, and you now have several days of reprogramming ahead of you.

At first everyone thought that memories would get wiped out because of "brown outs." In other words, when you start your engine, your voltage dips below 10 volts, and this must do something to the memory of some of your marine electronics. Not true. Why can you remove a piece of marine electronics from a boat without any power at all, and still have the memory survive? It does, so it's not voltage, or the absence of voltage, that causes memory loss.

It's those darn starter motor spikes. One company, Newmar (Santa Ana, California), plus several other marine specialty groups, have developed voltage isolator boxes that are tied into your ignition switch. When you turn the key, the box instantly switches over your marine electronics to a floating battery, independent of your ship's electrical system. Once the engine kicks in you release the key, and this little black box then puts you back onto your normal ship's power. An internal rechargeable battery not only recharges itself, but acts as a further buffer against any voltage spikes when the engine is running. These boxes may be a last resort when nothing else seems to work.

One final note on noise and ignition problems—if you have a marine electronics specialist install your equipment, make sure everything goes out for a sea trial. It's amazing how many things might develop when you are away from the dock that the technician might miss. If you're paying top dollar to have a professional marine electronics specialist install your gear, make absolutely sure everything is working properly before you pay your final bill. If it's a turn-key installation, make absolutely sure that when you do turn the key, all of those valuable memories won't get lost to starter and noise spikes.

CHAPTER 12

The Global Positioning System

by Freeman Pittman

Even before it has become officially operational, the Navstar Global Positioning System (GPS) is already the standard against which all other navigation systems in the world are measured. GPS offers instant position fixes that are more accurate than any other technique, electronic or otherwise. It maintains exceptional accuracy worldwide, virtually 24 hours a day, in any weather. With a GPS receiver in your hand or on your bridge, and with a government chart on your chart table, you have the most powerful tools for safe navigation available.

Even better, GPS is still evolving in the marine market. The receiver you need to tap the GPS network will cost less and become more compact and powerful in the next few years. In five to 10 years, GPS will be used for purposes we may not even have imagined.

The GPS project was started by the Department of Defense (DOD) in 1973 on the heels of the Navy's succesful Transit satnav system. Transit, the original satellite-based radionavigation system, was designed to help nuclear submarines position themselves accurately and quickly after long periods under water. Transit, though, contains only seven satellites and thus can't give continuous coverage. Time between fixes is between 20 minutes and six hours, though the average is close to two hours.

GPS satellites are not geostationary—they have inclined orbits that take them over any point on their ground track once every 12 hours.

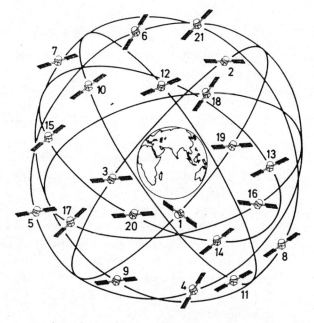

With a planned constellation of 21 satellites orbiting the earth in six planes, GPS was designed for full-time coverage (see above). It differs from Transit also in using signals from multiple satellites—not just one—to achieve a position. (In fact, GPS operates more like loran, with moving satellites replacing the fixed transmitters on the ground.) GPS adds a third dimension, altitude, and is thus useful in army field work or surveying in any kind of topography. And since GPS updates a position at very high speed (about one-second intervals for civilian sets), it is also used for navigating aircraft, even missles.

In 1992 Department of Defense plans called for the full 21-satellite constellation to be in place by the end of 1993. Skepticism would not be unwarranted given the system's track record on keeping a schedule, though with 19 working satellites at the time of writing, the DOD's prediction is pretty safe.

Don't take full coverage for granted until the system is officially declared operational, however, sometime between 1993 and 1996. Experiments, glitches, and other factors may still play a role in denying mariners 24-hour coverage until then.

How It Works

GPS satellite specifications

Weight: 1,900 lbs

Span across solar panels: 17 ft

Planned useful life: 7.5 years

Number in orbit: 24 (21 operating, 3 in-orbit spares)

Orbital altitude: 10,900 nautical miles

Orbital period: 12 hours

Orbital plane: 55°equatorial plane

Satellite distribution: 6 planes, 4 satellites in each

GPS is a ranging system. If your receiver hears a satellite's signal, records its arrival, and knows when the message was sent, it can measure the signal's time of travel and translate that to distance. Perform that process for three or four satellites in different parts of the sky at once, and you have a position.

Take a look at the figure below. Knowing the distance from one satellite would place you at some point on a theoretical sphere around the satellite (a). Knowing the distance from two satellites would further limit the area in which you could be—a circular line of position is created where the spheres for the two satellites intersect (b). The intersection of a third satellite's sphere with the other two will cut that line in one or two places (c). But since you are on the surface of yet a fourth sphere—the Earth's—any ambiguity over your position dissolves, since one of the two possible positions won't be on the planet's surface. A GPS receiver resolves all these mathematical problems and more in less than a second.

For a three-dimensional fix, four satellites are needed; for a two-dimensional fix, you would need three. The extra satellite measurement in each case is used to overcome receiver time errors.

Each satellite uses an atomic clock for the ultimate in accuracy and reliability. The clock generates a 10.23 MHz frequency from which all the satellite's signals are derived.

The satellite transmits on two microwave frequencies: 1575.42 MHz and 1227.6 MHz. The latter carries a coded signal for precision ranging

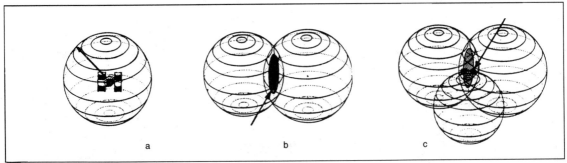

GPS uses ranges from satellites to determine the only possible position of the receiver. (Courtesy Trimble.)

purposes (P code). This P code, which is accurate to 15 meters, is used by the U.S. military and is thus encrypted. There is no receiver circuit for the P code on civilian sets.

The 1575.42 MHz frequency carries another code that can be received by civilian sets and used for ranging: the Coarse/Acquisition (C/A) code, which is repeated every millisecond.

When a receiver acquires a satellite's signal, it begins to generate its own copy of the code as well. The receiver shifts its replica code in time until the two codes are synchronized. The time delay between identical portions of the two codes is the time of signal travel. Then the receiver corrects its measurements of the satellite signal travel times to find the one solution that fits with all the satellites' known positions.

In addition to the ranging code is a continuously updated navigation message running at 50 bits per second. The message contains present satellite position, speed and direction, and time information, along with some data about health and position of all the GPS satellites. Borrowing from celestial navigation terminology, the former data is called ephemeris, while the latter is called almanac. The entire message takes 30 seconds and gives information a receiver needs to operate with the transmitting satellite for the next four hours.

The satellite's signal is broadcast at an extremely low power, so low that it cannot be detected against the backround noise without software that locates the rises and falls of the signal mathematically. Partly the low power is to frustrate enemy decoding, and partly it's to make the system very power-efficient. Naturally, this very low signal-to-noise ratio (SNR) has an effect on how receivers operate.

Receiver Design

The first generation of commercial GPS receivers is behind us. The scramble of manufacturers to come up with something—anything—to compete with the early leaders is over, and receiver design seems to be trending in fewer directions. Meanwhile, practicality and price are improved.

One of the major distinctions among receivers is how they pull the various satellites' signals from the air. The number of channels each set has, and how the receiver samples each signal are convenient ways to categorize GPS hardware.

We'll start with the simplest approach, and head toward the more complex.

Single channel, slow sequencing. A sequencing receiver tunes in to each visible satellite in sequence, ranging on a satellite's signal for up to a second before moving on to the next satellite. A three-dimensional fix, using four satellites, may take about four seconds of ranging, as well as eight to 10 seconds of listening to the satellites' location messages. Once the receiver has acquired the four satellites, a position can be updated in 12 seconds. Periodically the receiver stops ranging to update satellite almanac data for several minutes.

When introduced, the single-channel, slow-sequencing receiver offered low-cost GPS for the first time. But this has been superseded by faster ways to a fix.

Single channel, multiplexing. This is a high-speed receiver. Multiplexing means dwelling on each satellite's signal for between one and four milliseconds, then coming back to it after sampling each of the other satellites for an equally brief period. Since the satellite message is composed of digital data bits, and since each bit's modulations last about 20 milliseconds, the receiver can sample each bit of data several times before the next bit is broadcast. Assuming a strong signal, ranging on four satellites can be done virtually simultaneously on a single channel. The receiver is said to emulate multi-channel sets. Position updates may take only one second.

Why aren't all receivers single-channel multiplexers? Multiplexing has the disadvantage of a low signal-to-noise ratio. Since the signal is touched on so briefly, you may lose it if it's below the receiver's threshold for acceptance during that instant. Sequencing receivers listen long enough to distinguish the signal from the noise.

On a slow-moving vehicle with an unobstructed view—a perfect definition of a boat—the SNR problem is usually not significant. Most of the time, almost any GPS receiver will do a superb job of telling you where you are, though an onboard transmitting radar set, microwave transmissions from shore, or working with satellites close to the horizon could possibly affect reception.

On the other hand, in rolling seas, a GPS antenna at the masthead of a sailboat, or atop a high sportfisherman's tower might result in some odd speed numbers being factored into the receiver's calculations. The receiver should solve this problem by averaging the speed over a relatively long period. A multiplexing one-channel receiver will retail for $1,200 to $2,000, depending on its features. Assume 25 to 33 percent off at discount houses.

Multichannel, continuous tracking. Multichannel circuitry allows the receiver to listen continuously to more than one satellite at a time, lowering the time between fixes and improving the SNR even more. Some multichannel sets are the sequencing kind—the more channels you have, the less the need to multiplex. These are two- or three-channel receivers.

Then there are the multichannel continuous receivers, the five- and six-channel designs that dedicate one channel to each satellite needed while the fifth, sixth, or both, channels search for new satellites and perform housekeeping duties. These sets have the fastest update rates, the fastest time to first fix, and track satellites as close to the horizon as is possible.

Multichannel sets run the gamut in price from around $1,200 to $3,000 retail, depending on other features.

There are also a few other channel designs, such as the eight-satellite tracking Garmin handheld models, that defy easy comparison. The manufacturer won't describe the proprietary architecture, but says its channelizing is done with software, not hardware, and that it's not a multiplexing receiver. These receivers are competitive with the other handhelds offered.

In the final analysis, it's the receiver's performance, rather than its hardware, that is important to the user. As GPS receivers become more alike, most will probably be multichannel, continuous-tracking sets—because those will be made in such high numbers that they will be the least expensive to manufacture. This is a current trend, anyway, and new technologies always upset safe predictions.

Accuracy and Precision

In spite of its terrific potential accuracy, GPS does have its sources of error, as does every other navigation system. These can be classified as systemic, environmental, and receiver.

Some system errors are caused by the ever-changing satellite geometry. When two satellites are close together, the crossing angles of their LOPs are low, and the area of the fix is wide. When the satellites are farther apart, their LOPs cross at wider angles, and offer a smaller area where you could be. This phenomenon is familiar to navigators using piloting, celestial, RDF, or loran techniques. In GPS product specifications, this dilution of precision (DOP) may be measured in the two-dimensional mode (horizontal dilution of precision, or HDOP), the three-dimensional mode (position DOP, PDOP), or in four dimensions, including time (geometric DOP, GDOP).

Other system error causes are in satellite clocks and in the ephemeris data—the satellite is not quite where its message says it is.

Environmental error is what happens to the signal on its way from the satellite to your receiver. Being a microwave frequency, the signal follows a very straight path. However, it can be slowed by ionospheric activity, and by moisture in the air. It's also possible for the signal to bounce, causing multipath error.

Receiver error is due mainly to the programming of the set. The mathematical computations it performs could be carried to ridiculous lengths or rounded off for efficient operation.

Altogether, the errors in a GPS position are remarkably small. With the pre-operational system up and running almost continuously in 1990-91,

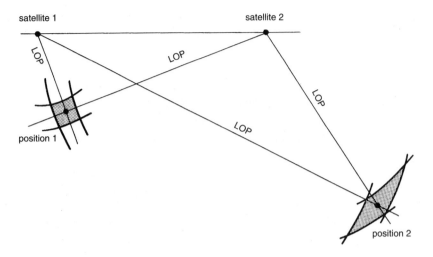

Dilution of precision (DOP) varies according to where the satellites you're using are in the sky. When crossing angles of lines of position (LOPs) are close to 90 degrees, DOP is minimized. When the crossing angles are more acute, DOP is larger. The shaded areas surrounding each position here are defined by the minimum and maximum ranges possible between each satellite and receiver. Though the minimum-to-maximum distance is the same for both Position 1 and Position 2, the area of uncertainty is larger in Position 2 due to the poorer satellite geometry. (Illustration courtesy Magnavox.)

users were finding accuracies well within 100 feet, and often within 50 feet. At that level, the accuracy of your reference points comes into question—a buoy's charted position isn't nearly good enough. Even the chart may not be precise enough to establish accuracy—until GPS-surveyed charts become widely available. However, as we're about to see, the civilian level of accuracy has proved to be too good.

After all the errors over which the system operators and hardware manufacturers have only partial or no control, there is one more—the biggest of all—that is intentional.

Selective Availability (S/A) is the Department of Defense's answer to an enemy's possible use of the civilian GPS code. As we have seen, the C/A code is nearly as accurate as the P code. So the military introduces errors that include satellite clock signal "dithering" and orbital disinformation to reduce position accuracy to plus or minus 100 meters, which matches the stated accuracy of the civilian system of 100 meters 95 percent of the time. Signal degradation is random or virtually so, which is intended to deter as well.

There has been much pressure on the Department of Defense to turn off S/A except in time of crisis, but so far, the Pentagon has resisted. After all, how could S/A foil a surprise attack if it weren't operating? Instead, the military will consider specific requests for civilian use of the Precision code.

And for the rest of us, there is another route to exceptional precision, one which we'll be hearing a lot more of in the coming years. More on that later.

2-D Versus 3-D

Is GPS more accurate in the three-dimensional mode than in two-dimensional? Theoretically, yes, it can be. In practice, it usually is not. In 3-D, an accurate altitude reading can improve horizontal accuracy. The rule of thumb is a foot of vertical error equals about a foot of horizontal error.

However, Selective Availability introduces error in all three dimensions. So the horizontal error S/A creates is compounded by the vertical error.

One manufacturer recommends that marine users manually input their antenna altitude (above sea level) as a constant, and operate in 2-D at all

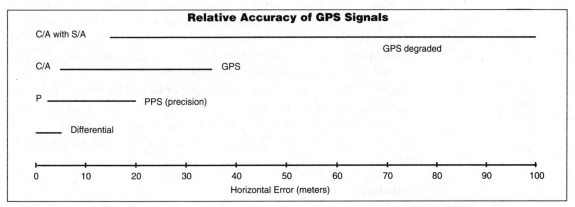

Relative Accuracy of GPS Signals

The P code, which can be received only by the military, is accurate to 15 meters. C/A can be received by civilian sets, and is almost as accurate.

However, S/A degrades the signal to prevent an enemy's possible use of the civilian system.

GPS Characteristics

	Accuracy*		Availability	Coverage	Reliability	Fix Rate	Fix Dimensions	Capacity	Ambiguity Potential
Predictable	Repeatable	Relative							
PPS**			Expected to approach 100%	Worldwide continuous that a 21-satellite constellation will be operating	98% probability	Essentially continuous	3D + Velocity + Time	Unlimited	None
Horz - 17.8M	Horz - 17.8m	Horz - 17.6m							
Vert - 27.7m	Vert - 27.7m	Vert - 11.7m							
Time - 100ns									

*Horizontal 2 drms **For U.S. and Allied military, U.S. Government, and selected civil users specifically approved by the U.S. Government.

These parameters are government specifications for GPS performance.

times. If you boat on the Great Lakes or other inland waters, be sure to include your height above sea level as well.

Features

Everything said about displays for loran receivers holds true as well for GPS. There is more variety in GPS LCDs, though, including a double supertwist version on the Magnavox MX 100 and MX 200 that has exceptional contrast for an LCD. The screen looks almost like black on white and works in both bright and dim conditions, but is relatively expensive.

Menu-driven displays, familiar to anyone who has used a computer, are popular on both loran and GPS receivers. For the first-time user, especially, they can make using the set easy. The menu shows a variety of modes of operation, and may show some of the functions available within each mode, too. When you hit a key for one or another mode, another set of options arises, along with some of the basic information you're looking for. With some sets you'll always have present position showing, no matter what other functions you're using. Getting back to the main menu is usually quite easy, too, as there's almost always an escape option.

Some GPS machines can operate in any of several languages. You want to be careful not to play with languages you don't know at all, or you could find yourself deep in some subfunction without knowing which word or character can get you out! Then you have to turn off the set to get back to English.

Readouts

An important aspect of GPS navigation, certainly until there is fulltime coverage, is the time of day you can get a position. GPS receivers have several readouts of satellite status, including whether any one is off-line, whether you are operating in 2-D or 3-D mode, and when the next up-time and down-time is for the day.

Some sets go further, with a few having bar graph readouts of coverage over 24 hours, with gaps in the bars showing when 2-D and 3-D coverage is lacking. Some of these sets also show an overhead look at satellites that should be above your horizon at the moment. With this, you can watch satellites coming into and out of view, getting a good idea of which ones give you the best geometry. If a satellite should be in view, but you're not receiving it, something is wrong with the satellite, or with your set.

Most of the navigation readouts available on a GPS receiver are familiar to loran users. Some manufacturers no doubt use as much of the same hardware and software in their loran and GPS sets as possible. There are some differences, though.

GPS receiver with navigation readouts for course over ground (COG), speed over ground (SOG), cross-track error (XTE), course to waypoint (CTW), and an off-course graphic.

Speed and heading, while available in both systems, are updated much faster in GPS. There is very little time lag in recording speed or course changes, so a GPS receiver can be used as a real-time speedometer and compass.

Course over ground (COG) and speed over ground (SOG) are standard names in the GPS industry for those two functions. However, you may find several names and definitions for speed made good. Some call it velocity made good along a course (VMC). Others use speed of advance (SOA) toward the next waypoint. At least one GPS reports the corresponding readout of waypoint closure velocity (WCV), along with ETA and TTG (time to go). You need to understand exactly how the terms used by your receiver relate to nautical navigation terminology.

Steering to a waypoint, you'll see readouts for course to steer (CTS), cross-track error (XTE), and an off-course graphic of some kind. Alarms sound if you wander more than a settable number of degrees or distance off course.

Dead reckoning (DR) will take over automatically on most sets if satellite coverage is insufficient. Or you can choose to navigate in DR mode, exclusive of satellites. You can update position, speed, and heading at any time to improve your DR, with each point at which you choose to input a change becoming, in effect, a waypoint.

Weather Resistance

GPS receivers are weatherproofed just like loran receivers. The same materials are used for the case, for the key pads, and for the seals and cable connections. Most GPS sets are built for cockpit mounting, so they're at least spray-resistant. A few can be immersed a foot or two and continue operating, but it's still not a good idea to drop them overboard.

Since there is no agreed-on definition of water resistance in the electronics industry, don't allow the set to stand in water, especially salt water, for any length of time. Rinse it with fresh water (not sprayed) and dry it off before opening it. If there is one, check the battery case for moisture, and the power and antenna connectors. Wipe them off with a damp cloth.

Handhelds

Unlike handheld loran sets, handheld GPS receivers came out early on, and a large percentage of GPS sales are in handhelds. They operate well with

GPS receivers are weatherproofed just like loran receivers. This module includes both the antenna and receiver circuits.

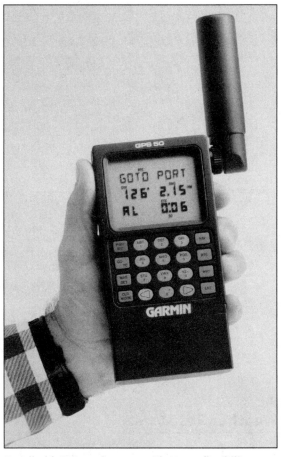

Handheld GPS receivers provide great flexibility.

their own antennas, and run on AA battery power, either alkaline or nicad, and on ship's power when put in their fixed-mount holster. Most use the same internals as permanent-mount sets, and they have at least one NMEA 0183 output port. The 0183 output feeds the GPS position, heading, and/or speed to an autopilot, radar, or electronic chart plotter. The only compromise may be the limited amount of data available on the smaller screen of a handheld, and the lack of plotting or steering graphics. Handhelds are competitively priced between $1,200 and $1,500 retail, and are invariably sold at less than $1,000—and as low as $800.

A handheld GPS is the electronic equivalent of the ship captain's personal sextant and chronometer. Its independence from ship power allows it to serve as backup navigator, or as the primary navigator on a small boat. You don't have to use it belowdecks in a nav station. You can carry it aboard a chartered boat, take it on a friend's boat if you've been designated navigator or if you just don't think much of your friend's piloting skills.

Handhelds have a feature that is maddening as well as sensible: In their power-saving mode they automatically turn themselves off after a few minutes if you don't hit the power button again. While this saves the batteries—some handhelds run for as little as an hour and a half on one set of AA-cells—you'll want some warning if you are still using the set. Find one with an audible alarm and visible indicator. You can also program the set for continuous operation, but then be very careful to use the set sparingly or you'll burn up the batteries fast.

For extended use, it's also a good idea for the set to float; otherwise, put a strap on it for on-deck use.

While lorans were first and foremost marine navigation devices, GPS receivers are routinely used for many other tasks. Some are programmed for aviation, survey, and backpacking work. A couple are even sold with an antenna you can stick to your car roof.

So far, the multipurpose sets we've seen don't impress for use as marine receivers. Trying to be all things to all users, they may have an undersized display, tiny buttons, limited memory, and an awkward shape. A handheld should have buttons large and spaced far enough apart that gloved fingers have no trouble pushing the right ones. It shouldn't be top-heavy in your hand, and its display should be readable at arm's length.

Interfacing

Interfacing GPS with an autopilot, chart plotter, or other electronic instrument is exactly the same as interfacing with loran. GPS sets, being newer, use the NMEA 0183 interface language almost universally.

Some sets will interface only with other products from the same manufacturer, Furuno and Autohelm Seatalk, for example. But both Furuno and Autohelm products also talk NMEA 0183, and that's the only one really needed.

Be careful when setting waypoints on interfacing electronics—such as a GPS receiver and a video chart plotter—that they number waypoints the same way. If one unit calls the present position Waypoint 0 and the other unit calls it Waypoint 1, you could be in for some potentially dangerous confusion over position and course to the next waypoint. Be sure you can program waypoints in a way that evens the score.

Using a computer's memory, you can create limitless waypoint and route libraries. You can hook up to a satcom terminal to automatically send your vessel's position back to a shore office or home periodically. You can also use the GPS's precise positioning to help run sailboat race tactics and performance analysis programs. The boat's position, heading, and speed are essential information for such programs. Tracking the boat's course over the period of the race or training session lets you see where you were on a race course when a burst of speed—or a case of the slows—occurred.

Most GPS receivers have a function allowing you to plot long distance courses—or short ones—over a rhumb line or great cirlce course. The great circle route may actually be a series of rhumblines between waypoints set along a great circle, but the extra distance traveled across an ocean compared to a complete GC is trivial.

GPS versus Loran

Which system to buy—loran or GPS? Loran costs less, is familiar to many boaters, and has repeatable accuracy to 50 feet. GPS has greater absolute accuracy, usually a shorter start-up time, and works where loran coverage doesn't exist.

How much more accurate is GPS in practice than loran? That depends on where you are. On Florida's east coast, loran coverage is not as good as in New England or the Great Lakes. Position readouts taken on handheld loran and GPS receivers at a well-surveyed reference point showed a ¼-mile spread for the loran positions in varying weather conditions. GPS readouts in the same spot were generally closer, and more often.

At a similar site near Boston, the difference in accuracy in clear weather was much less. Both sets were very consistent. As New England has excellent loran coverage, the choice would be a harder one.

Loran and GPS receivers have many similar functions. You have to weigh the currently higher price of GPS against its accuracy advantage in your area.

In 1989 Magellan brought out the first GPS receiver costing $3,000, which was about $4,000 less than any other set available at the time. In

1993, a better version of the same handheld set retailed at $1,200. In 1992, the first GPS receiver for less than $1,000, from Lowrance, came out. Of course, nobody pays retail for these sets, either.

Where will the downward price spiral end? Probably right about where loran sets are now—as low as $300 to $500 in the next two or three years.

Could GPS sell for under $100, as some predict? Nobody knows yet; it depends on markets far larger than our marine sport. But it's not impossible. So when do you buy your GPS receiver? It's inexpensive enough right now to be a bargain compared to every navigation device except loran in most areas. And wherever loran is weak or non-existent, GPS is the only game in town. If you want precision navigation in marginal weather and in unfamiliar waters for which you don't already have loran waypoints stored, GPS is an investment in safety you shouldn't wait to make.

If you do have good loran coverage, and you plan to stay in waters for which you have good loran waypoint numbers in memory, loran's repeatable accuracy of 50 feet is as good as GPS would get you for those particular spots. You can wait on GPS until your loran wears out, GPS gets so cheap that you can't resist, or differential GPS becomes available in your area. Differential, when it becomes widely available, will redefine accuracy once again.

Differential GPS

By the time GPS is operational, you'll be able to navigate along most of the coastal and inland U.S. waters with an accuracy that makes the 100-meter S/A resolution look crude. The reason is differential GPS (DGPS).

DGPS came along because, even without S/A, GPS is just not accurate enough for the likes of big ship operators in narrow channels and harbors. Even given access to the Precision code signal, many navigation experts feel GPS is inadequate. DGPS takes accuracy to a new level—within five meters.

It's not theory, either. If you enjoyed watching the America's Cup coverage in San Diego in 1992, you could not have missed the high-precision computer tracking of the competing yachts. The tracks of the boats, with all their wiggles and changes in course, were created using second-by-second positioning by DGPS. The Trimble company set up a temporary DGPS system for television and competitors.

Meanwhile, the Coast Guard has several experimental DGPS stations operating on the East and Gulf coasts and in the Great Lakes. More are planned, with full DGPS coverage of U.S. coastal waters the goal.

How does DGPS work? Differential refers to the difference between what a GPS receiver at a known site reports as the position and what a computer knows the position to be. A differential station is sited near a

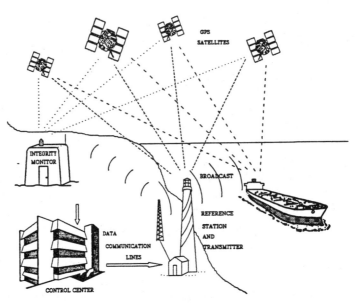

Elements of a differential GPS system. A carefully surveyed differential GPS reference station monitors ranging signals of the satellites within its view. A remotely located control center computes true satellite positions based on the errors noted and generates corrections to be added or subtracted for each satellite range signal. These corrections are broadcast by minimum shift key (MSK) modulation of a Coast Guard radiobeacon operating in the 285 - 325 kHz range, and are good for the area covered by the radiobeacon. User equipment consists of a GPS receiver with differential correction software and a radionavigation beacon receiver. A remote integrity monitor station acts as a user check on the system. It compares its known position with the DGPS position and alerts the control center if position accuracy falls below a set level. (Illustration courtesy U.S. Coast Guard.)

harbor entrance or important lighthouse. Its position is known to within inches, or better. Range measurements from all satellites in view are computed by the on-site GPS receiver, and fed to a computer, which compares them with what it is told the range numbers should be at that moment. These reference numbers come from a remote control center. The differences, or corrections, are transmitted via radio signal to all users in the area—up to 100 nautical miles or more, since the corrections are good within that range. The GPS receivers aboard vessels in the area add the corrections to their satellite ranging measurements, to come up with a final fix that is within 5 meters of true position.

Correction signals are broadcast over the existing Coast Guard radiobeacon network. You therefore need a radio receiver that works in the 285–325 kilohertz range, and you need a demodulator that turns the high speed correction message from a series of frequency shifts into a set of digital bits. These are fed into the DGPS receiver, which has the software to use the corrections.

Combination receiver/demodulators are available from Magellan, Magnavox, Trimble, and some others, and more are expected soon. Differential software is already being included in some of today's GPS receivers, which also have the data ports to connect to the demodulators. In the future, all the software and hardware will be available in a single package that will look just like any non-differential receiver, but with two antennas—one for satellite reception, and one for the correction signals. Costs will surely come down, as well, but DGPS will probably always be a relative luxury.

An alternative scheme to the Coast Guard radiobeacon system is Magnavox's use of the Cue electronic paging network to transmit differential corrections. This is a land-based system, and it's too soon to tell how well it will work for coastal boaters. It's a fascinating plan, however.

How can DGPS be useful to you?

Obviously, it can guide you among hazards in dangerous waters at night or in the fog. At that point, your greatest danger may be a chart that isn't up to date.

DGPS will also allow you to find fishing hot spots or dive spots with a minumum of hunting, saving time and fuel, and perhaps with less likelihood of scaring away your quarry.

You'll be able to find the right part of the bottom to anchor in time and again—hitting the deep, soft sand every time, rather than the reef or rock.

If you race your sailboat, you'll be able to take advantage of tactical software that only navigators at the America's Cup level have benefitted from heretofore. Software that gives you precise time and distance to the startline, to laylines, and to marks. You'll be able to instantly measure the advantage or loss of minor wind shifts in any direction, and determine whether to tack for the mark now, or wait until you have added enough distance to allow for current or tide.

From a safety standpoint, you'll be able to determine man- or gear-overboard positions more accurately than ever.

More uses for DGPS will undoubtedly come up as people begin to use it. In fact, GPS on its own is on its way to revolutionizing position-finding—on the water, and elsewhere in our lives.

Transit

Transit is the original satellite navigation system, dating back to 1964. In fact, since Transit receivers became affordable to recreational users 10 years

Text continues on page 178

ago, the system has simply been known by the generic name of "satnav." Now that GPS is the premiere satellite network, Transit is due for shutdown at the end of 1996. Nonetheless, there are thousands of satnav units operating reliably.

Why GPS is replacing Transit is basically twofold: higher potential accuracy and continuous operation. A Transit receiver will display your position within 100 to 200 yards in any kind of weather—not quite as good as GPS, but better in absolute accuracy than loran. It will operate anywhere in the world. Its biggest drawback is its lack of full-time coverage. For most of its operational life, it has had just six satellites in low polar orbit, meaning that, on average, a fix is available about every two hours. Using a single satellite tracked over several minutes for its fix, the receiver takes several minutes to perform its computations.

Ironically, due to the system's announced phaseout, all the spare satellites have been launched to allow for their use until the deadline. There will be eight orbiters available until 1997, the best coverage the system has ever seen. If someone offers you the use of a Transit receiver, take it. Though the technology has been overtaken by GPS, it's very reliable technology.

During the intervals between satellites, the receiver dead reckons your position, based either on manually input speed and heading, or on automatic inputs if your speedo and electronic compass can be interfaced with it.

Besides being an excellent DR computer, the satnav receiver can store waypoints and routes, though its memory capacity may not be more than ten waypoints. You can also call up Greenwich and local time, set position and time alarms, and do most of the other functions possible with a loran or GPS.

Some Transit receivers can drive an autopilot, but they will be doing it on dead reckoning, not on a succession of close satellite fixes, which is okay if you're confident of your position and course, or are traveling far from land.

Transit receivers have been bought more for long-distance voyaging, out of loran range. Since they've been used mainly where there's little to hit between fixes, they've worked admirably in conjunction with a loran receiver.

Now GPS is here, and there's no reason to buy a new Transit receiver. Think carefully, in fact, about how valuable a used one will be to you for the limited time it will function. If you're about to head off on a long transoceanic voyage, you need a good navigation receiver, and your bank is too broke for GPS, go ahead, buy a used Transit receiver like the Magnavox MX 4102 (by far the most popular model) for as much under $500 as possible. Anything over that won't be worth the savings, since the bottom for GPS is already under $1,000 and falling.

CHAPTER 13

Electronic Chart Plotters

by Freeman Pittman

One of the few genuinely new pieces of marine electronic hardware in the last decade is the electronic chart or fishing plotter. And there are lots of variations to choose from.

The most expensive are video plotters for commercial and recreational fishing, with memory for thousands of "event markers" to show where fish were found or traps were set.

At the other end of the price range are the LCD plotters often combined with fishfinders, lorans, or both. These record fishing spots and routes to them, but are much simpler, smaller, and have much less memory than the big commercial-grade fishing plotters.

In between are the most versatile electronic plotters—video chart plotters that show your position, chart features, and your track and route on a TV screen.

Any one of these plotters is a fascinating device that can make piloting problems soothingly simple, take the time and tedium out of laborious tasks, and possibly even reduce the chance of navigation errors.

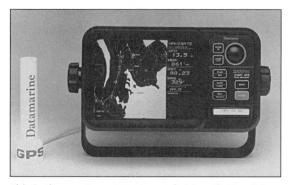

This is the most common type of video plotter. It has a 7-inch monochrome screen and shows alphanumeric data in a column on the right, along with the chart image. Note that while the screen image shows buoys, land outline, and the fathom and 2-fathom curves, it does not show depth soundings, nor other details, notes, or symbols. It takes one of the CD-ROM charts to show all details of a paper chart. The controls on this plotter are few and easy to understand; much of the work is done with the cursor trackball. This unit has an optional GPS sensor included to give position, speed, heading, and other information.

Here is the same plotter, but showing one of its other functions—a display for any of a host of integrated instruments. In this case, GPS satellite data has been called up to check the reliability of a fix. Data from log, sounder, other instruments, autopilot, and even radar can be shown in one place, and organized for optimum use.

Video Chart Plotters

A video chart plotter can perform a variety of services. For instance, you can:

- instantly find the position of, and range and bearing to, any point on the chart
- lay a course with as many waypoints as you like, instantly reading the position, range, and bearing of each
- track and record your boat's passage to compare against the plotted course while under way, and to store or print it for your log
- store courses and waypoints in memory for future trips
- set alarms to warn you when you reach waypoints or stray into hazardous waters
- access a far larger chart library, or database, than possible even with a nav station full of paper charts
- steer your boat by the instruments when visibility is impossible

There are other functions and ancillaries that add to a video plotter's value. And as more options are possible, the video chart plotter will become important in its own right, rather than as the electronic alternative to paper charts, dividers, and parallel rules.

Yet, as intriguing a gadget as it is, the video plotter has been no more than that to some navigators. Reasons? They consider it:

- A high-cost duplication of paper charts. The paper variety show as much or more detail and data than do most video charts, and cost much less, although the equivalent of many paper charts are stored within the memory of a video plotter.

- Not as reliable as paper. When the 12-volt power fails, your paper charts will still be there.

- Conducive to sloppy navigation. The argument here is that the video plotters are so easy to use, you won't bother to back them up with proper paper plots or log entries. More important, since most video plotters display much less than complete chart information, you can get into dangerous places by relying on them exclusively.

- Hard to read. This is most true for LCD plotters, but can also apply to video chart displays when put in the cockpit or bridge in bright sunlight. On the other hand, most of the time, these units are carried inside the boat. Few are designed for exposure to spray. Also, when paper charts are hard to read under a red light in the dark, video displays are bright and sharp.

Whatever you think about the validity of these criticisms, video plotters are here to stay. The moral for video chart plotters is obviously the same as for all navigation devices and techniques: Don't rely on any single approach. Use alternative means to cross-check your work, copy your plots, and be prepared to use backup systems.

What's clear about chart plotters is that to be worth owning, they need to offer things paper charts can't. Development of video chart plotters is proceeding in both the software and hardware theaters. In software, you have a choice of chart databases. In hardware, you can choose a system designed specifically for marine use, or a home computer that runs plotting programs. You can pick a permanent-mount or portable plotter, LCD or video screen, and stand-alone plotter versus combination plotter/loran/fishfinder. There are more options, still.

First, let's look at electronic cartography. This is the database on which almost all electronic chart plotters depend. The most complete and quickest way to digitize a paper chart—that is, to make an electronic version of it—is to put it in a raster scanning machine. Everything on the chart can be

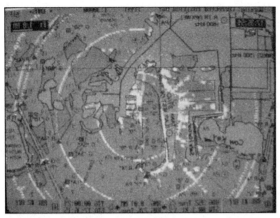

A full-color video chart (in this photo the darker shade is blue, the lighter, green; see back cover) shot directly from a paper chart is the ultimate in authenticity. Even what the government prints on its charts, however, is not all that can be shown on video charts. This version can be overlaid with a radar image to show other vessels and confirm your position in the real world. Other means of using electronic charts will evolve along with the technology. At the moment, charts on CDs, like this one, are more expensive to buy and operate than the vector-scanned charts used in most electronic plotters.

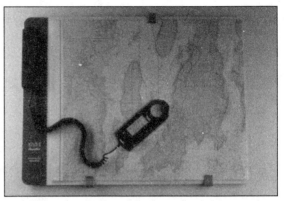

The paper chart can be used directly with electronic plotting power, as shown here. This system incorporates a digitizing tablet under the the chart and a mouse-like "puck" with readout and keypad to show position and waypoints. It's a powerful alternative to the video plotter for those who value paper charts

picked up by the scanner, in full color. The digital version is a complete video reproduction of the paper chart.

The preferred storage medium for scanned video charts is CD-ROM, or compact disk. Compact disks are rugged and waterproof, and they have high storage capacity—necessary when you're storing all the charts for a large piece of U.S. or Canadian coastline. That's what video chart manufacturers try to do. The two who offer raster-scanned charts on CD-ROM for use in compatible video plotters are Laser Plot of Auburn, Massachusetts, and Maptech of Ventura, California. Both companies also sell their charts as part of a system, including color monitor, processing computer, controls, and operating software.

More manufacturers will be offering raster-scanned CD charts. The quality of the image depends partly on the screen it's displayed on, and partly on the resolution (dots per inch) of the scanning machine. If you can, compare competing CDs on a single screen for color, brightness, and clarity. Take the image quality into account, along with price and computing performance.

Since these charts need so much memory, a faster processor in the display computer, with a lot of read-only memory, will result in quicker screen renewals when your position moves off the screen and onto a new portion of the chart.

The other way to create a digital chart is by *vector digitization*, a fancy term for tracing the lines on the chart with a handheld electronic recording device much like a computer mouse.

Rather than recovering every pixel of information, only the lines traced by the recorder and alphanumeric data selected by the manufacturer are put into memory. The largest purveyors of vector-scanned cartography are C-Map and Navionics, two Italian companies with U.S. subsidiaries. Each supplies a number of video plotter manufacturers.

Obviously the vector digitization process takes much longer than raster scanning, and can introduce slight errors into the digitized chart. (Theoretically, though, vector scanning can be more accurate than raster, if the vectorization is done from a larger scale original—say, a photograph—than is available in a paper chart.) Furthermore, currently available vector-scanned video charts carry only a fraction of the information of the paper chart. Generally, they provide a complete and accurate tracing of the shoreline, some depth curves, and navigation aids. But usually they don't have the individual depth soundings, chart symbols for rocks, grass, and so forth, or the notes for things like underwater cables or other areas to be avoided. They are, in fact, simplified versions of paper charts. However, they will continue to add information over the next few years. Furthermore, vector digitization has some important advantages of its own.

Since most vector charts present much less data, they take perhaps one-hundredth the amount of memory space of raster-scanned charts, allowing

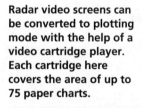

Radar video screens can be converted to plotting mode with the help of a video cartridge player. Each cartridge here covers the area of up to 75 paper charts.

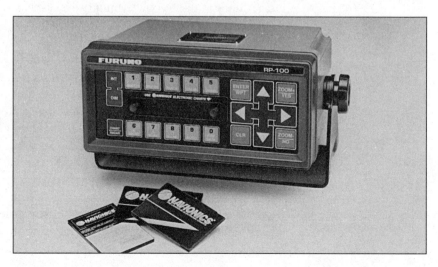

you to compactly store a far greater number of charts. In fact, no disk player is needed; up to 75 vector charts, for instance, can be stored on EPROM (electronically programmable read-only memory) microchips inside a palm-sized cartridge. Since there's less in memory, data processing is faster, most noticably in screen renewal time (when the boat moves off the screen and onto a new part of the chart).

At least as important, vector-scanned data can be processed. A raster-scanned chart shows you everything, and at times you may not want to see all that data and color on a small screen. Vector digitizing is like tracing data onto a series of transparent sheets over a chart—one for the coast and depth contours, another for depth soundings, another for buoys and lights, and others for notes, warnings, shore features. You can customize your display to show just the layers of information you desire, adding new ones as they become available, and using the information for other purposes. Custom print-outs of charts become practical, as well.

Both types of charts can be updated as easily, but while CD-ROM charts must wait until new government charts come out, vector-drawn chart cartridges theoretically can be reprogrammed as frequently as Notices to Mariners are issued. (In reality, they're updated at more like two-year intervals.)

Right now, most raster-scanned charts are presented in full color, while most vector-scanned charts are displayed in monochrome. Both types can be shown either way.

At some point, it may be possible to isolate selected data from a raster-scanned chart. Then the major advantage of vector charts will disappear. Meantime, raster charts will maintain unbeatable accuracy and faithfulness to their paper prototypes, while vector charts offer greater flexibility in data usage, along with less power-hungry, less expensive hardware.

Paper Charts From Electronic

Digital cartography is being pushed ahead by industry, while government chartmakers and mapmakers are still struggling with standards and procedures. When international standards for producing and using electronic charts come to pass, what will be the result? Will they impact recreational use? Time will tell. The currently agreed goal among hydrographic offices of governments worldwide is for a single, "seamless" database to be tapped by all users. This electronic world chart will exist in 1:1 scale in computer memory. Charts will not be restricted to a series of overlapping papers in a confusing range of scales; instead, any portion of the world chart will be viewable onscreen or printed out, and in any scale the user chooses. Paper charts will be made to order at the retail shop from a printer linked to the database, including whatever available data the buyer wants.

Such is the forecast of the system's proponents. Whether it happens by international cooperation or just happens, it's a likely scenario.

Video Plotting Hardware

Probably well over half of the video chart plotters now on the market use either the C-Map or the Navionics cartography. These two companies also make much of the hardware that uses their software. Both supply circuit boards, control panel options, and CRT that go inside the plotters sold by many of the best known companies. You can tell a Navionics package from a C-Map by the fact that the former usually has full-screen cross-hairs instead of the latter's flashing cursor; also, most C-Map displays include an alphanumeric data column on the right side of the screen that is always displayed, while Navionics shows words and numbers on the top, bottom, or in windows.

The two systems are quite similar; not surprising when you realize that C-Map was started by one of the founding partners of Navionics.

Individual Functions And Controls

In these systems you often see an eight-inch diagonal monochrome screen (green on black), usually with a membrane-type keypad to its right. There will be cursor movement keys as on a computer, with arrows pointing up, down, and to left and right. There may also be a track ball to move the cursor more quickly. The track ball is much handier than using the keys, and more fun to operate. However, a hole must be cut in the instrument's face for the ball, meaning it must be kept dry. Also, the ball can get oily and dirty, eventually gumming up the roller contacts that count its rotations. That calls for a cleaning by the local authorized service technician. Other types of cursor controls include joystick, as in a video game, and computer mouse.

A plotter with a sealed face may be exposed to sun and perhaps a bit of spray, but its case is not designed for a freshwater hose-down. It's best to keep almost all video chart plotters inside the boat.

It's worth knowing that you needn't be able to draw a straight line with any of these devices. You merely move the cursor from your last position or waypoint to your next waypoint and hit the enter key on the keypad. A straight line immediately connects the two points. Setting a course on screen takes seconds.

A few video plotters have what's called a "rubber band" function. With it you can adjust a course line between waypoints, in case you have plotted your course too close to a dangerous area. You hit the key for track functions, move the cursor to the safe side of the course and hit enter, and the course leg is pulled out into two new legs around the danger.

When you have completed drawing your course on screen, you can save it to memory as a route. Unlike operating a GPS or loran navigator, you don't have to manually input each latitude and longitude number for every waypoint. Since the plotter always knows the lat/lon position of any spot on the screen, each waypoint and route need only be marked on the screen, and when you hit the save or enter key, zap—it's in memory for recall at any time. You can put the route back on screen graphically, or you can call it up as a list of lat/lon coordinates for copying to paper chart and logbook.

Two other important keys comprise the zoom function. One key zooms you in through a succession of scales from continent-small to half-mile large. The other key zooms you back out. It's always possible to find the right scale for the kind of piloting you're doing. Try doing that with a paper chart.

You can call up range and bearing information from your boat's position to any place onscreen by hitting another button. You can also show the track of your boat as a separate, more meandering, line that can be compared with the straight course lines you have plotted. Observing the two lines at a convenient time interval gives you an excellent visual indication of the effects of current, wind, and leeway on your boat's progress.

Dynamic Plotting

Using a chart plotter underway to help you pilot your boat safely is one of the device's most powerful functions. This is the traditional task of radar, but sometimes radar doesn't define your location well. Low-lying land, similar looking channels, heavy rain showers blocking the radar's view of more solid targets can make positioning and piloting with radar chancy.

With a chart plotter, you have the benefits of radar's dynamic updating and paper charts' mapping accuracy. As long as you can trust your loran or GPS (which is usually possible to do by periodically comparing the receiver's position to the charted positions of deepwater buoys you pass), you can watch your position on screen in relation to well-charted features and nav aids.

A friend recently did a blind piloting test with a video plotter in some of the most congested waters in North America. Putting a hood over the windshield of a powerboat, he and his crew steered solely on instruments down Long Island Sound and through New York Harbor. A lookout on deck made sure there were no problems with passing vessel traffic but the plotter, being fed by a loran, kept the helmsman on the right path for the entire route.

What happens when you get to the edge of the screen? The plotter automatically redraws the next section of video chart ahead. As mentioned before, the simpler vector-scanned charts usually can be redrawn faster than can the CD-ROM raster-scanned charts. Redraw time is not an important factor in video plotter performance; unless you're racing an offshore powerboat, you're not traveling nearly fast enough to get far onto the next screen before it's complete.

Nonetheless, many navigators prefer to set up the plotter so the boat's position is always center screen, as on a radar set. That way, the charted picture slowly passes you by, rather than the other way around. Either way can be helpful in a given situation. You'll want to check to be sure the plotter allows you to choose the mode.

Special Features

Every plotter, whether C-Map, Navionics, or other type, seems to have features all its own. With one you can call up a window that enlarges the area just around the cursor or shows more navigation data. You can calculate fuel consumption over a route. And you can convert lat/lon readouts to loran TD. Another plotter displays strip charts of things like your steering over time—handy for optimizing the efficiency of an autopilot. You adjust the pilot until the zigzags on the chart are minimized.

There are varying waypoint capacities, from around 100 to several hundred. And there are different ways to mark different things. For instance, a circular symbol on screen might represent a waypoint, a triangle a nav aid, and a square an operator-identified event such as a fish strike, dive site, or anchor spot.

Screens

Most video plotters use a relatively small (eight-inch diagonal) screen, with 512 x 672 pixel resolution, or thereabouts. This makes them most viewable with fairly simple charts, in one color. Larger screened sets in full color are available, at a higher price. These also consume more power—not a concern for powerboaters, but worth considering for sailors. Some plotters can drive a remote monitor, such as a 19-inch screen for easier viewing, or for viewing at another helm station.

A couple of sets are available with touch screens, which make sense from a simplicity standpoint. In practice, touch screens have seemed to be less reliable, and slower to respond to commands than separate keypads. And you do have to clean the screen more often. Anyway, the option is there for those who prefer it.

The CRT screen is the most power-hungry part of a video plotter, and manufacturers are working with liquid crystal displays to develop more efficient, compact screens. CRTs are heavier and bulkier, but they're still much better for brightness, contrast, color, and wide viewing angles.

To date, LCD screens have not been too successful for electronic plotters. They seem to work best in low light, such as sailboat nav stations or

This is what an LCD chart plotter looks like. Given a large enough screen, an LCD can show as much detail as a video tube plotter, in a smaller, lighter package with less power draw and less RF interference to other instruments. However, the contrast and brightness can't compete with video plotters, and few manufacturers are offering full-function LCD plotters. That should change as the technology improves.

darkened bridges, where their backlighting feature can be turned on to make them appear more like a CRT. But you still have to be looking at them pretty much straight-on to get consistent contrast.

Outside, LCDs are either okay—if the light hits them right—or almost impossible to read because of too little sun or too much glare.

Color LCDs are available, and they'll help, but they're still prohibitively expensive for use with all but the most advanced computer-based integrated navigation systems.

On the other hand, there's one battery-powered laptop LCD chart plotter now sold, the Electronic Marine Chart View. It's possibly the only truly marinized chart plotter available, with impressive environmental specifications. And there are several smaller LCD screens on the combination units described later. These have simple graphics, and are okay for what they're supposed to do.

Computer-based Plotting Systems

While most video and LCD chart plotters are designed as such and sold primarily for that purpose, it's also possible, even advantageous, to run a charting and plotting program on a personal computer, either desktop or laptop. There are several systems that run on a PC right now.

You can buy chart and plotting software for both IBM and Macintosh computers. One program, called "Navigate!" uses the Macintosh-style menu system to perform virtually all plotting functions with only a mouse. It puts up a sharp and bright picture, in black and white or colors. A version of Maptech's Tru-Chart system is designed for use on laptop PCs.

Then there are the full-function programs—Maptech's, and Laser Plot's—designed for 386 model-and-up desktop IBM clones. We've already mentioned the CD-ROM cartography they use; a powerful PC with lots of memory makes CD chart usage quick and practical. With these programs, a large, full-color screen is used, and an incredible list of functions are available in menu, window, and graphic form. The emphasis is on full navigation system integration, so you'll be able to call up all the boat's instrument readouts on one side of the screen, while plotting continues on the other side. Readouts can be customized, too. Engine temperature, for instance, can be observed as a numeric or dial readout, or as a bar graph. Courses can be plotted, and then moved around the screen—useful to a sailboat race committee setting a racecourse so it always faces the wind.

These are just a few of the many things a computer-based plotting system can do. Because it's in a computer, it's not limited to plotting, or any other type of function. The computer can run a weather facsimile program one minute and call up a communication satellite the next. A well-used system may need more than one work station so different things can be monitored and worked with at the same time by different crew members. Some very large yachts are outfitted just this way, including one we know of that is set up complete with multi-task file server, several user terminals, and inputs from every instrument and sensor on the boat.

Electronic/Paper Chart Plotters

Many veteran navigators get very uncomfortable reading about this kind of centralization and electronic dependency. And with good reason. And a good many mariners simply like working with paper charts. Wouldn't it be nice to have the best of electronic plotting, but with paper charts?

Such a system is available, and works well, using a computer digitizing board beneath the chart. The palm-sized plotting device, or "puck," that slides around on the chart senses its position on the electronic grid inside the board. This corresponds to the lat/lon on the chart. The output of a GPS or loran plugged into the board lets you find your position in the same way it's done on a video chart. The difference is that you have to move the puck periodically to keep up with the change in your position while underway. In this way, the puck replaces the hand tools of paper chart plotting, as it helps you draw course lines and waypoints. The puck can read through the thickness of a whole chart book. With the chart securely clipped on the board, the plotter's accuracy is as good as you can achieve with a sharp pencil.

The puck is the positioning device, as well as the display and keypad. A two-line LCD gives lat/lon for whichever part of the chart the cross-hairs of the puck are located over. You can also enter waypoints, using current position or manually input numbers. You can get range and bearing from any point on the chart to any other point, and there are other functions familiar to video chart users.

And if the power gives out, you still have your course and the last fix on paper, ready for dead reckoning navigation with compass and log.

A couple of companies, the Better Boating Association and KVH, offer variations on the same unit that are extremely easy and quick to learn. BBA's Yeoman is designed specifically for its ChartKit chart books, with a companion GPS sensor available. KVH's version is designed to interface with its Quadro integrated instrument and navigation system. The BBA plotting board can be used on the lap, though it's pretty bulky and heavy. KVH favors a lighter flexible digitizing pad that grips the nav table well and works best with individual government full-size charts.

Generally, this type of plotter costs a few hundred dollars less than the video kind. It's an excellent solution for the navigator who likes many of the video plotter functions but prefers to operate on paper.

Integrating the plotter into a complete navigation system is the aim of many manufacturers. Sharing display screens, processing hardware, and

Combination plotters include a loran or GPS navigator and fishfinder, along with a screen that shows a boat's track, position, and waypoints. The screen can show any one function, or be split into two or three simultaneous functions. Combination units don't show chart features and are very limited for route planning and navigation, but can be useful for recording and returning to a number of fishing spots in a small area.

interfacing software with other equipment offers both efficiencies and enhanced capabilities all around.

We've mentioned the symbiotic relationship of a loran or GPS navigator and chart plotter. A chart plotter is only being used to a tenth of its potential without a position sensor feeding it.

A recent trend incorporates a GPS or loran receiver right inside the plotter housing—a handy way to fit two instruments into one space in the nav station, and less expensive than buying the two instruments separately (sometimes not, though). To be sure the navigation receiver's capabilities are maximized, all its functions should be available on screen just as they would in a separate receiver. The GPS or loran functions should not be subordinated to the plotter's. In fact, if the video screen doesn't make reading the receiver's functions easier, we would hesitate to purchase the units as one.

Video Plotters And Radar

Rather than having side-by-side CRT video screens for radar and chart plotter, some manufacturers have combined both functions in a single display. With these systems, one CRT calls up alphanumeric data from any sail or power performance-monitoring instrument, as well as alternating radar and chart images. It has not yet been reached, but the stated goal of manufacturers is for the charts to be enlarged at the same scales as the radar (¼, ½, 1, 2, 4, 8, 16 miles, etc), so you can toggle between the images to confirm landmarks on radar, and note targets not shown on the chart. These "points of interest" (POIs) will then be tagged on radar and the markers transferred to the chart screen. Each point will be thus more recognizable as a vessel, buoy, rock, or other object.

At least two manufacturers have chart control units that plug into their existing radars. With a single wire connection, the radar screen becomes a full-function video plotter. These conversion units don't affect the radar performance in any way, and they're less expensive than buying a separate video plotter.

Maptech's Tru-Chart, the high-end raster-scanned chart system for use on computers, is currently the only one capable of overlaying a radar image directly on a video chart. It takes complicated software to match the images, and to partly correct for radar distortion. The result is that you're able to see buoys and other nav aids on radar where they're supposed to be on the chart, as well as other vessels, plus other items that may not be on the chart. This is a fascinating feature that could prove very helpful in distinguishing types of radar targets, as well as clearly identifying radar land masses. The technology is not cheap, however, with prices running from $3,500 to more than $5,000.

Video Plotters And Autopilots

A video plotter and autopilot can be linked separately to a loran or GPS. Or the plotter may be wired between the electronic navigator and pilot. In one case, autopilot controls share space on the plotter control panel. You can set the course on screen and then engage the pilot without having first to dump the route anywhere else. Autopilot functions, including steering graphics, can be called up instead of the chart screen.

From the user's standpoint, it usually doesn't seem to matter much how the wiring goes, as long as all functions of all three instruments are conveniently available. Being able to do it all from one set of controls limits confusion and the possible inputting of wrong commands into GPS, plotter, or pilot. You do want to make sure that autopilot functions don't depend on having an operating plotter. You'll also find, unless you use one manufacturer's products, that some wiring adaptor plugs are needed.

The video screen is an irresistible attraction, to manufacturers as well as users. They are thus finding ways to offer every type of data possible from other instruments. Thanks to NMEA 0183, the navigation instrument interfacing protocol agreed to by manufacturers, you can call up boat speed and heading, wind information, and other functions. Be sure to ask the dealer how the plotter will integrate with other electronics: via NMEA junction box, data bus, or through just one or two NMEA ports? Is it possible to identify on screen anything that can be sent over the data line? Can you program the equipment to display what you want? Or will it take a professional to do that?

Since so many manufacturers are offering complete nav station systems, you may want to think about installing a single-brand system. This should maximize the interfacing flexibility, and minimize the installation. Many manufacturers find they can build more-efficient systems using an internal interface language of their own than by relying on NMEA 0183. They then use 0183 to connect to the instruments they don't make.

Cruising Information

Navigational and performance data are not the only information that can be transmitted via video. Of interest to cruising users is the new output available with C-Map cartridges—cruising guide information. Placing the screen cursor over one of several icons on a harbor chart calls up five lines of information in the alphanumeric column identifying the spot as a marina, yard, restaurant, or whatever. You can add your own information, for instance, detailing services and prices. It's a neat idea that expands the utility of the plotter. Just be aware that not many areas are well covered with cruising guide data yet. Nor is it possible for the chart cartridge manufacturer to keep current with all the changes in marina ownership, prices, and private buoyage in a given year to two. You'll still need local knowledge.

Long-Distance Routing

One of the most exciting offspring of integrated navigation is the routing system, which brings together elements of video charting, weather prediction, and boat performance analysis. Routing is the science of planning a long passage based on weather forecasts and a boat's speed potential in the expected conditions. Right now it's used exclusively by commercial shipping navigators and long-distance sailors, especially transoceanic racers. However, there's every reason to expect electronic routing to be beneficial to any boater, power or sail, who undertakes a major passage. Days can be shaved off a voyage, high and low pressure systems used to best advantage rather than blundered into unsafely, and a course set that combines comfort and speed.

Current routing systems consist of a computer with software offering small-scale (ocean-sized) charts for plotting purposes. Another program catalogs the boat's predicted sailing performance at every angle to the wind, and across a usable range of wind speeds. This is known as a velocity prediction program (VPP), and is covered more fully in Chapter 16. The computer also is linked to a weather facsimile receiver. Finally, the computer has a routing program to synthesize data offered from these inputs.

A routing system estimates the speed, time, and distance you'll make on any number of routes you test on screen, given your boat's speed for a given wind direction and strength. If the program worked perfectly, it would simply give you a best course to your next waypoint. Since it isn't perfect, and since conditions change anyway, it can be used most effectively to compare routes, such as a southerly versus a northerly route around a weather system. Or right through it. It gives the navigator many options to try, and a better feel for which is the fastest way to go.

The routing program takes wind information from an outside source, most often a weather facsimile map showing atmospheric pressure distribution at sea level. To enter it in the program, you either use a digitizing stylus and tablet and trace the isobar lines from the weather fax printout, or, if the program accepts it, just save the map to the screen.

From this, the program creates a wind field for the area, taking into account pressure gradient, latitude, variation of pressure gradient over time, air/water friction, and other factors. The result is that for any place on the screen, you can get a readout of expected wind speed and direction.

Now the routing program synthesizes boat performance and the weather.

It puts your boat in the onscreen wind field. You use a mouse to set up a series of test routes to see which one is fastest. One program draws lines representing the distance traveled in any direction for a given amount of time. These lines are analogous to the boat's polar curves, but as the wind changes throughout the field, the lines are much less regular.

The program makes a lot of assumptions about the quality of your VPP and of the weather report, although it does allow you to try cases where, for instance, expected weather arrives earlier or later than predicted. Successful sailboat racing navigators have found the way to use it best is by comparing a series of routes in one direction against a series of routes in another. You then go in the direction with the best odds.

These routing systems are highly specialized, and the software alone can cost in the thousands of dollars. More sophisticated programs for less money are sure to come along as interest expands. Video navigation systems will want to incorporate this kind of software, too.

Plotting Tomorrow's Course

This is only the beginning. Soon you'll be able to tap the Coast Guard's Notices to Mariners database via computer bulletin board to your personal computer. PC-based chart plotting systems allow you to update some electronic charts manually. At some point, you'll be able to enter these chart updates directly to a dedicated chart plotter's database, even if it doesn't run on a PC.

At sea, a satellite communications link will make it possible to receive the latest updated harbor chart for the boat's destination while still at sea. You'll be able to send faxes of your chart screens to show other mariners where you've been, where you've caught fish, and what the safe passages are, or are not.

For several years, offshore racing sailors have been looking at video plotters for their potential as a full-function race computer. Integrated instrument systems are already displaying useful wind and boat speed derivations of all kinds (see Chapter 16). Tactical racing software is available to run on a laptop; it is used by many course racers at the America's Cup level. A few very expensive laptop plotters have been developed that show the boat's track and predict speeds made on alternate courses to a mark. Bringing together these elements of polar prediction, wind and current over time, and tactical considerations will make for a powerful electronic racing tool.

So the potential for video charting and plotting is enormous, and substantial steps toward fulfilling the promise have already been taken. For video-geographers, paper charts won't be made obsolete, but they'll become more like the hard copy you keep as insurance against system failure.

Commercial Plotters

They look like video chart plotters, and they operate like them. So what's different commercial plotters?

It's what kinds of operations the user emphasizes. Rather than being used primarily to navigate coastal and inland waterways, commercial plotters are used for professional navigation, and to record fish catches, and trap and net drop points. As a result, memory capacity for chart features is limited to the simplest coastal outlines. No depths, no filling of land masses with color. Ports may be noted. Instead, you mainly see latitude and longitude lines, route and track lines, position coordinates, speed, heading, waypoint locations, and range and bearing information.

And waypoints, lots of them. Commercial plotters can store 2,000 or more waypoints and event markers, and label each one for what happened there, i.e. "crab pot number 35," or "tuna."

Markers come in different shapes and sizes for various purposes. A net perimeter can be noted with a properly scaled circle. Most of these plotters have large screens, with different colors assigned to different functions. Resolution is generally excellent—no fuzzy numbers or wiggly lines.

With some plotters you can superimpose color radar, and the radar targets can be assigned identifying numbers or names that stay with them as they move across the screen. You can put a tail on each target, or leave it off. This traffic monitoring can get even more sophisticated, resembling what goes onto a radar screen in an airport tower.

A truly dedicated sportfisherman may want to look at one of these plotters, but they're big, power hungry, and very expensive, in the tens of thousands of dollars. There is a trend to putting commercial features in smaller sets with cartography familiar to recreational users, but these units will always be for the specialist.

Using A Video Chart Plotter

An electronic plotter generally performs in one of three modes: tracking underway, range and bearing navigation, and trip planning.

The simplest, possibly most valuable function of a video plotter is automatic. When you plug in the GPS or loran, your boat's position moves across the screen at a heading and speed in scale with the boat's speed over ground.

You can show the vessel's track versus the planned path to watch for steer-

Text continues on page 196

ing irregularities and the effects of current and wind.

When observing the lat/lon position onscreen, you need to be aware of one thing, though. Is the unit displaying the boat's position, the cursor's position, or the position of some other point, such as a waypoint or buoy?

Normally, the default setting is for the vessel's position. And most plotters show the vessel's position at all times, in addition to any other. But if you, or someone else, has been working in another plotting mode, you could temporarily mistake the readout, especially as you come on watch in the middle of the night.

To avoid this kind of simple but potentially costly mistake, develop a routine for using the plotter. Regardless of how you've been using it, whenever you sit down to work with it, always start by keying in the basic chart and data display. Note the position, course, heading, speed, time, and other essentials in your paper log, and go on from there.

Setting A Course

Whether using a trackball, mouse, joystick, or keypad to move the cursor, you'll find course setting an amazingly fast routine. On a paper chart, it's common to set a course directly from buoy to buoy. When you're working with a plotter plugged into a navigation receiver and possibly an autopilot as well, you'd do well to use caution and set your waypoints well clear of the objects you're going to use as turning marks. While the nav receiver and the plotter will both sound an alarm when at a preset distance from the upcoming waypoint, if the receiver is off, the first alarm you hear could be the buoy you're about to hit.

You can also set alarms to sound if you stray from a safe course. Some plotters allow you to draw lines onscreen that parallel your course. If the vessel's screen marker hits one of the lines, the alarm sounds.

A nice feature for DR navigation is the bearing function. When you want to determine the safe moment to turn into an unbuoyed channel to an anchorage, you would likely look at the chart—paper or electronic—for a landmark or buoy to take a bearing on. When the buoy bears a particular number of degrees, you've reached the point where it's okay to make your turn. On a paper chart you would use parallel rules or triangles to move from the buoy to a compass rose to find the bearing. On a video plotter you put the cursor on the turning point along your course line. Then move the cursor to the buoy, and press the range and bearing key. Now read the bearing. Press the appropriate key for the reciprocal bearing to set your course back from the anchorage to the course line.

CHAPTER 14

Radar

by Gordon West and Freeman Pittman

At night or in the fog, marine radar will show you where you are, where you have been, and where you are going. It will let you spot surrounding dangers—buoys to starboard, the jetty to port, or other boats around you in the thick of the night or the height of the storm. More radars have been installed by sailboat and powerboat owners during the past few years than ever before, convincing evidence that the advantages of radar for piloting and safety are now being recognized by an increasing number of mariners.

For years, radar (an acronym that stands for RAdio Detection And Rangefinding) was considered an expensive proposition—cumbersome to install, heavy on the electrical system, and difficult to use. In the last 10 years, however, radars have made a quantum jump in technology (and popularity) with price levels dropping significantly. Quite simply, you now get almost twice as much radar for the buck as you did ten years ago, and your boat's electrical system will love it—the new sets draw about half the power of the older ones.

How It Works

Marine radar works on essentially the same principle as echo sounding. Radar pulses in the X band (3 cm, or just under 10,000 megahertz) of the microwave spectrum are generated by a magnetron in the antenna's transmitter. The pulses are, in effect, timed as they leave the antenna, bounce off targets, and return to the receiver portion of the antenna. From there they are amplified and fed to the display unit.

Unlike the depthsounder transducer, which points only downward, radar signals are beamed out by a rotating antenna. The beam sweeps a continuous circle, allowing direction to be computed as well as range. The beam width is a function of the antenna width, which, in turn, is a function of the signal wavelength. Practically sized small-boat radar antennas require a microwave signal.

Inside the radar is a timing device that measures time in microseconds (millionths of a second). At close to the speed of light, a radar pulse will travel 328 yards in one microsecond. If one microsecond passes from the time a pulse is transmitted to the time its echo is received, that burst of energy has traveled 328 yards—164 yards out to the target and 164 yards back. The radar displays the target distance as 164 yards from your boat's present position. The antenna's angle in relation to the bow at that moment is also relayed to the display unit, so that not only the range but the precise bearing of the target is displayed on the scope. Finally, the signal strength of the target on the scope is an indication of its size and density.

The basic components are the antenna unit, with the transmitter and receiver circuitry built into it, and the display unit, which contains the timing and computer circuits, the cathode ray tube, and the power supply. In recreational boat–sized systems the transmitter, receiver, and antenna system typically are housed in a 20- to 60-pound package measuring from 18 to 48 inches. Antennas can be much larger, of course, for big yachts and commercial vessels. The display unit is a lightweight, compact package sized like a small-screen TV—with which it has some parts in common. A one-inch-diameter cable connects the antenna unit with the display unit, and the display unit gets its power from a relatively small pair of 12-volt wires.

The antenna typically rotates at 24 to 40 rpm. It may be enclosed in a round fiberglass or thermoplastic "radome," or it may be an "open array" scanner rotating on a pedestal that houses the motor. Choose the former type if you are going to be mounting it aboard a sailboat halfway up a mast, since sails and rigging would foul an unenclosed antenna. In either case the assembly consists of a horizontal reflector that transmits and receives the radar pulses and echoes.

Small-boat radars can be defined as those transmitting at 5 kilowatts or less of peak power. The most common power choices are 1.5 kw for the smallest, lightest sets designed for mounting on sailboat masts, and 3 or 4 kw for the majority of powerboat (and many sailboat) applications.

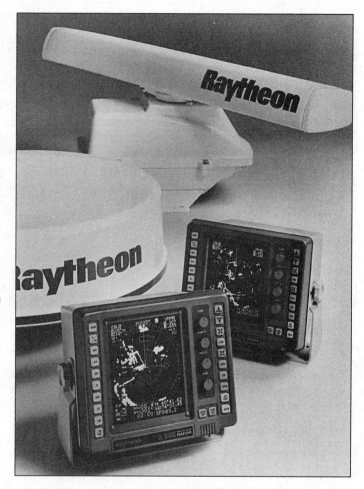

The antenna receiver section, meantime, is capable of detecting signal echoes as low in intensity as 1/10 microvolt.

Transmitting power is important because it can make weak targets visible. Tests of two identically sized antennas, one a 1.5 kw model and the other a 3 kw, showed that the more powerful radar displayed a small outboard boat clearly at 1 mile range, while on the low-powered set it became intermittent at .5 mile on and disappeared altogether at .75 mile.

On the other hand, if you're a sailor you may be concerned with power consumption under sail, and may opt for the lower-powered set, since the lower speed of your boat will give you more time to avoid targets that only show up at close ranges.

To save power, most radars come with a sleep mode that allows you to turn on the transmitter for a few sweeps periodically to check your environment, between which times the radar stays warmed up but at a low draw.

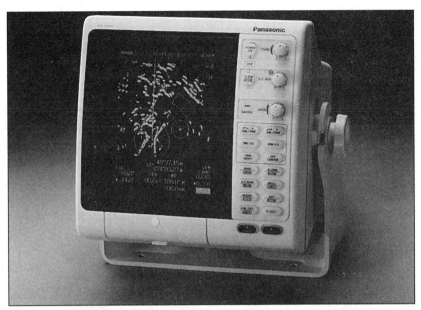

This display shows several of the popular radar features. For starters, note that the image is temporarily offset to show more at the top of the screen—the direction in which the boat is going. Dotted lines on the screen perform several functions. The dotted electronic bearing line from screen center gives bearings to any point and also is used to define two sides of a guard zone. The other two sides are created by the variable range marker, the dotted circle around screen center. The separate circle on the right is a guard zone around a point the navigator wants to avoid; the VRM can also be used to determine distance between any two points on the screen. Along with the picture and numeric readouts of range and bearing, speed, heading, and loran or GPS position can be displayed, with the proper instruments connected.

At least one model offers an additional power-saving mode, in which it turns off only the display while continuing to transmit, to warn you if a target enters a predetermined "guard zone" around your boat.

The transmitter section inside the antenna generates energy pulses on a frequency near 9,400 MHz. To be effective at widely varying distances, each pulse of energy should be made longer or shorter, and modern radars can generate between two and eight different pulse lengths. Pulses might be as short as 0.05 microsecond to differentiate closely separated targets when the radar is in a short-range (¼- and ½-mile) mode. The pulses may be as long as 1.0 microsecond for strong returns at long ranges (4 miles or more).

Pulse repetition rate is directly linked to pulse length. With each pulse, the antenna alternates between being a transmitter and its own receiver. A long pulse requires a relatively long reception period, which limits the number of pulses which can be transmitted and received in a second. This is fine at long ranges, where target resolution is not important. In its longer-

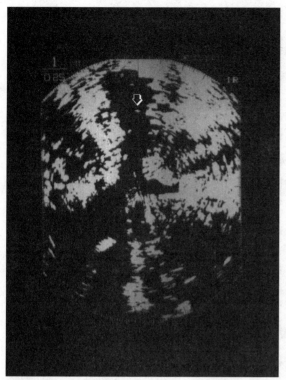
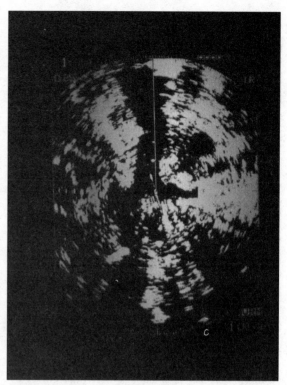

The effect of power on otherwise identical radars is shown here. A 17-foot runabout with radar reflector ran away from the radars until it disappeared from the screen on the right at .77 mile. This screen was attached to a 1.5 kilowatt antenna. At over a mile, it was still visible on the screen at left, served by a 3 kw antenna. Note that the 1.5 kw scanner gave a better picture close in, however.

range modes the radar will automatically slow down to approximately 800 to 1,200 pulses per second.

On the other hand, short pulses can be sent at a high pulse repetition rate, perhaps 2,000 or 2,500 pulses per second, which allows for finer target resolution; essential for distinguishing a boat from a buoy near to it.

A modern, microprocessor-based radar automatically selects the optimum pulse repetition rate and pulse length, depending on which range you have selected.

Most modern radars offer a minimum of five selectable ranges, the shortest of which will be ⅛ or ¼ mile and the longest 16 to 20 miles. There are radars with more power and longer range, but long range is the *least* important feature for a small-boat radar system. Since radar waves don't bend over the horizon, it makes no sense to buy a 40-mile radar when you can only mount it high enough to put the horizon 8 miles distant. If you are planning to operate along coasts with high mountains close by the shore,

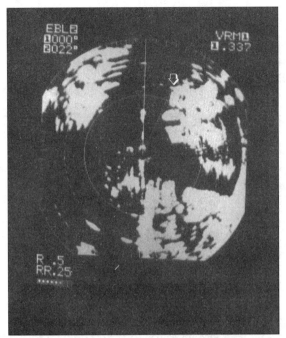

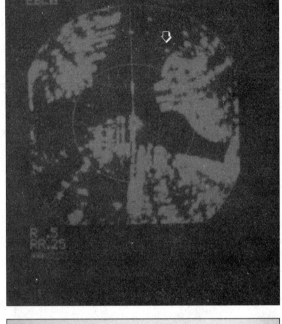

Antenna width, and its inversely proportional beam width, affect target discrimination. The left-hand screen, fed by a 24-inch diameter antenna, shows the runabout as a blob connected to the nearby land mass, while the right-hand screen, fed by a 46-inch scanner, shows the boat as a distinct target. The photo shows how far the boat was from the land in reality.

you might choose one of the longer-range radars, since the mountains will show up over the horizon. Remember, though, that for a radar to detect a target at a maximum range of 20 miles, your radar antenna must be 10 feet or more above the water and the land mass must be more than 170 feet above sea level.

The diameter (width, or span) of the antenna is an essential factor in radar performance. Depending upon the width of the antenna, the RF beam width may be from 1½ to 5 degrees in the horizontal plane. The narrower the horizontal beam, the better the discrimination between targets.

Open array antennas are commonly two feet wide, yielding a horizontal beam width of about 5 degrees, but a wider unit (four feet, for example) will concentrate radar energy in a tighter horizontal beam, say, 2 degrees wide, giving you greater target definition. The 18- to 24-inch antenna

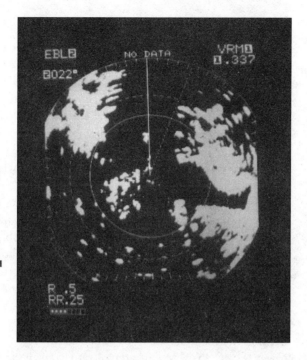

The effect of moderate heel is shown on this radar screen. The maximum most radars can be heeled without some image loss is 12½ degrees. The antenna feeding this screen is heeled 17 degrees. Compare with the screens in previous photos; much of the land on the low side at the bottom of the screen is missing, while targets on the high side have lost definition.

assemblies enclosed in radomes, while they are very compact, might show two fishing boats close together at a range of five miles as a single echo on the scope, while the slightly wider, open antenna would show the vessels as two separate targets. Wider antennas lead to better target definition.

Antenna assemblies are designed to offer reliable operation even when your vessel is rolling or heeling. The vertical beam width of most radar signals is greater than 25 degrees, so roll or heel angles of up to 12 degrees will still give you a full image on screen. However, any angle beyond that and the picture on your screen can be seriously degraded, including blurred targets on the side the radar is pointing down toward, and little if any picture on the side that's pointing skyward. Sailboat owners and owners of displacement powerboats that can roll a lot in a sea should seriously consider a mechanical means of leveling the radar antenna. One company offers a radar mast with a hydraulic ram that tilts a radome back to level on a heeling sailboat. Another company sells a hydraulically damped gimbal mounting for mast, backstay, or post. Either device is expensive, but the alternative is half a picture, or worse, in a seaway.

In heavy seas you may notice that a distant target "disappears" while you're in the trough of a wave. Such intermittent targets in heavy seas are probably small boats a few miles away.

You may wish to mount the antenna unit as high as practical to increase the maximum realizable range, but remember that while it might be nice to have the antenna halfway up a sailboat's mast, it's not really necessary for good coastal navigation and short-range ship detection. Antennas just 10 feet off the water will give you a good view of breakwaters, ships, and any other targets within four or five miles, and it's what is happening in your immediate neighborhood that concerns you most.

Also, the lower the antenna, the less violent are the effects of rolling. Radar displays electronically damp out most of the effects of the motion, but some picture degradation is possible. Besides, the weight of the antenna itself adds to a boat's heeling and rolling moment when it's mounted well up the mast.

When an antenna is mounted down low, there is always some concern over the potential harm to the crew from the transmitted microwaves. Many installations on powerboats put the antenna assembly directly in front of the operator on the flying bridge, or just behind and above him. While we know of no reported adverse effects, no efforts have been made, scientifically or otherwise, to find any relationship between antenna placement and radiation-related illnesses.

Probably the intermittent sweeping of nearby radar waves is no more harmful than standing beneath a large commercial broadcast station antenna tower setup. But since no type of radiation in excess can be beneficial to the body, it would certainly be best not to have the radar setup just a short distance away and sweeping by at eye level. The sensible approach is not to court trouble: There's enough radiation in the slotted antenna reflector to heat up a bologna sandwich. Mount the antenna assembly well above all occupants on the vessel and you can put your mind at rest.

The display unit is the component that has seen some dramatic improvements. At 20 pounds or less it's quite lightweight, with its internal power supply fully transistorized and with new circuitry in place of heavy transformers. The display unit also houses the microprocessor electronics that allow you to select the many different modes of operation for the radar.

The traditional radar scope utilized a cathode ray tube with targets and range ring information displayed as bright orange or green "returns" on the plan position indicator (PPI) scope. Your vessel was located in the center of the picture and emitted a faint scanning line that swept around the scope every couple of seconds, in synchrony with the antenna rotation. When this scanning line detected incoming signals, it painted a picture on the scope showing the bearing and range of the target and its relative intensity on that sweep. The targets were reilluminated with each rotation of the antenna. Fast-moving targets appeared to leave a phosphorous wake as you watched their progress across the screen.

Though you'll still see it operating reliably on older vessels, this display system is no longer offered on radars today. It had two main drawbacks:

First, the picture would begin to fade as soon as the cursor line passed over the target. Second, most presentations were impossible to read in daylight; a hood was required for viewing.

Ten years ago, a new type of display was introduced that solved both these problems, and made possible a host of extremely valuable features to boot. Today, "raster scan" displays are the standard. The raster scan display digitally processes radar returns so they may be displayed for the duration of the cursor line sweep, and with a brightness that can be seen in most conditions short of sunlight reflected off the screen into your eyes.

Raster scanning is the name of the process whereby your television converts analog signals taken from the air to digital information used to construct a picture. The digital signal determines which of the thousands of dots on the screen, called pixels (short for picture elements), are activated at a given moment. In the same way, each pulse echoed to a raster scanning radar is converted to a digital message good for one revolution of the cursor line.

Between 400 and 700 horizontal and vertical lines on the screen create the electroluminescent grid that defines the pixels. The number of screen lines is the screen's resolution, expressed as 480 x 640, or 610 x 486, for example. The number of pixels illuminated in one part of the screen corresponds to the intensity of the radar return. Weak targets may only illuminate two or three pixels, while large targets may illuminate a block of twenty.

Early raster scan radars had low-resolution screens, resulting in a blocky image that, though it lasted, was not nearly as natural and identifiable as on the old PPI screens. Today's raster screens have better resolution.

The first raster radars also had what is known as single-level quantization. This means that, regardless of the target's strength, all targets showed the same level of illumination. If a target was too weak, it didn't show. Most, if not all, radars nowadays have multi-level quantization, showing anywhere from two to eight levels of illumination according to the strength of the return. This is an advantage pre-raster radars once held over the newer sets. But no longer.

Some manufacturers have followed in the steps of video depthsounder makers and have assigned different colors to different echo intensities. However, color-coded quantization has not proved to be very useful, and is downright confusing to some operators. Color is better used to differentiate the types of information on screen: red for stationary targets, yellow for moving ones, blue for range rings, white for alphanumeric data, and so forth. Most users find that's not enough of a reason to pay the extra cost for color. But as more and more navigational data becomes available onscreen, color will gain in popularity for its organizing ability.

We have already discussed the range scales available in most small-boat radars. To choose a range, you either twist a knob or press a button as many times as needed.

A radar set offers other controls besides the range selector, of course. For instance, an electronic bearing line (EBL) radiates from your location in the center of the screen, just as the constantly sweeping cursor line does. Pressing a button, though, you can rotate the EBL to put it in line with a target, and the target's relative bearing will then be displayed in a corner of the screen. With this feature, you can plot the bearings of landmarks, nav aids, and other vessels in your vicinity, and you can watch other vessels' movements. If another vessel draws progressively nearer along the cursor line, you are on a collision course.

EBL bearings vary in accuracy, depending on the horizontal beam width. The EBL itself reads to 1 degree, but you can't be sure the target is accurately sized or located. So use the EBL readouts as close approximations of bearing.

Some sets come with two or more EBLs so you can track multiple targets more easily, or leave one EBL on a mark you want to keep at a constant bearing, while the other EBL is free for other targets. A few radars even have EBLs that can work from any target or other point on the screen. The functionality of this is mainly to help set up alarm zones around hazardous points, as described below. It's strictly a feature of secondary importance.

The electronic variable range marker (VRM) is another extremely useful function. Instead of having to estimate the distance to a target by interpolating between the fixed range rings that match the range scale you have selected, you can electronically expand or contract the circular range ring to coincide with the distance to a target. The range (to as close as $\frac{1}{10}$ mile) is displayed digitally. It's quite accurate.

Most radars combine the EBL and VRM functions to let you set up guard zones. Move the EBL to 90 degrees port and press the guard zone button. Rotate the EBL to 90 degrees starboard and press again. Move the VRM to two miles out and set the guard zone feature once again. Now, when any target, moving or otherwise, gets within two miles of you on any point ahead of your beam, an alarm will sound.

With some radars you can set multiple guard zones, or a single all the way around you. Guard zones alert you to vessels coming close, or to the fact that the wind has shifted during the night in your anchorage and you're now drifting close to shore or to a neighboring boat.

Guard zones are simple to set up and are an excellent safety feature. Be sure to try out the EBL, VRM, and guard zone functions on two or three radars before you buy.

In that the radar can almost always see farther than is visible onscreen, manufacturers have added a screen offset feature on some sets to let you look farther ahead, astern, or to one side. Hit the appropriate button and your boat's position moves out of the center of the screen, say to starboard, opening up your view to port as you motor along with the coast on that side.

Naturally, you lose that much image to starboard, as well. There's not much the offset function can do that you can't also do simply by moving to the next smaller scale.

Some radars have a function that shows moving targets' former positions in a slightly dimmer shade. The positions add up to a track, or trail, showing their recent course history.

Using this feature is easier than covering the screen with grease pencil marks, and alerts you to sudden course changes among your neighboring voyagers. If you boat in crowded waters, however, it may be difficult to distinguish among many moving targets. Try the feature on a working radar to see if you like it. And remember, you can always turn the function off.

Conventional radar display is with your boat at the center of the screen, always heading toward the top of the display. However, if you interface an electronic compass with a radar designed for it, you can have a north-up display. In this case, the display reorients itself to be viewed as you would a chart and the radar boat, still at screen center, moves at whatever heading your real vessel does. Rather than the image constantly sliding off the bottom of the screen, it now disappears on your back bearing.

North-up display is handy for comparing with charts, but you've got to maintain your own bearings when you use it. It can confuse someone just coming on watch at midnight.

North-up is necessary for same-screen viewing of radar and electronic chart images, and is used with big-ship–style radar plotting consoles. Unless you have plans for one of these systems, north-up is an unnecessary extra. For that matter, the compass will cost you several hundred dollars, too.

The radar screen is being used increasingly to display other information than just an electronic picture of your surroundings. Alphanumeric data from GPS or loran, compass, and speedometer are all possible to call up on a radar with NMEA or proprietary interfacing capability. Usually, the data is shown in a box in the corner of the screen.

Several video plotting systems already can share a screen with radar. Actually, alternate on it is more accurate; at the time of writing only one system allowed the radar and video charts to share the screen simultaneously. The others don't have common scales, and as noted above, north-up capability is a must to avoid disorientation. Most of these systems are still rather crude, but the leaders show what is possible and, in fact, inevitable.

Don't wait for these improvements, though. Radar's power alone is reason enough to get it on your boat as soon as your budget can afford it. Everyone who has it says they won't do without it again.

Prices for radars have been holding steady for the past two or three years at $1,500 to $3,000. Don't look for any dramatic price drops in the near future. Instead, more and more features are being made available for the money. This trend is likely to continue.

Operating Procedures

Before turning on your radar, doublecheck your marine radiotelephone license and see whether or not it has been endorsed for 9,400 MHz (9.4 GHz) radar operation. If it hasn't, you must fill out a new Form 506 and specifically request radar frequencies from the FCC. As soon as you drop this form into the mail, you can start operating the unit. When your license comes back, you will have the same radio call sign, but with additional frequencies allocated for radar use. You are not allowed to operate radar without the FCC frequency endorsement on your marine radiotelephone license.

Begin using your radar in daylight and note how the objects around you appear on the screen. You will notice that radar doesn't see over large ships or around islands to show smaller targets close behind them. Nor will it pick up low-lying rocks at distances greater than three to five miles (less if there is a sea running).

The type of target will influence its ability to reflect radar signals. Sailboats with sails set are poor radar reflectors. Radar waves simply penetrate sails, and an aluminum mast reflects radar signals in scattered directions. The effect is akin to bouncing a tennis ball off a round pole.

Some targets will make huge presentations on your radar scope. Supertankers turned broadside are an example, as are buoys with radar reflectors. Anything comprised of flat metallic surfaces that intersect at 90 degrees will reflect radar signals with great intensity. This is the benefit of mounting a radar reflector on a vessel.

Since fiberglass is a poor conductor except when wet, fiberglass boats are not good reflectors of radar waves. You will notice, too, that different shorelines give readouts of different intensity. Low, sandy beaches barely show up until you are almost on top of them, while sharp cliffs reflect signals with tremendous intensity. Low, rolling hills give only fair echoes, and sandbars will give almost no return echo at all.

Never tune the intensity (identified on some radars as "brilliance") up too bright. It should be just bright enough for viewing. The phosphorous cathode ray tube displays, especially, are easily damaged by a too-high brilliance setting.

Heavy seas may reflect radar signals, causing confused readings at times. This is known as sea clutter. There is a control to help eliminate sea clutter.

Rain clutter can also cloud your screen, making it impossible to see solid targets. An adjustment knob or key will solve this problem, too.

Rain is usually something you want to be able to see coming. Turning the rain clutter filter down will let you identify approaching storms, fronts, and attendant squall lines. Practice this function as often as possible so you'll be able to recognize fast-moving foul weather in time to do something about it.

One form of interference on a radar will tell you when other vessels using radar are in the area. Spiral interference traces will appear on your screen with every antenna revolution. The pattern can be tuned out using the interference controls.

Once you have gained confidence in detecting targets, the next step is to learn to use radar to avoid groundings and collisions. If you carefully align the EBL over a target, you can watch its progress and ensure that it is not on a collision course with you.

You can safely navigate within a harbor using the radar on its shortest range setting. Enter the harbor a few times in the daylight with the radar set on, and you should be able to rely almost completely on radar for a nighttime approach. Consult your chart for the buoys that appear as targets on your scope as you approach the harbor. Watch the shorelines or breakwaters as you pass through the entrance, and then look for small craft that might have been "hidden" behind a breakwater. As your skill increases, you'll be able to spot and negotiate the appropriate channel in a crowded anchorage, coming within 30 yards of your dock on the basis of radar alone.

At sea, you can use a radar for position finding by measurement of distance and bearing. Spot large headlands or points on your charts, and locate these landmarks on your display with the radar set to one of the longer ranges. Distant peaks will appear as small traces toward the scope perimeter. Use the EBL to develop lines of position and the VRM to give range.

By extension, radar can also be used to determine speed over bottom or vessel drift. Take your radar bearings for a fix, then do it again on the same or other recognizable shore features a half hour later. Plot your course and distance between the two fixes for the time period and calculate your speed.

The U.S. Coast Guard has made it a bit easier to identify a few important targets by equipping them with racon devices. Assume you are entering an important commercial harbor and need to ascertain which target is the main channel buoy; you'll be in luck if that buoy carries a racon device. It will paint a coded signal on your radar set, removing all guesswork. In the manner of the air traffic controller "squawk" signals that identify aircraft, racon buoys and shoreside racon installations mark the exact spot of a reflected signal. You can expect to see more of these devices in the near future; however, they probably won't ever be widely used.

Installation Tips

You must really see a radar set to judge it, and for that reason, particularly if you do not plan to install the unit yourself, you would be wise to purchase it from a specialty marine electronics dealer, one that is an authorized sales and service agent for that particular unit. You'll want someone local in case the radar should require service, so that a technician can be brought aboard for the work. Most of the electronics are in the antenna unit, which is not easy to dismount for repair off the boat.

Radar sets require high voltages, and high-voltage circuitry is inherently more prone to malfunction. This is another reason why many radar sales still take place at the dealer level rather than through mail-order sources. It takes a skilled technician at a hefty hourly rate to work on your radar, but if you develop a service contract with the marine electronics dealer that sells you the equipment, you can save yourself some money down the road. Most radars require service at least every two years due to their high operating voltages as well as the sensitivity of the magnetron transmitter output tube. If you use your unit a lot, it will require annual peaking and tweaking. For best results, this can only be done right on your boat by an experienced technician. Buying from a specialty dealer—and insisting on a firm service contract—is the surest way to a long and happy relationship between you and your radar.

If you *do* decide to install your own radar, follow carefully the instructions in the manual that comes with the unit. Unless the manufacturer includes an FCC certificate in the packing case, it will be necessary to have a technician "sign off" your installation and make an entry in your radiotelephone and radar logbook as required by the FCC. If you buy the unit through a mail-order house, be prepared for this added, not insignificant expense. The local marine electronics specialty dealer from whom you *didn't* buy the unit may not be eager to send down a technician to sign you off for just a few bucks. Indeed, he may charge you a couple of hours of service time for this sign-off procedure.

A few marine electronics mail-order companies will certify a radar before it is shipped to you. If this can be done, it will save you some money once everything is aboard and operating. Radars are so sophisticated and self-adjusting that a do-it-yourself installation is feasible *if* you are good with tools and can devise an appropriate antenna-system mount. Some manufacturers offer brackets for mast-mounted antennas, and there are countless other possible approaches.

Remember, though, if you're going to mount the antenna high above the deck, that there may be tremendous stresses on the installation when your vessel is pitching in heavy seas. Since the antenna unit contains almost two-thirds of the radar's electronics, make sure it's bolted down firmly. Replacing it would be expensive.

Remember, too, that the cable from antenna to display is long and bulky. Stuffing it down a mast filled with halyards and other cables may not be easy. This is one situation in which a professional can save you time and money in the long run. The cable connections between antenna and display unit are straightforward; you can hook it up yourself simply by following the directions and screwing in the wires by the numbers. You do want to screw the leads to the antenna and close up the antenna housing ashore before you climb a mast or tower, though. The job can be quite awkward at 30 feet up. Do a dry run ashore at least, to see what we mean.

When you buy the radar, you buy it as a complete setup, so you needn't worry about matching the antenna assembly to the radar. If you're given a choice of antenna lengths, try to accommodate the slightly longer antenna for better target discrimination.

Maintenance

Unless the unit is specifically guaranteed to a reasonable level of water-resistance, keep the display out of the weather to protect the delicate circuitry within. Don't leave it in a damp flying bridge for any length of time. If you're going to be storing the boat for some time, take the display unit home to store in a dry place. Never seal it in a plastic bag—that only collects moisture.

Now and then, you can rinse the antenna radome or open array scanner face with fresh water. Radar waves have a hard time sounding through accumulated soot. Never paint the antenna dome or scanner face—lead-based paints, especially, will literally soak up radar signals. If the radome is discolored have the dealer clean it, or buy a new cover.

For more on radar, pick up a copy of Jack West's *Boatowner's Guide to Radar*, which clearly and concisely covers all the general principles of radar use and interpretation, the limitations of bearing and range resolution, and the nuances of target resolution. The 128-page paperback was published by International Marine in 1988.

CHAPTER 15

Autopilots

by Freeman Pittman

Autopilots are inventor Elmer Sperry's gift to pleasureboaters—or they are a pain in the neck that don't work when you really need them. Skippers' reactions to them are based on experience, and when the system is a good one, it's not easily forgotten. The sensation of feeling a boat moving surely and economically with no one at the helm makes you glad to be born into this technological age.

When the experience is a bad one, you remember that, too. A good deal of the resulting unhappiness often stems from not having known enough about what you were getting into before purchasing and installing the hardware. The autopilot is one of the most complex systems on the boat and takes up a good deal of the available space and power. Discovering the strengths and weaknesses—as well as the idiosyncrasies—of each model that interests you will go a long way toward ensuring the reliability and good performance of the pilot you finally choose.

Autopilots have grown immeasurably sophisticated in recent years, and yet the least expensive electric pilot on the market costs around $350, a much smaller percentage of today's resources than were the less capable models of old.

On the other hand, a thorough, permanently installed belowdecks system costing several thousand dollars can keep you on a compass or windvane-directed course with an accuracy of plus or minus 1 degree in good weather, compensating for yaw, leeway, an imbalanced sailboat helm, and even (when a loran or GPS is tied into the system) current set and drift. And it will do all this while using little more of a sailboat's precious electrical power than does a cabin light. Powerboat autopilots, by the same token, today deliver more power from lighter, more compact systems than ever before. Trim, torque, or poorly synchronized engines can be offset by these pilots, too.

How They Work

Years ago the crudest autopilots simply zigzagged the boat across a chosen course, using electrical contacts touching the heading sensor's compass card as the limiting switches. Because of their behavior, these basic pilots were dubbed "hunting" or "bang-bang" types.

Miniaturization of components and the development of highly efficient, solid state electronics have made autopilots viable for small craft. The first big improvement was the incorporation of a "deadband" in the system. The deadband, whether mechanical or electronic, is the narrow pie-slice of water down the middle of which the boat's course is set. As long as the boat's heading stays within the deadband, say 2 degrees on either side of the course, the autopilot takes no corrective action. In a manual steering system, the total play is its deadband. Wiggle the steering wheel a half inch or so and you may feel no rudder movement. The boat is free to wander within that range.

Obviously, allowing the boat some free rein saves energy. Within the typical 1- to 5-degree deadband width current autopilots allow, the boat, if it has been trimmed and balanced, will wander back to course a fair amount of the time. Making the pilot work only outside the deadband lessens the amount of electrical power needed to drive the motor that turns the rudder.

Deadband used to be a manual adjustment, and it still can be on many pilots. It is often identified as the "sea state" control. However, today's microprocessor-controlled pilots incorporate a higher level of sophistication. This is known as "proportional response." Proportional response means the rudder is turned at a particular angle (and, on some pilots) rate for a given course error. Less rudder is needed for a small error, more for a large error. The proportional pilot applies the right amount for each, in contrast to simpler systems that react with the same amount of helm correction for all course deviations and conditions.

Most pilots today, in fact, include still more inputs and feedback circuits (such as heading, sea state, gain, rudder angle, rudder rate, counter rudder, drive unit load, and polarity), and manage almost all of them automatically, so you can't monitor even a fraction of what is going on inside. The result is a system that's too complicated for most manufacturers to explain. They may use general-sounding terms like "adaptive control" to distinguish current hardware/software pilot systems from older electromechanical types. The bottom line, however, is autopilots that are simple to operate, and with fewer electromechanical parts to wear out.

Heading Sensors

Regardless of the principle of operation, an autopilot works only on the command of its lookout. For the powerboat, and generally for a vessel under sail, too, the lookout is the "heading sensor." For many years, autopilot systems have incorporated a modified card compass as the heading sensor. In a typical system, an electrical "pickup" coil carrying a low voltage placed above or below the compass card is aligned with the field created by the compass's magnets. As the compass card turns, the magnets affect the voltage and cause a signal whose voltage and phase are converted to left-right steering instructions. Several manufacturers still offer the pickup coil sensing system or something like it.

Another effective sensing system uses a photocell to detect a light beam that passes through a compass card divided into clear, partially shaded, and opaque sections. If, through rotation of the card due to course deviation, either the opaque or clear portion swings into the path of the light beam, a signal change is generated that activates the pilot's drive motor. This system, too, still has a few adherents.

Most manufacturers today have turned to a fully digital electronic heading sensor, the "fluxgate compass." You don't see numbers on a card with the fluxgate; you may not see any heading readout at all for it, although all but the least expensive autopilots do include the digital display.

The fluxgate sensor ("flux" for the earth's magnetic field and "gate" for the type of electronic circuit used) was originally (and still is in some fluxgates) a set of four ferrite rods in the form of a cross, each wound with copper wire to create four small coils. A toroidal, or ring-shaped sensor has since become more popular, but it functions the same way. With a low-voltage alternating current fed to the coils, the earth's magnetic field distorts each coil's voltage output. The amount of disturbance varies with the coil's angle to the field. A given voltage output and AC phase correspond to a particular compass heading. Many fluxgates included in autopilot systems have a digital LCD readout, allowing them to be used as an alternate to the ship's steering compass. A visual display is not needed for autopilot work, though, since the sensed signal need only be transmitted to the autopilot control unit for amplification.

The fluxgate system is not subject to the oscillations and overshoot of a card compass with an electronic repeater. It also uses less power. Some fluxgate compasses perform better than others: absolute accuracy is from less than 1 degree on the best models to 2- to 3-degree accuracy on the worst. Equally important is heeled accuracy. Gimballing designs differ: most brands use a universal joint from which the sensor element dangles inside the compass housing. Some hang up more easily than others in a seaway. The sensor element may float on oil in a sealed chamber, though most fluxgates are "air-damped."

Electronic damping, or averaging, is required with all fluxgates. The sensor's signal may be sampled every ¼ second, but that update rate would drive the autopilot crazy. Given all the movement of the sensor and its sensitivity to heel error (typically 3 degrees of error for every 1 degree of heel), averaging adjustment can be between 1 and 40 seconds. If you have programmed in a lot of averaging, you'll get slower response to off-course headings, and the pilot will take longer to catch up to your new heading when you change course. That can make for very slow sailboat tacks. The adjustment is usually quite easy to tailor to the conditions, however.

With a fluxgate, or any electronic compass, of course you'd better have a mechanical steering compass as a backup.

Steering a sailboat need not be by compass alone. The sails and helm can be set to hold a course relative to the wind's direction. Some autopilot manufacturers offer a windvane option that can take over from the heading sensor when you're sailing on the wind. This is simply an electronic apparent wind angle sensor like the indicators in many sailboat instrument packages. You set up the boat so the rig and helm are balanced, and dial in the relative wind angle you want to sail. The wind direction sensor takes over from the compass sensor and the boat will stay on a heading relative to the wind, rather than a compass course.

If the windvane is well-integrated with the autopilot logic, it is a feature worth having, especially when you are sailing on the wind while crossing an ocean and must take time off to rest. But not all windvane-steering autopilots are created equal. Experienced transoceanic sailors say they have not yet found a windvane system that reacts quickly enough to wind shifts. They say pitch and roll of the boat can affect the pilot's idea of the boat's heading relative to the wind.

It is also possible for a system to react too quickly, turning the boat without waiting to see if the wind shifts back to its original relative angle. The key here is how often the pilot samples wind readings, and how much it averages them before acting on them. Having a manually adjusted averaging rate might solve the problem momentarily, but since wind strength and direction are always changing, the right rate now might be the wrong one in five minutes.

At least one line of pilots incorporates a different solution to this problem. In these pilots the windvane does not totally preempt the compass, but only updates it from time to time. Still, nobody has a system that works on every point of sail, in any wind and sea condition.

Pilots for cockpit mounting typically employ a windvane on a shaft that can be clamped to the stern rail when in use and stowed below at other times. Ideally, you would have two vanes, one on each side so you could always plug into the windward one. A stern-rail vane mounted on the centerline or to leeward gets dirty air off the sails and gets hopelessly confused.

Some pilot systems can also be tied into the electronic wind indicator instrument mounted on the masthead. Although you might think this would offer cleaner air and more accurate readings, there is far more motion aloft, and the wind indicator can send the pilot steering data based on wild gyrations. Most of the time, wind sensed from the weather side of the stern gives the best steering results.

Controls

A heading error signal from the compass or windvane sensor goes to the autopilot's control unit. There it is processed and amplified in order to command the actuator motor that turns the rudder. The control unit may be better envisioned as a control group; it performs a number of functions, and not all its components necessarily reside in one housing. The amplifier in one manufacturer's system is in the actuator motor case. Several systems put the buttons and knobs in a compact control panel that's easy to locate in the nav or helm stations, while placing all the microprocessors, switches, and other electronic components in a separate box that can be mounted in the location best protected from interfering electrical fields.

However the parts are packaged, the control unit in a permanently mounted system contains an amplifier, logic circuitry, a junction box for all the plugs and connectors going to and from other components, as well as the dials, buttons or knobs with which you operate the system. Portable cockpit-mounted pilots may be completely self-contained, with compass sensor and drive unit included, or they may have the compass in a separate case you can mount below decks.

Unfortunately, you cannot rely on the manufacturer's literature to help you understand what all the control unit functions are, since the terminology is not yet standardized. The following explanations should help to resolve confusion.

Yaw (variously called sea state, sensitivity, response, or deadband) sets the deadband width on a rudder correction. The control may be totally automatic, but in most pilots it's a mechanical one inside the pilot that you set once for your boat's characteristics, or else a keypad or dial adjustment you can make at any time to suit the sea conditions. A wide deadband lets the boat react to momentary influences such as individual waves in heavier conditions. A narrow deadband keeps the boat on a straight course in smooth water. Given heading sensors with plus-or-minus-1-degree accuracy in smooth conditions and drive motors able to make small corrections with minimal time lag, today's autopilots offer a deadband as narrow as 2 degrees (1 degree to either side of course) and adjustable to as wide as 5 to 8 degrees.

The most automated of autopilots do away with deadband control by feeding a nearly constant stream of small power pulses to the drive unit, instead of fewer but larger bursts in response to wider yaw angles. For these pilots a low-pass filter, which won't allow momentary errors from individual wave impacts to be signaled to the drive unit, offers the damping inherent in deadband systems.

The *gain control* (rudder, ratio, P-factor) adjusts the proportion of rudder response to course error. For a given error on a light sailboat with a spade

Contemporary autopilot control panels are a far cry from those of 10 years ago. There are fewer buttons, often no dials to twist. Instead, there are large LC displays with computer-style menus you scroll through to reach the function you want to turn on or adjust. The buttons on this panel change purpose, depending on the menu page selected. The panel is styled to match the manufacturer's other instruments. Most permanent-mount pilots include a choice of several electric and hydraulic drive systems.

rudder separate from the keel, or on a planing powerboat, the gain might be set low, since little rudder movement is needed to make the boat change course. On a heavier, long-keeled boat with an attached rudder, or on a trawler-hull powerboat, more helm might be needed to make the boat respond. In that case, a higher gain setting would make the rudder turn farther for the same degree of heading error. In a proportional-response pilot the gain may also control the speed, or rate, at which the rudder is turned in relation to the rate at which the boat falls off course.

Essential to a proportional-response system is an indicator that signals rudder position to the control unit. On most proportional-rate models the *rudder-feedback unit* is a potentiometer (the rheostat for adjusting a dining room light is also a potentiometer) attached to the rudder by a small tiller and tie-rod; the potentiometer feeds a higher or lower voltage to the control box depending on whether the rudder is hard over or nearly centered. Recently, some of the newer, solid-state pilot systems have offered an alternative to the electromechanical potentiometer with its corrosion-prone contacts by including a circuit that simulates rudder angle signals. Such a circuit senses the strength and polarity of signals sent to the drive motor. Comparing these values to those assigned to a neutral helm, the circuit determines rudder angle. Although this system may be more reliable mechanically, it has not proven as accurate as the potentiometer. Now some manufacturers of simulated feedback systems also offer a mechanical feedback unit.

Counter rudder, another function increasingly being automated, is tied to the amount and/or speed of rudder response. Counter rudder is designed to keep a pilot from overshooting the course while making a heading correction. Some pilots still have a manually adjustable counter rudder function to cope with various sea and load conditions. Others are set once for a particular boat's characteristics. Most microprocessor models have an automated counter rudder circuit that is proportional to the error, just as the rudder response is. In most cases (except when the error is a very large one), the pilot reverses the drive motor long enough to keep the boat from crossing the course line when it is returning from its off-course angle. In general, the lighter and shallower the hull, the less need there is for counter rudder.

Trim (bias, offset) compensates for a persistent heading error, such as from extreme weather helm, only one of two engines working, or a strong, steady wind blowing the bow off to leeward. Some pilots have a trim adjustment that alters the control unit's sense of proper heading to a position slightly off center. It makes the unit think a slightly turned rudder is actually amidships. You make the adjustment based on visual references outside the boat, or on experience. You can't feel the tiller or wheel for wind or for

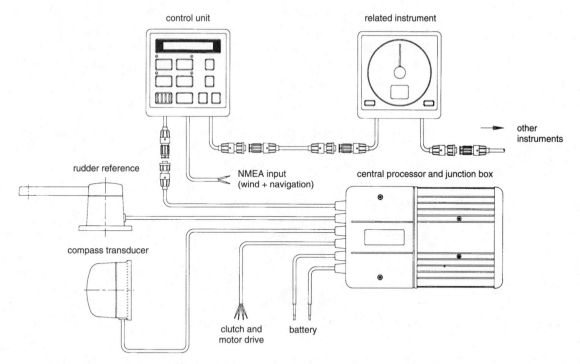

control unit

related instrument

other
instruments

rudder reference

NMEA input
(wind + navigation)

central processor and junction box

compass transducer

clutch and
motor drive

battery

Most pilot systems feature modularity, so plugging in additional items such as a control unit in a second steering station, or a loran or GPS requires little work.

weather helm, because the pilot has taken over. Other pilots have an automatic trim circuit that deals with accumulated error by sampling errors over a period of time, and applying the rudder if most of the errors have been to one side of the course.

Trim corrections cannot deal precisely with the effects of current- and wind-induced leeway. The boat may keep to its set heading, yet still drift off track. To cope with these influences, an outside position-finding device such as a loran or GPS must be incorporated into the system. Many permanently mounted autopilots have a nav unit interface as an option. And because the industry generally has agreed on a standard interface (National Marine Electronics Association 0180 or 0183), many lorans and GPS receivers can be plugged right into the pilot.

Depending on the pilot's sophistication and the nav receiver, different receiver inputs offer more than one kind of steering. The receiver outputs heading, and the pilot can simply substitute the receiver's heading signal for its own compass. In this case you do not benefit from the position finder's ability to compensate for set and drift.

The pilot can also follow a course you set in the receiver. In this case, the course is a continuous string of waypoints, and the heading the boat will be steered to will be whatever the nav receiver demands to hold to the plotted course. This is an invaluable safety feature that can keep you off rocks and out of busy shipping lanes.

The third common way the nav unit can drive the pilot is to a waypoint. In this case, a heading or course is not held, but rather, the bow of the boat is always aimed at the waypoint. In open water aboard a powerboat, this is a sure way to get to your destination, but it may not be the most efficient. If the waypoint is to windward, a sailboat, of course, could not operate in this mode.

Different pilots and receivers may interact in varying ways, and the above descriptions may not apply exactly to the equipment you're looking at. Be sure you know which mode you're operating in, and what that means for the systems you're using.

And here's that standard warning about NMEA interfacing again: not all so-called compatible navigators and pilots really do interface. Check with the manufacturers of the equipment you're considering to be sure their products are on speaking terms. Read the chapters on loran and GPS for more on NMEA 0180 and 0183.

Pilot Configurations

The innards and functions of an autopilot may be nearly identical within two or three of a manufacturer's models, but how they're packaged determines the boats they can be used aboard.

Compact dashboard models for small motorboats have been made, but they have not been successful. Self-contained much like sailboat wheel-steering models, they slip over the steering column and bolt to the dash. The steering wheel goes over the pilot. Some dashboard instruments may have to be repositioned to accommodate the pilot box.

The more recent autopilots for hydraulically steered sterndrive- and outboard-powered craft have conventional pilot control units to mount on the dash or bridge. Drive units offered range from a small hydraulic pump to connect with the sterndrive's power steering lines, to an electric linear drive operating the power-steering pump, and to a clamp-on hydraulic linear drive for an outboard. These systems range from $2,000 up at retail.

Sailboat tiller-steering pilots may be the best bargains among autopilots. They are compact, simple to operate, extremely power-efficient, and when removed, leave no other hardware to impede hand steering or crew movement in the cockpit.

Tiller pilots universally incorporate a fluxgate heading sensor, controls, drive motor, and rack- or screw-type drive shaft. The least expensive models don't have a heading display; all the rest do. Higher-cost models have heavier-duty motors, a stiffer chassis, better bearings, and more electronic functions, such as wind and nav receiver interfacing. A few can also integrate with entire instrument/navigation systems made by the pilot's manufacturer. More and more of this will be coming.

Manufacturers assume these pilots will be put aboard smaller cruising boats (25 to 40 feet), and power consumption is as important as steering power. However, if your boat is in the overlap range between pilot sizes, always opt for the bigger motor if you have the chance. It will still be very efficient, and you'll never be underpowered on the helm.

Tiller pilots have to be water- and shock-resistant to survive for any length of time in a sailboat cockpit. Almost all have plastic cases, but these are tough enough to resist beating with a winch handle. Water-resistance is the biggest challenge. While the case can be pretty well sealed, the end where the drive shaft comes out is bound to let at least small amounts of moisture in, and damage to seals is always a possibility, too. This all makes a case for annual or biennial return to the factory for inspection and cleaning if needed.

Priced from $350 to over $1,000, tiller pilots probably won't last as long as your non-mechanical electronics, as they're stressed a lot more. Still they're invaluable to the shorthanded.

Sailboats with wheel steering do not necessarily need expensive under-deck autopilot systems. Cockpit wheel steerers feature motors that mount easily on the steering pedestal base and drive a detachable sheave on the wheel through a belt. Using the mechanical advantage in the ship's steering system, these units can be smaller than the powerful underdeck drives yet still control surprisingly large boats. For day-to-day cruising, these pilots are recommended for sailboats up to forty feet.

Most wheel steerers have a control panel, a drive motor, and a belt-driven sheave that clamps to the wheel. The motor has a bracket that screws to the steering pedestal or cockpit side, with a foot-operated clutch lever to engage or disengage the steering wheel.

Most wheel pilots sold use a grooved or toothed belt made of flexible reinforced rubber. These belts used to wear prematurely, but now are more dependable. You'll still want a couple of spares (around $25 each) aboard, however.

The grooved belts can stretch and slip, and tension adjustment should be a simple screwdriver job. Compare this feature on the models you're considering.

Pilot speeds of between 3 and 6 rpm are possible on the belt drives, depending on the model, but be sure to compare torque as well. Gearing can make for a quick turn, but not if the motor is overwhelmed by the boat's displacement, rudder, sail area, and winds.

If you find the wheel speed too slow or too fast, at least one manufacturer offers a choice of wheel sheaves, eight-inch for high-speed turns or twelve-inch for easier ones. If you have a heavy-displacement boat and plan long passages in steady tradewind conditions, a fourteen-inch sheave is available.

Many boatowners like the belt drive units, but want something a little more bulletproof and protected. At least one model is now available with the motor mounted just below the compass binnacle on the steering pedestal, driving a belt inside a plastic ring. This saves the belt from exposure and puts the motor in a spot where it's less likely to be engaged or disengaged accidently. However, it may now be too close to the boat's mechanical steering compass. You'll have to check how the compass reacts to having the motor turn on and off at different points of sail, and either make up a new deviation card just for when the pilot is activated, or disregard the steering compass at those times and rely on the pilot's compass readout or a handbearing compass.

Another system uses a stainless steel chain drive. It's a very robust alternative to belts.

All wheel steering pilots present a potential danger to the crew. Whether belt, chain, or geared drive, they all can smash fingers caught in the drive sheave. They can catch hanging sunglass straps and jacket cinch cords, too. Unlike underdeck pilots, which can be fitted with a clutch to disengage the steering wheel, they also don't care if someone gets caught in among the wheel spokes. An arm could be broken between spoke and pedestal. Beware these dangers before buying, especially if you have small children. Check that the pilot can be disengaged instantly, and that all your crew know how to do it.

Most wheel pilots can be integrated into compatible navigation and instrument systems. A control panel can be below deck in the nav station, where the navigator can choose the course and monitor the pilot's performance vis a vis the GPS's routing directions, but you should always have at least pilot engage-disengage and emergency turning capability by the wheel.

More complicated but more weatherproof, and in any event necessary for boats too big for cockpit pilot motors, is an underdeck system with the drive unit next to the rudderpost, driving the steering quadrant via linear drive shaft and tiller or through gears and chain via rotary drive. The layout of the boat's structure, the position and angle (vertical or raked forward or aft) of the rudderpost(s), and the type of mechanical components used (cable and sheaves, push-pull flexible cables, rack and pinion gear, or even worm steering) determine whether a given unit will fit. This is where a professional installer is invaluable. He has seen many installations, knows what various manufacturers have to offer, and can help you select the one that delivers enough power and fits the space with a minimum of parts and labor.

Naturally, underdeck systems are not the self-contained units the cockpit systems are. But most offer more functions and custom programmability. They have larger displays with steering graphics to show how far left or right of course you are. They often have interfacing capability as standard, where it is an extra-cost option on some cockpit pilots. They often can handle a wider range of heading sensor inputs, including gyrocompass on big-boat models.

All the control functions described earlier are likely to be included in the control unit, along with other things such as:

- rudder stop adjustment (a narrower range of movement at higher speeds, wider at harbor speeds)
- a selection of standard maneuvers (circle, U-turn, loop to reciprocal course on same track)
- and a host of alarm functions (off-course, watch, waypoint, malfunction, etc.)

An important feature for multihelm station boats is the ability to connect several pilot control units, any of which can access all pilot functions. You'll also want the ability to lock out any units you're not standing in front of yourself, just to make sure nobody starts driving the boat without permission.

Handheld Remote Controls

At their simplest, these have a switch to take over control temporarily from the main pilot, and another to dodge left or right of an obstruction. They're connected by cable to the main unit.

However, of late these hand remotes have sprouted more and more functions. Some let you set the pilot mode from compass to wind or NMEA sensor, enter a command to tack a sailboat, set the deadband, alarms, or input current position as a waypoint, especially if you lose something overboard at this point, such as a crewmember, and you want the pilot to reverse course and head back to it.

The most sophisticated hand units give you access to other instruments in an integrated system, allowing you to change the displays or settings of your GPS, speed, depth, and other electronics, or put some autopilot functions on display on LCDs elsewhere on the boat.

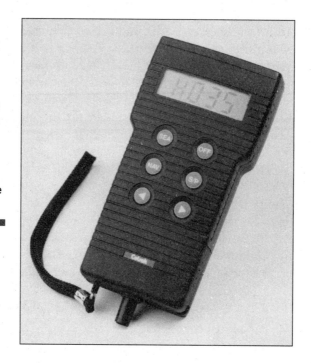

A handheld remote control usually looks simple, but some do more than just the traditional manual override function. This one also lets you set the heading, adjust for sea state, or tack a sailboat. The hand remote must be splash-proof, and it needs a cable about as long as the length of the boat.

It's all very handy, but don't let the functionality get away from you. The main function of the handheld is to let you move to other spots on the boat where things need doing, while maintaining control of your steering. Everything else on the hand remote should be subordinate to that.

Actuators

After all the processing, modifying, and overriding done by the control unit, the result is an amplified signal that powers the drive motor actuating the rudder. The actuator turns the steering wheel or tiller in the case of a cockpit-mounted pilot; the rudder cables, quadrant, or steering rack in an underdeck system; or a hydraulic pump in a hydraulic steering system.

To adapt to the countless types of possible installations, there are four basic actuator configurations—mechanical linear and rotary, and hydraulic linear and rotary. Manufacturers offer one, two, or more types, depending on the extent of their product line.

All tiller-activating cockpit pilots have screw-type linear drives in which a servo motor (a small, high-torque motor often used to move aircraft control surfaces) turns a long threaded shaft. Riding the shaft is a collar to which the tiller is attached.

Many linear-drive units for belowdeck steering are no different, and usually they are attached to a small dedicated tiller fitted to the rudderpost.

Rotary-drive actuators are offered by many manufacturers. They can usually be mounted in tighter places than can the linear type, since without the long throw of a screw shaft to accommodate, they're more compact. And they don't have to be positioned next to the rudder post. Installation may be more complicated, though, requiring a chain to be

A beautifully simple setup is a tiller-driving autopilot that can be rigged or taken below in a minute or less. Some models come with the heading sensor separate from the drive unit, so it can be mounted below out of the weather. Most portables range between $400 and $800.

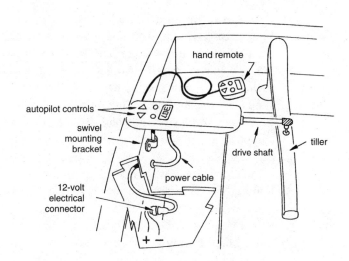

hand remote

autopilot controls

swivel mounting bracket

12-volt electrical connector

power cable

drive shaft

tiller

A common system for pedestal steering in sailboats, as well as for any cable-driven rudder, has an electric or hydraulic linear drive attached to the rudder post by its own tiller arm. This is a clean installation, and keeps the manual and automatic steering systems as separate as possible. In a sailboat this is important to maintain good helm feedback when hand steering. In any boat, it makes for system redundancy, always a good feature.

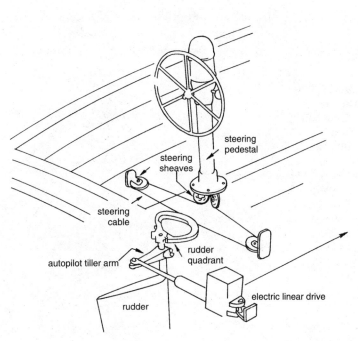

steering pedestal

steering sheaves

steering cable

autopilot tiller arm

rudder quadrant

rudder

electric linear drive

spliced into the steering cables, the addition of a new sheave or two, and perhaps more structural modifications for mounting the new hardware.

It is possible to mount a rotary drive unit so as to operate as a linear drive does, by fitting a toothed rack to the quadrant and a pinion gear on the drive shaft. Edson Corporation's curved rack segments for mounting on the rudder quadrant is a workable variation, though all the rack systems tend to add weight and friction.

A less common drive in sailboat autopilot systems, though often the most sensible choice for powerboats, is the hydraulic actuator, in which the motor drives a pump tied into one of the boat's hydraulic steering lines. Few sailboats have hydraulic manual steering due to the lack of feel inherent in such a system, but this doesn't preclude the addition of a separate hydraulic system for the autopilot alone. In fact, hydraulic drives can be less of a drag on your manual steering than mechanical systems. And some hydraulic components can be much easier to find room for than for a large mechanical linear drive.

In a powerboat with anywhere from two to four steering stations (pilot-house, flying bridge, tuna tower, and cockpit in a big sportfisherman, for instance), hydraulics are far preferable to a forest of cables and sheaves. There are plenty of hydraulic actuators available, since hydraulics are common aboard fishing and work boats.

A hydraulic system offers flexibility of installation. Fluid lines can be routed around bulkheads and previously fitted equipment. The electric pump doesn't have to be mounted right with the cylinder at the quadrant. Boats with twin rudders can have one pump driving two compact cylin-

Hydraulic autopilot installations are quite flexible. The drive unit need not be at the rudderpost. Clutches disengage steering wheels from the system. Hydraulic pilot gear runs $2,500 and up.

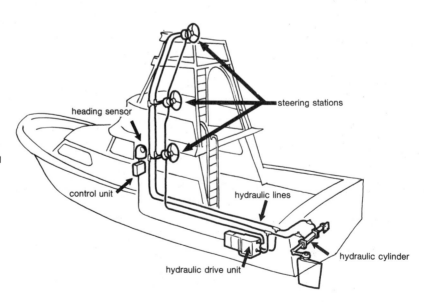

ders. The autopilot system also serves as a complete second steering system, separate from the cable steering gear. There are potential fluid leaks and bubbles to contend with, instead of loose or corroded wire connections.

A linear hydraulic drive is a pump clamped to, or feeding by hose, a hydraulic cylinder that drives the steering quadrant. Many powerboats with room in the lazarette carry this system since, in many cases, it can be simpler to install than a rotary drive. In fact, most sailboat belowdeck installations now include a linear hydraulic activator. There are no performance advantages either way; choosing a linear or rotary system is a matter of installation opportunities.

Some pumps work at one speed in forward and reverse, receiving longer or shorter duration commands from the control unit. More expensive pumps work at variable speeds, increasing or decreasing fluid flow as needed depending on the degree of course error and how slowly the rudder responds to correction. Both types of pumps do the job; the variable flow rate models do it more efficiently.

How much power will you need? Drive units are catalogued along rough guidelines according to boat length, but hull shape, displacement, rudder efficiency and helm-balancing ability, as well as likely cruising conditions, all play a part.

Manufacturers rate their products in terms of thrust (in pounds) for linear drives, both mechanical and hydraulic; in torque (pounds-inch or pounds-foot) for rotary mechanical drives, and pressure (in pounds per square inch) for rotary hydraulics.

There's little you can do to outsmart the manufacturer's representative or dealer in spec'ing the right size pilot for your boat. The only danger in getting an undersized unit is if you quote the boat's design displacement, which may be way under what the boat weighs as built, and as loaded down with all its gear and all your toys. Doublecheck with the boat's designer and builder before offering the autopilot man a displacement figure.

Part of the power of the drive unit is converted into speed through the manufacturer's choice of gearing.

The hard-over-to-hard-over time listed in linear pilot specs is usually quoted for no-load situations; that is, the unit is simply bench-tested without being hooked up to anything. When comparing hard-over times between products, be sure you're comparing for equal stroke, or factor for the difference.

The corresponding figures for rotary mechanical units is shaft rpm; for rotary hydraulics it's flow rate. In both cases, assume no-load unless stated otherwise.

With a light boat, you would tend to look for better rudder-turning speed and not worry so much about the maximum power of the drive unit.

A heavy boat with a big, hydrodynamically unbalanced rudder demands a powerful autopilot, and not so much speed.

Just as important—to the sailor, at least—as rudder turning power and speed is power drain. How many amperes will the pilot suck out of your batteries while steering the boat? The answer will vary once again according to boat design, pilot installation, and sea conditions. While on standby, the pilot should draw a negligible amount of power, just enough to sense heading or wind direction. A typical draw for a pilot on course and not driving the actuator is 0.10 amps. Under "normal cruise conditions," which few manufacturers define, tiller-drive pilots draw from 0.20 amps to 0.33 amps. Momentary peak loads might call for three to five times as much power, but in such conditions you will be shortening sail and retrimming to reduce the steering effort anyway.

Makers of permanently mounted pilots list a wide range of power drain figures, from as little as that required by the cockpit-mounted models to 10 amps or more while on "cruise." Some drive motors are rated much higher, but the rudder may well be hard over and stalled before the limit is reached. In any case, quoted power drain figures are only of value in comparing spec sheets when you know the numbers are obtained in the same way. How much power the system will use on your own boat is best estimated by the dealer or manufacturer, who has installed his pilot on similar boats and tested it with an ammeter. Be sure you know your batteries' amp-hour capacity when you talk to the dealer.

Installation

Installing any pilot other than a cockpit-mount model may involve more work than you think, especially if you have the manual steering system already in place. The simplest mechanical tie-in would be a rotary-drive actuator turning your boat's steering wheel shaft directly. Often there isn't room under the dash or bridgedeck of a powerboat for a big drive unit.

Your boat may well need structural reinforcement where the drive unit is to be located, as well as a mounting stand or bracket. Connections and the surrounding structure must be able to withstand as much power as the autopilot drive can apply to the rudder. Be prepared to modify your existing steering system to accommodate the new components. You may have to reroute cables so the pilot drive chain can be spliced into them. You may need a new steering quadrant that can carry both manual and autopilot cables, or a second quadrant dedicated to the pilot. A clutch will have to be installed in the manual system to deactivate the steering wheel and keep fingers from getting stuck between an unstoppable spoke and an unyielding steering console.

Potential Problems

Once the system is installed, what kind of problems might be expected to crop up? First are those stemming from the installation itself. There may be binding of the moving parts under stress that would not show up at dockside. This will cause an excessive power drain and mechanical wear.

Then there may be electromagnetic and radio interference problems. Even a well-installed autopilot can't be expected to work unaffected by noisy electrical systems nearby. Radio, navigation gear, stereo, instruments, and ships' systems such as the generator, bilge pump, battery charger, or even wires carrying current to light fixtures, can cause the compass to deviate from magnetic north. So can metal objects left too close to the heading sensor. A thorough trial period during which the pilot is directed on cardinal and intercardinal courses while each of the electrical systems is turned on and off is the surest way to avoid surprises later. Once again, this is where the experience of the professional installer pays off.

The other major worry concerning an autopilot's reliability is its water resistance. Cockpit-mounted pilots are most vulnerable to spray and boarding seas. With membrane keypads and good 0-rings they can be well sealed, except where the drive shaft exits the case. This end can be better protected by adding a cloth, leather, or rubber bellows over the drive shaft. This won't keep all the water out, but it will help.

A more dramatic solution is to install your tiller-steering cockpit pilot underdeck. This may seem to contradict the reason for buying such a pilot, but many boats have the rudder post accessible through a cockpit locker or lazarette, so rigging or stowing the pilot would not be more trouble than it's worth. A separate tiller underdeck would have to be installed.

Pay careful attention to construction details prior to buying a cockpit-mounted pilot. Consider, too, the number of years the pilot you're looking at has been marketed. Five years should be enough time for the manufacturer to find out what works and what needs upgrading.

Out of sight must not be out of mind when installing a belowdecks system. Components should be in well-ventilated but dry quarters. External gear, such as plug outlets for a handheld remote control unit, must be cleaned regularly. Don't expect to be able to fix all the failed components yourself, either. With the shift to integrated circuits has come Mr. Fixit with his black briefcase full of miniature tools and spare processor boards.

Autopilots are a real boon to mariners who can't or shouldn't have to stay behind the wheel the entire time at sea. Just remember that the best autopilot is no match for the human hand on the helm when judgments have to be made. The autopilot can follow orders just fine, but it can't see for you or think for you. You're the captain, and you're responsible.

CHAPTER 16

Performance Instruments

by Freeman Pittman

As with fishfinders and some of the navigational gear described elsewhere in this book, instruments—particularly sailing performance instruments—are no longer a case of one function, one dial. The range of capabilities available from a variety of equipment is so wide as to be impossible for most of us to master.

Your choice in types of systems is growing faster than most people's understanding of them. There are the familiar single-function speed, depth, wind speed and wind angle, temperature, and heading instruments. There are systems that combine some of these functions to achieve a new set of numbers, called true wind and velocity made good (VMG). There are also some highly complex systems that synthesize a great deal of information from dozens of sensors, and integrate not only all the above inputs, but also information from navigation electronics and from portable computers. It's sometimes hard to distinguish the subtle variations between instruments of one category and another. How much number-crunching power will you need in the system you choose? Do you want speed, time, and heading only for your dead reckoning calculations? Do you want that information to be available should you want to use it to compute speed made good to windward? Do you want a system that has potential far beyond what

Today's digital instruments offer dozens of kinds of information, in large digital and graphic formats. The problem now is no longer how many instrument displays you can fit in your cockpit, but how to easily manage all that data on just a few screens. One method is the separate hand controller at lower right.

you think you need right now, or do you want a modular system that grows only as fast as your needs? Getting familiar with the terms and options should help you make the right decisions.

Speedometers for Power and Sailboats

Along with a depthsounder, the most basic instrument you're likely to need is the speedometer, or log unit. It displays two basic functions: speed and distance. Many speed-logs also offer time functions, allowing you to make your computations any way you choose.

Here are the readouts for a typical low-priced digital speed-log:

- choice of nautical or statute miles or kilometers
- speed through the water
- average speed over trip
- trip and sum (cumulative) logged mileage to 9,999
- trend in speed (acceleration or deceleration)
- elapsed time up to 99:59 hours
- countdown to race start or any other event

Obviously, you can get much more for your money than just speed and distance.

The guts of the unit may differ according to manufacturer, but almost all modern speedos share certain features. The through-hull unit that generates the electrical signals used to calculate speed is normally a small paddle-wheel impeller in a cylindrical housing. An amplifier sends the signal through a shielded cable to the display unit, where it is timed against a crystal oscillator, averaged, and displayed on a digital liquid crystal display (LCD) or on an analog (pointer-type) dial. The log portion of the display unit may be a separate mechanical readout like your car's odometer, or it may be a digital display that comes up in place of the speed readout when you press the keypad.

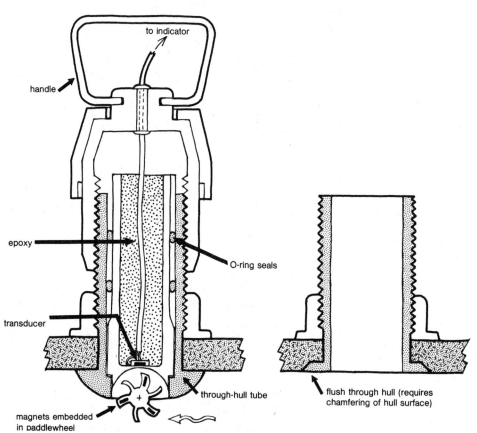

A paddlewheel boat speed transducer in its through-hull tube (left) and a flush mounted through hull (right). Mounting the paddlewheel at the end of a protruding through hull can lead to some distortion of water flow, but the instrument's calibration will overcome most inaccuracies. Most through-hull units nowadays are plastic and must be mounted with compatible adhesives. They are also more vulnerable to damage than bronze tubes, but they present a small target. The boat speed indicator, paddlewheel, and through hull plus 50 feet or so of cable can cost as little as $200 or as much as $800.

Though most are similar in form and operation, transducers are the weak link in the system. There are a number of reasons why they can't be as accurate as they ought to be to keep up with the other electronics aboard, and there are several ways they can fail altogether. Many are the solutions that have been tried, but the vast majority of speed-logs employ the reasonably trustworthy and surely simple paddlewheel.

The plastic paddlewheel rotates on an athwartships axle. Molded into the paddlewheel, or glued to it, are magnets, and inside the through-hull unit just above the impeller is a sensor—an AC generating coil, Hall-effect semiconductor, or electrical reed switch—as part of a circuit carrying a small but constant voltage. As the magnets in the impeller rotate past the sensor, they generate a pulse that is amplified and passed on to the indicating unit for processing. One way to understand what's going on is to envision the paddlewheel rolling its way along a nautical mile. An impeller with a three-inch circumference will make four revolutions per foot, or 24,320 in a 6,080-foot nautical mile. Two magnets on the paddlewheel will result in 48,640 pulses per mile, assuming an ideally efficient rotation through the medium. Of course slippage must be expected, so speed-logs have rather wide calibration ranges, from 20 to 40 percent higher or lower than the displayed figure.

The above explanation is really more valid for the old-fashioned mechanical taffrail log, the spinner on the end of a rope dropped over the stern. In fact, electronic log manufacturers all have gone to microprocessing. Datamarine's Corinthian speedo, for instance, treats the transducer signal as an electric frequency, with about 4 cycles per second (4 hertz) equalling 1 knot. (To be sure they got it right, Datamarine engineers calibrated the transducer in a U.S. Navy flow chamber.)

Using the impeller's motion to generate its own signal without a current applied from ship's batteries is quite possible, and you can buy an inexpensive speedometer that does just that. The impeller and through hull operate as a small generator to power an analog speed display. There is no log function, and 12-volt power is still required for night lighting, but for under $200 list, you do get basic performance recording.

With any paddlewheel, there are limitations on accuracy. In the case of a sailboat beating to windward, the boat's leeway combines with the asymmetric shape of the heeled hull to cause water to flow over the impeller at a different angle than while the boat is sailing upright. This crossflow makes for slower impeller speed. On the other hand, if the impeller is too close to the boat's keel, water around the keel's leading edge can accelerate flow over the transducer. Then there is the pitching and heaving of the hull, which make an impeller mounted too far forward vulnerable to breaking out of the water on wave crests. If the impeller is mounted in any spot on the hull that experiences frequent water turbulence, accuracy must suffer. And if it is on one side of the hull rather than on the centerline, it will probably read differently on one tack than on the other. This is a necessary compromise if the hull layup is too thick at the centerline for a through-hull installation. The obvious if somewhat expensive solution is to mount an impeller on either side of the hull, with a mercury or pendulum gravity switch to change automatically from one impeller to the other. In any case, the sailboat through-hull unit should always be mounted forward of amidships, preferably away from the keel or underwater fittings, so it will be in smooth water.

Displacement powerboat hulls don't create heeling, tacking, or leeway error (except when crabbing against a current), but they, too, need clean water flow over the transducer. Transducers on planing hulls should be mounted well aft, since the bow sections frequently operate in a lot of spray, and sometimes even in daylight.

One other factor often brought up when discussing the paddlewheel or other impeller types is the "boundary layer," the water closest to the hull. Due to the hull's natural surface friction, a certain amount of water tends to be dragged along with the hull as it passes through the medium. An impeller operating within this layer will read low. How far from the hull the boundary layer extends depends on speed, the shape of the hull, and location on the hull, but if a sailboat speedometer impeller is mounted correctly it should protrude far enough into clean water to be accurate through most of the boat's speed range. Powerboats, with their much wider speed ranges, can expect greater accuracy problems at either end of the scale. At zero to three knots this is not a concern, but at forty to fifty knots it is.

Manufacturers recognize the aforementioned factors and have ways to deal with most of them. Most speedometers have either a calibration knob or screwdriver hole on the back of the box or, more commonly, a programming button on the front that lets you change the displayed speed for a given frequency of impeller rotations. To find out what the right frequency ratio is, you run a measured course and compare it with the distance logged on your speedo. Use landmarks for course markers, since buoys can drift, and make your run when the tide is slack or the current is steady. Steer your boat on a straight course at a constant speed, as near as possible to its cruising speed under power or sail. Mark the measured distance after running the course, and then run the reciprocal course. Add the two distances and divide by two. Compare with the charted distance and adjust your speedometer, according to the manufacturer's manual, to resolve the difference. Errors of 2 percent or more can be eliminated in this way.

What can't be adjusted for is an impeller fouled by marine growth or floating debris. Mount the impeller where it's easy to reach for inspection, and check it occasionally. Clean as needed. Some units are painted with antifouling paint at the factory. This can be renewed, but check with the manufacturer as to what paint is compatible with the plastic, and be careful not to gum up the works.

Some boatowners routinely pull the speed and depth transducers from their housings when not in use, sealing the housings with the factory supplied screw-on caps. Only a cupful of water enters the bilge if you're quick with the cap.

The coaxial cable carrying the transducer's signal can pick up interference from other electronics if it's cut or damaged. Don't cut it to length without first reading the manufacturer's instructions—they may warn you not to cut it at all, but simply tape the excess in a coil and secure it. Good-quality instruments have the transducer and cable end potted in epoxy, from which the cable runs about 10 feet to a connector. The connector enables you to remove the through-hull fitting if needed without having to cut or pull out the main run of cable. There should be a connector at the indicator unit end of the wire, too.

Racing sailors, along with cruisers of both sailboats and powerboats, will appreciate a timer function in their speed-log. If it has a countdown function, it can be used for racing starts. As a chronometer for navigation, it should be able to give elapsed time, and should be easy to synchronize with radio time ticks.

Wind Instruments

While every mariner should learn to judge wind speed by how it affects the water's surface (the Beaufort scale for wind force) and be able to feel where the wind is coming from without looking, an electronic wind speed meter can measure puffs and lulls your eye and skin can't always distinguish. And while every sailboat should have a nonelectronic masthead fly such as a Windex to show apparent wind angle, a wind angle indicator in the cockpit provides an excellent fine-scale guide to wind shifts and shows clearly which tack is favored upwind. At night, when your own senses are limited, wind instruments become more valuable.

Some big motoryachts and sport fishermen have begun to wear wind-speed and angle sensors. The indicators help the skipper dock in crosswinds, and give useful meteorological information for trolling.

The wind speed and bearing you feel, which your boat's instruments measure in raw form, are called "apparent wind" functions. They are trigonometric results of the true wind speed and bearing combined with the boat's speed and heading. The resulting apparent output is very useful for gauging boat performance and weather trends, and is more than adequate for most cruising sailors.

A combination digital and analog wind instrument. Apparent wind angle is shown in 10-degree increments relative to the boat's bow. Apparent wind speed is shown digitally, in knots. The readability of an analog pointer has yet to be beaten by LCD graphic imitations, although very small wind shifts can be transmitted by numeric digital displays, which can read out to a degree. Having the wind speed display in the wind angle dial makes it easier to note when an apparent wind shift is actually due to a change in wind velocity.

But if you're interested in keeping up with the competition on the race course, or have a more rigorous means of testing your speed relative to the true wind, you may have to start looking at some more precise, computed wind data. When you decide to use this "true wind" and "velocity made good" data, you enter a world of sailing performance technology and philosophy perhaps unlike what you're used to. We'll show you a bit of this world later, but first let's look at the hardware used for all wind measurements.

Wind speed instruments (anemometers) have much in common with speed-logs. Instead of having a rotating impeller underwater, they have one aloft, in the form of three little black cups spinning in the breeze, or, on one Swedish masthead unit, a propeller like an airplane's. Either device spins a rotor that creates electromagnetic pulses with the same hardware used in the water-speed through hull. Inside the rotor housing, the sensor may be a Hall effect microchip or micro-generator. Or a photocell may be used to count flashes from an LED as seen through gaps in a fitting that spins with the rotor.

Sensitivity is a source of pride for top-of-the-line race gear makers, whose sensors are claimed to begin turning in half a knot of wind. That's not enough for anyone to sail with, so it's not that important a number. What's more important is how strong the masthead unit is. Can it withstand winds to 100 knots? It's not unusual in many places to have at least one day a summer of wind gusts at least half that, and on the East Coast hurricanes are to be expected about every five years. If a hurricane is coming, though, you'd better take the masthead unit down!

Accuracy for windspeed indicators is rarely given by manufacturers, but plus-or-minus 4 percent is a typical figure.

The transducer is normally mounted on the end of a stalk projecting up and forward from the masthead. This gets it out into clear air and away from antennas, halyards, and sails—especially the spinnaker—which might otherwise foul it. You might be surprised by the amount of aerodynamic interference other hardware aloft—including even the wind unit's own stalk—can develop. This is more likely to affect the wind angle vane than the anemometer, however. The masthead unit must be robust, but with very light moving parts, and it must be corrosion- and waterproof.

The masthead unit installation requires effort and care. Be sure the unit is securely positioned on the fore-and-aft axis and that it indeed extends forward from the mast, unless the manual specifically states that you can mount it facing aft over the mainsail. The wind speed unit won't care, but the wind angle indicator that usually comes with it may not operate properly unless it's facing forward.

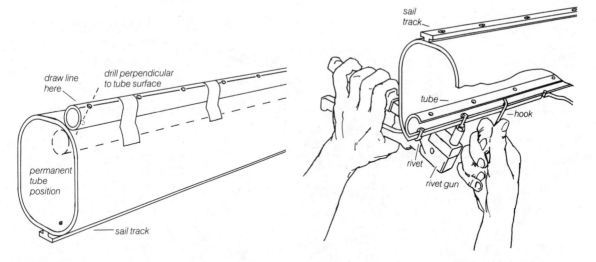

Installing a PVC conduit for electrical wires within the mast. Left: firmly tape the PVC tube to the outside of the mast just where it will be permanently on the inside. Draw a guildeline for drilling on the tube 180 degrees from the line of contact between mast and tube. Drill perpendicularly through the tube and mast.

Right: Use hooks to align and hold the tube for cutting exit wire holes and for riveting. Wiggle the hook in the hole next in line to the one being centered. Use the hook to hold the tube snugly against the mast, and rivet. (Courtesy SAIL magazine.)

If you are lucky, your mast will have a dedicated tube inside for running electrical wires, and if you are thoughtful, you will have a permanent messenger line inside the mast or tube to draw new cables from deck level to the masthead. Owners of boats without a dedicated tube may want to add a PVC conduit on the inside of the mast, as shown in the accompanying drawings.

The cable can also be secured to the outside of the mast, but that exposes the coax to the elements and ensures a short life for it. If possible, have the cable exit the mast below the deck but well above the bilge. When planning this arrangement, be sure the cable and its connectors will pass easily through the mast partners when it's time to pull the mast out of the boat.

For many wind speed sensors on the market there is no calibration circuit, since there is no hull or boundary layer to affect fluid flow around the sensor.

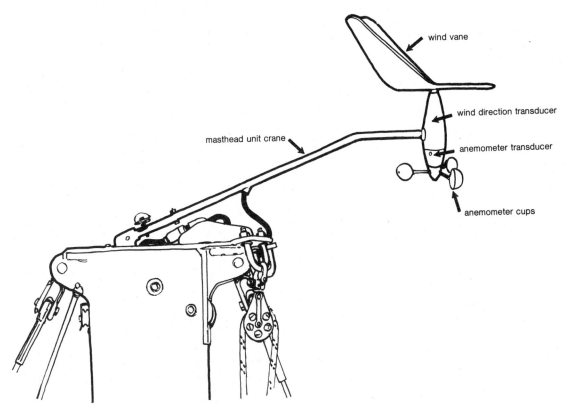

A masthead combination speed-wind angle unit extends forward of the spar into clean air. Components are lightweight aluminum or plastic for low inertia, but they're easily damaged. Connections must be well sealed here or you'll spend a lot of time in the bosun's chair.

Calibrating a wind speed sensor is possible with some of the integrated instrument systems. It can be done with a handheld anemometer you know to be accurate. You have to go aloft and hold it near the masthead unit. Do it on a day with variable winds, to get a range of wind speeds for comparison. Someone on deck records the readings from the masthead unit as you note the anemometer speeds.

Almost always on the same stalk as the anemometer sensor is the vane sensor for the wind angle indicator. The windvane's shape varies with the manufacturer's aerodynamic theory (or lack thereof). There's no way of telling in the store whether the vane you're inspecting is going to fly well on your boat.

In the past, most vanes were made of thin aluminum; now they're almost all molded plastic. A few of these plastic vanes, molded in black to ensure good visual contrast against the sky, have been known to sag in the heat of the tropics. Ask your dealer for his recommendations on this score.

The wind angle vane rotates on a precision bearing, and for even wear the vane's weight should be balanced over it. You can tell whether it is by holding the masthead unit tilted to one side, as it would be when heeled. The vane should not rotate. On some models the nosepiece is adjustable for weight distribution, but most are carefully designed and balanced at the factory. It's best not to mess with either the weight or the aerodynamic balance.

To generate electrical signals the windvane likely has a metal wiper or two fitted to its shaft inside a housing just below the vane. The wipers sweep a potentiometer coil wrapped around the shaft. Varying resistance around the coil results in different voltages for the various angles sent to the display unit on deck, and these are converted to specific readouts.

The potentiometer in such a masthead unit is likely to wear out after five seasons. From the moment it's installed it is working, and salt air eventually finds its way in to corrode the contacts. Some manufacturers, therefore, prefer a non-contact circuit that uses a magnet on the vane shaft to change the voltage in a coil surrounding the shaft. More expensive, but it has several advantages. One, the friction from the contacts is eliminated. Two, the case can be filled with a light oil to damp the vane's movement. Three, the system allows full 360-degree readings. With most potentiometers there's a gap of 10 or 20 degrees to either side of dead ahead that simply doesn't register. This may manifest itself as a jump of the display unit's pointer across the dial from port to starboard, or as a dial whose degree marks aren't where they should be. Check this out on the store demo unit before you buy

On the other hand, if the needle moves from one angle to the next in discrete steps like the second hand on a clock, it probably has a stepper motor in the display case to track the signals from the masthead unit. That's what the Datamarine company has put in probably more wind indicators than any other brand and it's a precise means of repeating what's happening at the masthead.

Wind angle indicator accuracy should be good to within 2 degrees. Consider the unit's accuracy when you decide to tack on a small windshift. It may be even smaller than you think.

Calibrating a wind angle unit can be tricky. Assuming the display is adjustable, sail the boat at a steady speed on both tacks, at equal heel angles, in as steady a breeze as possible, on flat water. Note the corresponding wind angles and adjust the display by half the offset. You'll probably need several tries to get a reasonable estimate.

Display Unit Packaging

The display unit, whether for boat speed, wind, water depth, heading, or other data, takes one of several shapes and forms. There are the traditional barrel-shaped models with a flange or bezel for mounting through a four-inch-diameter hole in a bulkhead. Other models are similar but with a square bezel. Many today, though, are nearly flat units that mount on the bulkhead. These do not require cutting any major holes in the bulkhead for mounting; you need only drill holes big enough for screws and wire connectors.

There are stand-alone wheelhouse units with trunnion brackets for dash or overhead mounting in powerboats or pilothouse sailboats. The nice feature about these displays is that their viewing angle can easily be adjusted for taller or shorter helmspersons or to counteract glare.

There are display units that combine several instruments in one housing, either with separate displays for various functions, or sharing a single readout. This usually doesn't allow for as much flexibility in installation as do individual instruments, but it sometimes makes for a lower package price.

Do you want analog readouts or digital? The choice is personal, but digital displays can give more discrete readings, and most people prefer them. Many digital speedometers read out in tenths of a knot, and some even in hundredths. That implies greater absolute accuracy than the system is capable of producing, but for the racer interested in seeing trends displayed, tenths are certainly a worthwhile feature. Though a given readout may not be precise, the numbers are consistent, and accurately signify the magnitude of speed changes. This level of precision isn't possible on an analog pointer and dial.

The only instrument for which an analog display is preferable is wind angle, although here again a finer reading is had with a digital display. Some

Instruments can be packaged in different ways. This compact display lets you choose any four main and secondary pieces of data. The single display does not mean that the data is integrated, only that the measuring circuits and controls share a single readout.

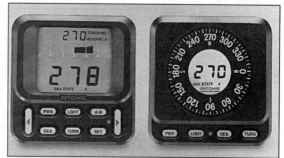

Digital and analog readouts for a fluxgate compass. The large LCD on the left offers an off-track steering graphic along with the heading; readout damping rate is shown in small type. Some helmsmen prefer to steer to a traditional compass rose, and a fluxgate sensor can drive one of those, too (right). For good measure, there's a digital readout in the middle. Correct damping is important for a smooth readout with minimal compass lag, so an easy means of adjustment is a good feature.

digital displays emulate the wind pointer with liquid crystal graphics. These can work well. Just try viewing whichever indicator you're interested in from eight feet away or so to see how good the display is.

Every point made in previous chapters about LCDs holds true for speedometers and wind instruments. In any LCD, contrast and clarity in bright sun depend very much on the quality and cost of the liquid crystal specified for the instrument. Also pay attention to how wide a viewing angle the display has. LCDs are not noted for showing much unless you're looking at them nearly head on. If you steer from the windward or leeward rail, as do many sailors, the instruments will have to be mounted well ahead of the helm or in one of the swiveling instrument pods you can get for steering pedestals from the Edson Corporation.

Digital character size is becoming an adjustable feature on some LCDs. You can customize some displays to show four normal-sized pieces of data, two jumbo readouts, or one number big enough for the crew on the boat next to you to read.

Instrument lighting is something you don't often get to judge in advance, but do try. Some rather expensive electronics have amazingly uneven lighting. Or the lighting may be too bright, and you can't look from the instruments to the horizon at night without waiting for your eyes to adjust. A brightness key on the instrument should have as many increments of adjustment as possible to give every user the optimum readability.

The other aspect of readability you don't get any indication of in advance is resistance to fogging. If the instrument has a sealed double-layer lens or is hermetically sealed with nitrogen, you should have no problems. Not many units have these features, however.

Electronic Compasses

Electronic compasses are a common element in autopilots, radar systems with north-up displays, sailboat performance instrument systems, and simply as a steering compass aboard powerboats, especially high-speed ones.

Electronic compasses, in particular the solid-state, digital types, needn't suffer from the lag and overshoot that card compasses do when you turn the boat quickly. Their damping is electronic, and you can adjust the averaging, or the time the compass readout takes to catch up to your new course to suit conditions. If you're running fast on smooth water, you can get near immediate updates of your heading. If it's rough out, you can slow down the averaging so the numbers read out in a steady, progressive way.

Electronic compasses have the potential for greater accuracy than most card compasses, and in most instances they are more accurate. A large, well-damped card compass can offer a visual resolution of 1 degree. With careful compensation for deviation and variation, you might be able to translate that 1-degree visual precision into 1- to 2-degree accuracy for navigation calculations.

But most pleasure-boat card compasses are not big enough to allow 1-degree visual discrimination. And variation, deviation, and dip errors all affect the accuracy of what you see. The best fluxgate compasses claim 1-degree accuracy or better, eliminating dip error and compensating automatically for deviation.

From a manufacturer's viewpoint, the solid state compass is the most efficient type for integrating with other electronics. There's no need to convert an electric signal from analog to digital for processing by a nav device's computer. Today's digital compasses are extremely power-efficient, and put out a signal that can be used for many more purposes than just which way you're heading.

By far the most common electronic compass is what's called the fluxgate. The term refers to a gate circuit passing a signal created by the earth's flux, or magnetic field. Rather than aligning itself along the local magnetic field, as a card compass does, the fluxgate measures the voltage generated in an electronic sensing coil. The earth's magnetic field creates electricity in the coil the same way that a moving magnet creates electricity in a generator. Using two coils oriented 90 degrees apart allows determination of the magnetic field's angle and thus your heading.

An alternative is to make the coil toroidal, or doughnut-shaped. Advantages claimed for the toroid by those manufacturers using it are that differences in the core material within the coils are eliminated, as is the need for the coil rods to be absolutely square to each other.

In practice, these considerations need not be a significant factor. A good fluxgate can be built either way.

How the sensor is gimballed and damped, and what to do with the alternating-current signal developed by the sensor, are where differences among brands can result in performance advantages. A good gimballing system is essential to fluxgate accuracy, as every degree out of level results in a 3-degree sensor error. Some fluxgate sensors are gimballed in an oil bath as card compasses are. Others hang dry from a universal joint and are damped electronically. Averaging periods may vary between ¼ second and 20 seconds. The only time a really high averaging period is noticeable is when you make a fast or extended turn. Gimballing typically works to plus-minus 45 degrees of heel.

Some brands have sophisticated compensation programs for deviation, while others require that a deviation card be made up just as you would for a conventional card compass. A compensation program usually requires you to put the compass into the compensation mode and then steer your boat in a slow circle. Once you have done this, the compass should continue to correct itself until you decide it needs recompensating. Anytime you add electronics, electrical gear, or big metallic objects or move any of the above on your boat, it's time to make that slow circle again. Compare these compensating programs before purchasing. Some are more tolerant of inexact circling than others.

One of the most popular uses for a fluxgate on sailboats is as a racing tactical compass. It helps you read windshifts with minute accuracy. Some displays identify the windshift for you as a lift or header, in case you haven't been paying attention. (Beware the velocity lift, however, wherein a seeming lift is in fact a puff. The compass alone doesn't identify the puff as such.) You reset the compass at any time for new wind conditions.

Another use for the fluxgate is, of course, as a steering compass. The LCD graphics on some fluxgates work as an off-course indicator.

Compasses interfaced with other electronics need common interfacing language. Among the outputs offered by fluxgate compasses are sine/cosine, N+1, NMEA 0180, and NMEA 0183. The first three of these are used virtually exclusively for driving autopilots, which need only simple instructions.

Some fluxgate systems come with a certain level of memory, so a series of

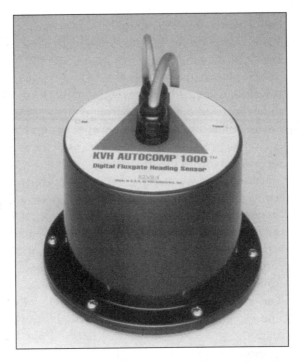

A fluxgate heading sensor is hung inside a protective container. It may be damped in oil, or its wiggles filtered out electronically. The sensor must be mounted in the part of the boat with the least motion, away from electrical and metallic influences, whether they be engine, wires, radio, or tool box.

courses can be entered. This was designed to give racing sailboat crews the course to the next mark as they round the one before it, without having to consult the race circular or chart. But it's handy for any navigator.

Installation of any fluxgate sensor is mostly a matter of finding a place close to the boat's centers of pitch and roll, and at least three feet away from electrical equipment and wiring, as well as from ferrous metals such as rigging, engines, iron keel, steel tanks, tools, galley utensils, and so forth. It's not the sensor itself that is affected, but the local earth's field that is bent. Whether the sensor container has magnetic compensators or an automatic correction program to deal with interference, you need to be sure that objects like stereo speakers or a tool box aren't put near the sensor after you have corrected for deviation. And, just to be sure, after installation and correction, turn on each electrical and electronic device (radios in transmit mode, autopilot in motion) on board and check the compass readout again for errors.

Integrated Systems

Nowadays the name of the game in instruments is networking. Both power and sailing craft benefit from the integration of performance and systems monitoring instrumentation, though the movement started on the America's Cup racing scene over ten years ago and is still being fueled by developments there. Let's focus on these sailing-oriented systems first, and on the functions they can provide.

From the basic wind, water, and heading sensors can be derived what are called computed functions, data that are the result of combining wind and water inputs and adding a dash of trigonometry. The most important of these computed functions are true wind speed and true wind direction, and to a lesser extent, new ways of measuring speed, such as velocity made good (VMG).

True wind direction and speed, the values you'd measure if you were sitting atop a buoy rather than on a moving boat, are, if not critical, indeed worth having for the sake of safety and good seamanship. If you are sailing directly downwind with the apparent wind indicator at fifteen knots and the speedometer at eight, you know the wind is blowing twenty-three knots true. That means you'd better have your heavy headsails ready to hoist and a reef or two in the mainsail before turning upwind. This calculation is easy to make dead downwind or directly into the wind, but at all other angles it takes some fancier thinking than most of us could do while steering and keeping watch.

True wind direction means you can select the right sails more easily before heading off on a reach. Will you be far enough off the wind to set a spinnaker, or must you keep the genoa up? Or perhaps the reacher and a staysail make the right combination. This judgment is not easy to make before you've actually turned onto the new course, and if you've guessed

Knowing what wind angle indication you're reading can be confusing. Note that "true wind" as defined in some sales literature is not related to true North at all, but may be a bow angle corrected for forward speed.

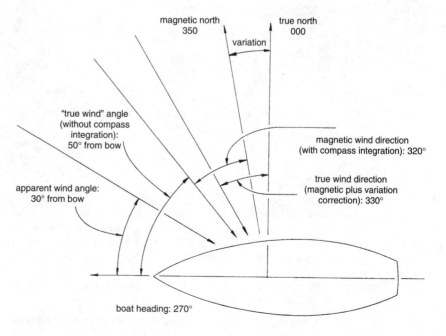

magnetic north
350

true north
000

variation

"true wind" angle (without compass integration): 50° from bow

magnetic wind direction (with compass integration): 320°

apparent wind angle: 30° from bow

true wind direction (magnetic plus variation correction): 330°

boat heading: 270°

wrong, you must go through a needless sail change. True wind direction is a certain guide to use in conjunction with a polar chart or table of wind angles to match the sails in your inventory to the expected conditions.

Velocity made good tells you which course and speed are the most efficient for getting to a point directly upwind or downwind. Will pinching the boat higher and trimming the sails in tight result in a net gain to windward even if you're going noticeably slower on the boat speed meter? Or should you slack sheets a bit and foot off faster on a course not so close to the wind? VMG tells you this, as well as the best angle at which to reach broad off the wind, and more.

All these functions are useful, but they're impossible to solve in real time without the power of a microprocessor to bring together wind speed, wind angle, boat speed, and for some functions, compass heading, on an ongoing basis.

There are more than a dozen network systems that can calculate these functions by combining sensor data. If you expand the definition of an integrated system to include any that can incorporate navigational functions (position finding, radar, electronic plotting, and autopilot) and systems monitoring, there are even more.

The systems are becoming more capable each year; even so, most offer more information than most crews can use meaningfully. Some functions

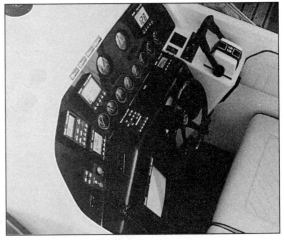

The square instruments in each cockpit are linked via coaxial cable, and communicate in a common language; they are integrated. Each instrument shows a lot of information; even so, finding room for the many displays is becoming a challenge. Instrument pods over sailboat pedestals are becoming larger every year, while powerboat helm stations are easily mistaken for aircraft cockpits. Note the multi-function video screen next to the wheel in the powerboat; it runs radar, charting, and, soon, fishfinding displays.

aren't even very useful. Yet their ability to be customized to the needs of any navigator, helmsman, sail trimmer, or other crewmember, along with their expandability and a few really good functions, makes the network systems look good to just about any boatowner who can afford one.

Affordability has gotten better, too, over the last few years. Inside most systems, there is no exotic hardware, and even much of the software is fairly simple. As the systems become more popular, volume component buying by the manufacturers makes integrated instruments more price-competitive with stand-alones.

What are the important features to consider in an integrated system?

- expandability for additional functions you may want as your needs change
- ease of learning and operation
- visibility and lighting of displays
- system flexibility
- ability to interface with other systems, such as navigation and autopilot
- computing power and speed
- precision and accuracy of data
- installation and calibration ease
- ruggedness and water resistance
- dimensions and power specs
- special features and functions
- cost, initial and thereafter

The traditional minimum sailing instrument package includes depth, boat speed, apparent wind speed and angle, and compass. As described earlier in this chapter, all these functions are available in discrete or in stand-alone instruments, and if they are all you want, you can save money by buying them that way. Much of the saving comes from buying a mechanical compass, which can be less expensive than the electronic type needed for an integrated system.

But if you buy these basic functions as parts of an integrated system, you immediately get the bonus readouts—true wind speed and true wind direction, and speed made good (VMG) to windward or to leeward. VMG, first thought to offer a new way to sail for speed, has proven to be a function of marginal use around the race course. It can be helpful for periodic navigation and strategy updates over a long leg of a race or passage, but not useful in the short term the way boat speed is.

The term VMG, by the way, is used with respect to other measurements of speed, and it can confuse the most learned navigators. VMG to the next mark or other waypoint, for instance, is almost never directly upwind or downwind. If you want this function of speed made good over a course, any loran or GPS can calculate the value, which is more correctly termed VMC, or velocity made good over a course.

Integrated systems are available in many price ranges, and some offer similar-sounding functions that are not. One of the most important distinctions is between *true wind angle* (TWA) and *true* or *magnetic wind direction.* TWA is a function of the apparent wind angle and boat speed through the water. True wind angle is thus the wind angle off the boat's bow (which is 000 degrees). This can be helpful for sail selection right now, but not for choosing the sails for the next leg of the course.

To do that, you need the magnetic wind direction, and to get that you need an electronic compass. Magnetic wind direction is the direction the wind blows to a stationary sensor, as related to magnetic north. The advantage of magnetic wind direction is its constant north reference. Choose your "true wind" instrument package accordingly.

Note also that magnetic wind is still not true wind as referenced to true north. For that the system would have to incorporate a correction for variation, which is feasible, but certainly not necessary for racing—or non-racing—purposes.

After the basic integrated outputs, there are a number of interesting secondary functions to consider. These will relate more specifically to the type of boat and type of performance sailing you do. If you're into racing tactics you may want to know, besides countdown and countup time, things like current, the boat's leeway, course on the opposite tack, time or distance to laylines, and which end of a starting line is favored. The more sophisticated systems offer these and other outputs.

If you sail to velocity prediction program (VPP) numbers, that is, you attempt to reach speeds a computer (and/or experience) says the boat should be capable of at different wind angles and strengths, there is a host of outputs to consider. Several systems allow you to enter a table of VPP numbers into a processor unit, giving you a target speed to steer and trim to and letting you monitor your percentage in terms of a percentage of the VPP (when you hit over 100 percent consistently, it's time to update the VPP table).

If the crew can stand it, you can compare helmsmen's average speeds or the speed through a tack using different techniques.

Because sensor precision, especially for the wind instruments, is critical to an integrated system's accuracy, a few systems offer corrections for heel, upwash, and even mast angle if the mast is a rotating one. (Upwash is bend-ing of the flow of air by the sails before it reaches the sails. The effect can extend to the vicinity of the masthead indicators.) There are also readouts for rudder or trim tab angle and for electronic solid state load cells that measure tension on headstay or elsewhere.

There are lots of navigation outputs, such as course deviation, DR range and bearing to the previous and next waypoint (sometimes calculated on a linked nav receiver and displayed on the instrument system), and a man-overboard panic button that overrides the waypoint library by instantly entering the event as a waypoint to steer to.

There are also environmental outputs for sea and air temperature, as well as condition readouts for engine, fuel, and electrical systems.

Virtually every readout an integrated system can generate can be recorded on computer disk or on a printout for further study. The system must have an RS-232 computer interface for these options. The most advanced racing systems, as used almost exclusively on America's Cup boats, can send large amounts of data ashore to mainframe computers via telemetry. Woe to the analysts staying up all night to report the new genoa was slow.

Most integrated systems are very easy to use, as each display is limited to one category of readouts, such as speed and log functions or wind functions only. Most keypads are also laid out with three to five buttons, each of which has two or more functions, depending on how many times you press it.

Some instruments have "soft" keys; that is, those keys' functions change, depending on what mode the instrument is in. The specific use of a soft key is identified on the display screen adjacent to it. Soft keys usually are found on instruments that are designed to display a wide variety of, or virtually any, data the system can generate. They thus have to be flexible.

One system, in a way, is the simplest of all. Each display is identical, and totally "dumb"; it displays whatever it is told to, according to individual plastic function cards slipped into it. Each card has small magnets that connect reed switches in the display to select the function called for on the card. The approach works, though you have to keep track of the function cards, and the number of functions displayable at once is limited to one item.

Be sure to try out a functioning system aboard someone's boat (best) or a dealer demo system (next best) to determine how well you like the keypad functionality and feel. An audible beep confirming each key pressing is a nice feature. And don't think that the fewer the buttons, always the easier the operation. You may have to memorize many keystrokes to call up information you could get with dedicated keys on another system.

Good visibility and lighting are as essential for integrated systems as they are for individual instruments, so inspect each system's readouts according to the same criteria mentioned earlier in this chapter.

System flexibility is a somewhat nebulous term, but it can be defined as the ability to display any function on as many displays as needed while also allowing for distinct, parallel operations. The ability for the navigator to operate the system in a tactical mode while the helmsman or trimmer are reading boatspeed and heading numbers is obviously important; you should understand before buying just how far your system can go, and how many displays and other components are needed.

As mentioned at the beginning of this section, there are two ways of defining an integrated system. Our discussion focuses on performance-based systems, as opposed to navigation-based systems, whose interfacing abilities and needs are covered in the chapters on navigation receivers. For nav electronics, wind, water, and heading instruments need not be the integrated type beyond having an NMEA 0183 output for use on the nav devices. The main instrument outputs needed are boat speed and log, apparent wind, depth, and heading. A loran, GPS, radar, video plotter, and/or autopi-

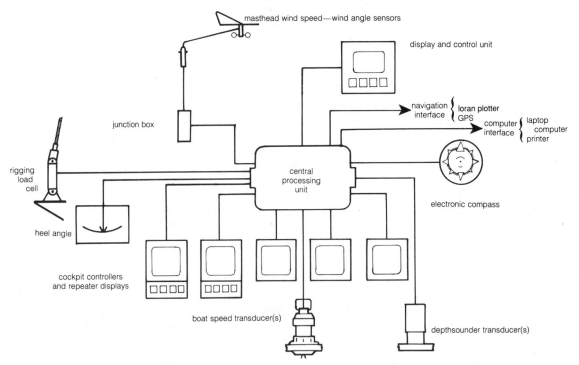

Network-type integrated systems transfer data along a common connector strip or cable, which is basically open ended. Limited only by the power of chips within the processor units to communicate with one another, any number of processor units and displays can be added, each working independently as well in conjunction with others.

lot will use these outputs for dead reckoning, north-up radar display, and steering direction, among other purposes.

Most integrated performance systems, however, need the outputs of a loran or GPS to calculate leeway, current, course and speed over ground, and whatever tactical functions the system can call up. Fortunately, just about every loran and GPS (and autopilot) now made has the standard interface for marine electronics, NMEA 0183, so two-way data sharing should not be a problem. Just check with the manufacturers involved to ensure a match.

Can your system be overwhelmed with too many functions? Manufacturers all say their microprocessors (typically 8-bit, though one or two use 16-bit) and memory chips are underutilized. Instead they say limiting factors on a system are most likely to be the update and damping, or averaging rates.

The faster systems update every quarter second or so, which means the numbers on the display will appear to change smoothly and quickly, though the digits to the right of the decimal point may distract you with their constant fluttering. Slower systems update more like once a second, meaning displays won't respond as quickly, but they'll still be fine for most purposes.

Damping, or averaging, is done using different computing processes, depending on the output needed. Heading and wind direction need the most sophisticated averaging algorithms; temperature and depth less so. Damping differs from updating in that it takes a given number of data points and averages them for a more readable display. Damping can be adjusted on most instruments through the keypad.

Installation and Calibration

The high-end integrated systems are best installed by professionals familiar with each brand. There are many components to connect and many tests to run throughout the process. But other systems, those aimed at a wider market, are designed for owner installation. Some include cables with BNC or waterproof plastic connectors already added, so it's a matter of drilling small mounting holes, screwing the sensors and displays in place, installing the sensors, running the cables, and plugging the system together.

Calibration is the key to any instrument's performance, and with an integrated system it's both more difficult, and more important than with stand-alones.

All sailboat electronics have improved immensely in seaworthiness in the last decade. What's worth knowing about the system you decide on is whether its components are sealed, and if not, whether any maintenance, such as baking dry a silica gel pack or cleaning the circuit boards, is needed.

You'll also want to know which components must be housed in relatively dry, vibration-free quarters below deck.

The connections may be the most vulnerable to water-induced corrosion; check the installation manual for advice on whether grease or water-displacing lubricants are indicated. And made sure the connectors are not at the bottom of a bight of cable, where water collects.

Today's instrument displays are compact and easy to find room for. Few require large mounting holes in bulkheads. Some are flat-backed, needing only holes for fasteners and cables.

What you'll have the most trouble fitting will be the processor and junction boxes below deck, so make sure you know just how many black boxes there are to go along with the handy displays.

All the systems on the market are power-miserly. The large-format mechanical repeaters are the biggest power drains; the newer jumbo repeaters, with LC displays, consume much less 12-volt power.

Special Features

Many of the more exotic readouts have already been mentioned, but an increasingly important feature is the ability to interface with PC laptop-run programs. A tactical program can use instrument system outputs to tell

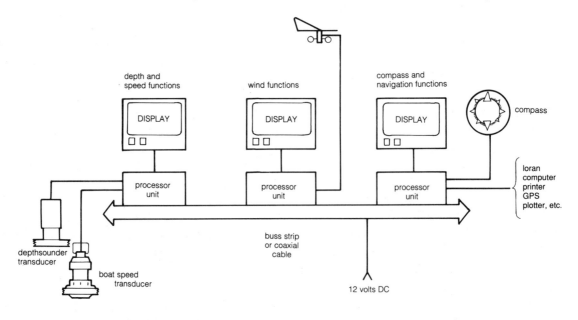

A printer designed to give periodic readouts of selected functions from an integrated system. This one plugs directly into the manufacturer's network; other means may require hooking up a computer with appropriate software between instruments and printer.

you things like position, starting line, and layline information. Just as useful, potentially, the program can feed back in polar data updates and almost any imaginable readout to the instrument displays. Time allowances on competitors, speed to sail to beat them, buoy identification and which side to round on, weather data—the possibilities are limited only by your, or your navigator's, programming skills.

Short of this, most systems have features all their own. One has an easily set up graphing function. Another can do the same if you add the system's video monitor. Yet another network integrates nav functions like radar and video plotter, along with any digital readout, on its monitor.

The most expensive racing-oriented systems have long lists of outputs and can transmit them via radio to ship- or shore-based computers. They are equipped for PC interfacing, and at least one also has its own printer that plugs right into the system, for periodic printout of key functions or strip-chart printing.

Some systems offer great circle and rhumb line courses to steer. Several systems have a trend, or trim, indicator to show acceleration or deceleration—useful in some situations as a guide to whether you're trimming the sails right.

Cost

When you come right down to it, you can choose and customize a system to perform almost whatever function you can think of, if you have the money. But the nice thing about integrated systems is not that they're getting more sophisticated, but that they are becoming affordable to more boat owners.

They can also be confusing in the extreme to compare before purchase. To lessen your aggravation, first determine all the functions you need now, and then those you may want later. Give the list to the dealer of each system, and get an itemized list back of all the hardware and prices needed to perform the functions. This will ensure you aren't surprised later with additional costs, after you have carefully compared brand A with brand B.

Also get an estimate of installation cost, whether you plan to have it done professionally or not. This figure will be an indicator of how complicated the system is to install. By this logic, the more costly installation is probably the one better left to the pros.

To get the full benefit of the system, flawless installation and calibration aren't the end of the exercise. You need to update your polar data as your crew becomes more proficient and you get better sails. You need to practice sailing the boat in a way that maximizes the system's power. All this work is bound to pay off in better boat speed, better crew work, and better tactics and navigation. And at that point, you'll be back to using the instruments as you did preintegration—as reference checks to seat-of-the-pants know-how, but at a higher level than you thought your boat capable of before.

Buying Tips

There is a wide range of choices in instrumentation, just as with any other piece of marine electronics. Prices vary, and so do accuracy, ruggedness, and dependability. At one time the cheap stuff was easy to spot: it had the plastic indicator housing and through-hull unit. Now almost every manufacturer's electronics come in plastic cases, only the material is now touted as lightweight rather than economical. Plastic has its advantages, though. It is a better choice for a watertight keypad than is aluminum or bronze with rubber seals, and for ease of maintenance. Bronze still makes for a more rugged through-hull tube, though.

Can you tell anything about an instrument by picking it up and looking at it? Sometimes. Does the transducer paddlewheel or spinner rotate freely? Blow on it. How much breath is needed to make it start to turn? Are the paddles well molded and balanced, with the magnets molded in and not just glued on? Is the transducer well potted in epoxy inside the through-hull tube? Are there connectors in the coax cable five to ten feet from the through hull as well as at the indicator unit? Is the indicator itself well gasketed where it must face the elements? Are circuit boards inside coated with a waterproof sealer? Is matte safety glass used for the dial, or else a high-impact plastic such as Lexan? Does the masthead wind speed and direction unit rotate at the faintest breath of air, or take 2 or 3 knots of wind to get cranking? How does it register on the indicator—instantly and wildly, or after a slight delay for damping and averaging? Are damping and averaging rates adjustable? Does the indicator give full 360-degree wind coverage?

Some integrated instrument displays are so flexible they can call up numbers in different sizes or change to a graphic readout, depending on what information is required. Here the display is a depthsounder; press one or two buttons and it's a wind indicator, compass, or speedo.

Jumbo, or maxi-sized, repeaters show standard readouts in a size everyone on deck can see.

You can compare spec sheets, too, of course. Power draw is usually expressed in microamps. Accuracy is most often seen as a percentage of true speed (such as ±2 percent) or in degrees of wind or compass angle (±1 degree). Sensitivity—how light a breeze or how low a boat speed is sufficient for reliable readings—depends on bearing quality and weight of moving parts. For masthead components, especially, this is important.

Dependability is best determined by looking at instruments aboard other boats in your harbor and asking the owners for a brief operational history. Be specific about failures, causes, repair time, warranty, and cost. Surveys of this type are more illuminating than all the dealer assurances you can get.

Where should you buy instruments and sailing computers? Is there any advantage in buying from a discounter? The question applies only to the simple, single-function equipment. This stuff is sold in large enough quantities to be offered at less than full markup. It is simple to install and test, and just about anyone can do the job. It thus makes sense to look for the lowest price on basic speedometers and wind instruments, assuming you're buying a well-known brand such as Datamarine, Standard, or Signet that's supported by the factory should something go wrong. For the more specialized gear, those electronics that require exceptional care in installation and calibration, it's worthwhile having a dealer around to help. Anyway, the integrated systems as a rule don't get discounted. Only two mail-order sources offer B&G, for instance. Pay the retail price, and expect retail service.

Some Integrated System Outputs

Performance
Boat speed
Average speed
Target speed
Polar speed
VMG upwind/down
VMC
Speed over ground

Navigation
Total log
Trip log
Time
Countdown/up
Elapsed time
ETA/time to go
Heading
DR course, distance
Distance made good
Course made good
Leeway, current
Depth
DR to man-overboard
NMEA navigation interface

Wind
Apparent wind angle
True wind angle

Magnetic wind direction
Expanded wind segment
Apparent wind speed
True wind speed
High/low wind speeds
Upwash
Heel
Pitch

Tactics
Tacking angles
Opposite tack/gybe course
Time, distance to laylines
Distance/speed lost
Distance/speed lost to tack
Favored starting position
RS232 computer interface

Other
Air temperature
Sea temperature
Rudder angle
Headstay load
Engine, fuel condition
Electrical condition
Large digit displays

Handheld Fluxgates

Some fluxgates combine sensor and display in one unit. By eliminating things like interfacing ability and, in some cases, gimballing, a small, inexpensive (under $200 at street prices) unit can be built for use as a hand-bearing compass. These fluxgates may have timing and memory functions to let you mark the time and record the bearing of a series of visual sightings. One very good one is combined with a three-power monocular and range-finding function.

Watch out for the non-gimballed handbearing models. They're inexpensive, and can work well, but you must hold them absolutely level to achieve accurate readings. That's easier said than done on a rocking, pitching platform like a small boat.

Two kinds of fluxgate handbearing compass. The one shaped like a potato also has a three-power monocular range-finding function and count-up, countdown timer. Its fluxgate sensor is gimballed in the belly of the scope. The card-like compass has a timer, as well as memory for the most recent nine bearings. Be careful to keep this one dead level when taking bearings, though; the fluxgate is not gimballed.

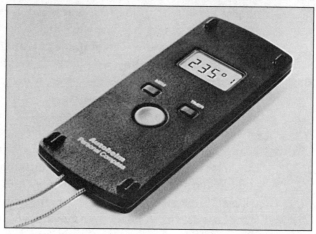

CHAPTER 17

Security Systems

by Gordon West

Boat break-ins and thefts of marine equipment are on the rise, and statistics from law enforcement agencies make it clear that marine electronics items and fishing gear are popular targets. Because marine electronic equipment has become ever smaller and more portable, it can be removed in a matter of seconds. Trailered boats are particularly susceptible because a burglar has only to unsnap the canvas boat cover and he is in, hidden from view and able to take his time while methodically disassembling every piece of electronic gear and searching for anything else of value. Anyone who keeps expensive equipment on his boat would do well to consider a security system. Many such systems, specifically manufactured for the marine market, sell for under $200, and experience has shown that they are effective in protecting a boat and its contents.

A word of caution: Most home security systems have no place aboard a boat. For example, inexpensive ultrasonic home security alarms are great for their purpose, filling a room with ultrasonic waves that will trigger an audible alarm if disturbed. Let anyone enter the room, and the alarm is tripped. On a boat, however, use of an ultrasonic system will lead to constant false alarms. A boat cover moving with the wind, the wind currents themselves, hot air funnels, a tinkling of keys, high-pitched disc brakes

Marine security alarms take on many sizes, shapes, and capabilities. Marine alarm systems are strongly recommended for all boats with installed marine electronics onboard.

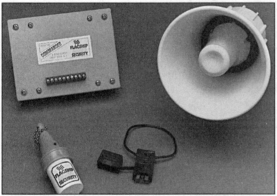

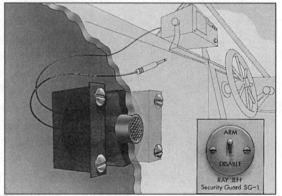

near the dock, mechanical emergency vehicle sirens—any such disturbance could trigger a response.

Another type of home alarm sometimes installed aboard small boats uses radar waves rather than ultrasonic acoustical waves to guard an enclosed space. In a home, these work quite nicely, even sounding through walls—and there's the rub. The radar waves just as readily sound through a fiberglass hull and can detect the relative motion of pilings as the boat moves up and down, or boats passing by, or other movements remote to the boat itself. After a few of the resultant false alarms, neither the local harbor patrol nor your neighbors will be overly pleased with your new system.

How a Marine Alarm System Works

Probably the best sort of alarm for small-boat use—and certainly one of the least expensive—uses small wires to protect everything on board. Two

Open-loop system— two wires to each sensor.

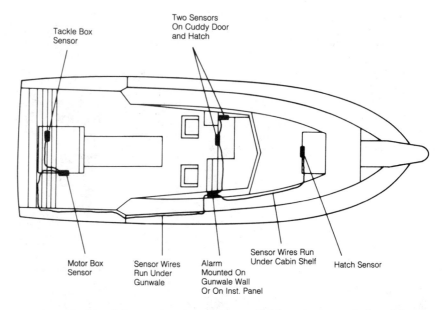

Tackle Box Sensor

Two Sensors On Cuddy Door and Hatch

Motor Box Sensor

Sensor Wires Run Under Gunwale

Alarm Mounted On Gunwale Wall Or On Inst. Panel

Sensor Wires Run Under Cabin Shelf

Hatch Sensor

generic varieties of these wire alarms are available—open- and closed-loop systems. Both work well.

The open-loop system is normally wired so that the alarm sensors are kept open until something is disturbed. Most manufacturers use hatch-mounted magnets that energize small, wired microrelays. The magnet keeps the relay open until the hatch is opened, at which point the weighted relay snaps shut and the open-loop alarm system is triggered. In one variation, a special sensor snap is used along with the usual snaps on the canvas cover of an open boat. When the boat cover is buttoned up, an open circuit is created; anyone pulling apart the snap while trying to unbutton the cover will automatically set off the alarm system. The sensor snap should be placed in a part of the cover through which a burglar would be likely to enter. Individual instruments can be protected by snap switches if fitted with canvas covers. The switch is mounted on the bottom half of the snap.

Other types of open-loop intrusion detectors include concealed sensors that close a connection should someone walk on a pressure-sensitive mat, and sensors that are triggered when gear is moved out of the magnetic field that holds the sensor open.

The closed-loop security system strings its sensors in series, like Christmas tree bulbs, and will protect everything within this "chain." The closed loop is easy to set up: Pass a single wire through every piece of electronic gear you wish to protect, and terminate the wire at the security alarm master unit. If anyone cuts the wire, the alarm immediately goes off. Alarm sensors that normally remain closed may be wired in as desired. As soon as

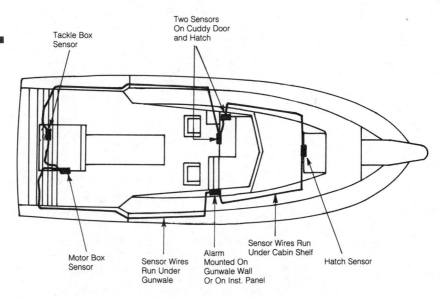

Closed-loop system—sensors wired in series.

Tackle Box Sensor

Two Sensors On Cuddy Door and Hatch

Motor Box Sensor

Sensor Wires Run Under Gunwale

Alarm Mounted On Gunwale Wall Or On Inst. Panel

Sensor Wires Run Under Cabin Shelf

Hatch Sensor

a magnetized object is moved away from one of the sensors, it will trigger the alarm by opening up a contact.

The merits of open-loop versus closed-loop systems are much debated among security manufacturers; in practical use, both systems work extremely well. In fact, since both are universally accepted, most alarm systems incorporate contacts on the back of the control box to accept either configuration.

With either type of system, the control box must be mounted where no burglar can easily get at and disarm it. Most control boxes allow placement of a remote key switch so that you can turn the alarm off before stepping aboard your boat. In some systems, a remote keyboard with numbered keys that must be pushed in the correct sequence accomplishes the same purpose. The switch or keyboard should be completely weatherproof.

The alarm control center should be wired directly to the vessel's 12-volt battery system, allowing the alarm to function even after an intruder cuts the 12-volt wires at the fuse panel. Some alarms feature a built-in rechargeable battery that will power the alarm even when the ship's battery supply gets cut off from the alarm box, and a few will sound off automatically if the 12 volts is disconnected. The control system usually features a delayed circuit, allowing you to place your turn-off switch somewhere inside the cabin. This gives you, normally, about thirty seconds to enter the boat and turn off the alarm. If you exercise this option, make sure the control center is well hidden from a burglar to keep him searching a good deal longer than the delay time.

The control center accounts for the big price differences among alarm systems: the more features it offers, the higher the price. Any good marine system should have the following accessories and capabilities:

- automatic alarm if voltage is removed
- normally open and normally closed compatibility
- terminals to enable wiring of a remote outside key control system
- an optional plug in the AC power supply with float charger for a stand-by battery
- an adjustable exit snap bar allowing delayed entry time of ten to sixty seconds
- adjustable siren alarm time of two to twelve minutes
- automatic alarm shutdown after ten minutes of sounding
- optional outputs to turn on lights, strobes, and auxiliary sirens
- optional output to a radio transmitter

As the list illustrates, while the basic operation of an alarm system is quite simple, options are plentiful.

Most mariners opt for an audible siren, which is enough to scare almost anyone away from your boat. The siren should shut down automatically after a few minutes of sounding; in some states, this is a law. No one likes listening to an audible alarm for more than a few minutes at a time. Some alarms yield a constant 12-volt output when triggered, permitting a broad choice of sirens (including a voice-synthesized alarm that yells "Burglar, burglar"). Strobe lights are also effective, and assist the harbor patrol in tracking down the boat. Alternatively, some alarms will flash your spreader lights, masthead light, or anything else that takes 12 volts.

Some alarms have dual 12-volt outputs, one to trigger another alarm such as a speech-synthesized horn that yells "Fire, fire." With this arrangement you can wire in fire sensors; the control box will know whether it is detecting a fire or a burglary and will sound the appropriate alarm.

Installation of an alarm system is rendered simple by the manufacturer's suggestions. Again, the control box is usually hidden below decks, out of the weather and out of sight. Feed 12 volts directly from the ship's battery to the control box, and keep the 12-volt wiring out of the way, so no one can detect and cut It. (Even when the system includes an automatic alarm when the 12-volt source is removed, visible wiring would help an intruder locate the control box.) Once activated, the system draws only about one-fiftieth of an amp; you could leave the system activated for months on end without pulling down a regular 12-volt battery.

Run normal, two-conductor No. 14 or No. 16 wire to the sensors or through the various pieces of electronic gear to be protected, keeping the wire as neat as possible. You needn't worry too much about whether or not the wires are exposed. Most burglars won't cut alarm wires, because many alarms need to see a normally closed circuit, and cutting a wire could thus trip the alarm. Furthermore, the metal wire cutters used to slice through each pair of cables might accidentally trigger the alarm. Indeed, burglars usually shy away completely from a boat with alarm wires visible.

The idea when arming a boat with alarm wires is to keep every sensor point as simple as possible. Connecting a sensor improperly can result in an inoperative alarm. If your vessel uses a normally open circuit, you should be able to inspect every sensor easily. In a closed-loop system, you get an immediate indication that everything is armed from the alarm status light. The light should come on when you set the switch. A great advantage of the closed-loop system is the ease of doublechecking that everything is indeed activated.

When the system is installed, have a friend try it out. See how long it takes him to set it off accidentally, and how long it takes to find the source of the noise and disable it.

If you use a siren, make sure it can't be tossed overboard easily or otherwise deactivated. A plastic siren that makes a lot of noise inside a cabin can immediately be silenced by ripping it from the wall and breaking off the wires. Locate an alarm horn or siren in a hard-to-reach place.

Police reports indicate that most thieves will immediately high-tail it if they hear an alarm that they can't easily disable. The reports also indicate, however, that cheap alarm systems are immediately detected and destroyed by a thief, who then goes about his business.

A relatively new innovation in marine security alarms is the completely waterproof keypad controller. This eliminates the need for fumbling for the right key when you plan to go aboard your alarmed boat. The controller also gives you some nice options, such as "temporary authorization" to come aboard.

Let's say you are going to be leaving your boat for several weeks, but a marine electronics technician needs to come aboard and replace a scratched faceplate on your radar setup on the flying bridge. Since your flying bridge is alarmed with a pressure-sensitive pad, the technician would need to have your secret security disarm number. And you also remember that a carpet-layer is going to come in and trim the edges of the new carpet down in the galley.

The technician will probably be aboard the boat several times during your absence; the carpet layer, just once. What can you do to make sure they don't come back at a later date, and use the same disarm number to help themselves to everything on board?

The new marine security system controllers allow you a limited number of times access code for specific workers. The code might let them on the boat one or two times, or for the carpet layer, just once. They could not deactivate the alarm after they have exceeded the number of times on board. This is sort of like a one-time combination.

This same principle is also being used by selected marinas throughout the country. You and your guests are issued magnetic card gate entry passes. Not only does the card get you in and out of the dock area, it also electronically records when you were there, how long you stayed, when you left, and every time you went in and went out of that particular gate. At the end of the month, you can look at the computer and see how many times you went up and down the gangway!

If it's been several months since you last paid your dock bill, the marina may want to get your attention to have you come to the office to settle up. A few keystrokes on the computer, and presto—you are locked out. This may get your attention real quick.

Some mariners don't like the idea of "big brother" having a record of how many times they've been back and forth to the docks. But nonetheless, it's the latest security measure in marina management.

So whether it's a sophisticated marine security management system that keeps out the thieves—or a smart marine alarm system aboard your boat that keeps the thieves out—you can be assured that there are now marine electronic security systems specifically designed for the wet environment. Put one on your boat now, and quite possibly you might even enjoy some lower-cost insurance rates if you can prove that your marine alarm system is specifically designed for boat protection.

Summary

Keep your marine electronics investment safe. Use your marine electronics often. Review our maintenance tips, and we wish you continued safe boating with marine electronics on board.

Ham radio. *See* Amateur radio
Handheld units, VHF radio,
54–56
Heading sensors, autopilots,
214–216
Hyperbolic navigation, 139–140

Indicator unit, depthsounders, 11
installation of, 29
types of, 20–21
INMARSAT equipment, satellite
communications, 68–72
Integrated systems, 244–252
buying guidelines, 254–256
cost factors, 253–254
important features of, 247
installation and calibration of,
251–252
outputs, types of, 256
performance-based systems,
250–251
special features, 252–253
true wind angle, 248
true wind direction, 245–246
velocity made good, 246–247,
248
velocity prediction program,
248
International voice channel designators, 98–99

Laser Plot, 189
LCD display units, 241
LCD graph recorders, 23–24
LCD loran, 145–146
LCD screens, electronic chart plotters, 187–188
Licensing
amateur radio, 100–104
single sideband radio, 95
types of licenses, 101–103
VHF radio, 57–58
Loran, 132–153
additional secondary factor
correction, 142, 144
buying guidelines, 143–150
compared to global positioning
system, 174–175
future view, 153
hyperbolic navigation,
139–140
installation of, 150–151
interfacing problem, 148–149
LCD loran, 145–146
NMEA 0180 standard,
148–149
position fixes, reliability of,
133, 141–142
scope of coverage, 132–137
secondary stations, 140–141
steering graphics, 146
troubleshooting, 152–153

waterproofing, 147–148
waypoints, 145

Manuals, for equipment, 8
Maptech, 189
Marine electronic equipment
buyer's checklist, 8–9
installation, 5
quality of, 7–8
sources for, 1–6
warranties, 6–7
*Marine Radiotelephone User's
Handbook*, 97

National Marine Electronics
Association, 2, 7
Navigate!, 189
Navionics cartography, 185
NAVTEX receiver, 117–118
Noise
common problems, 154–155,
156
locating source of, 155–156
and single sideband radio,
94–95
sources of noise, 156–161
Novice license, 101–102

Paddlewheel, speedometers,
233–234
Potentiometers, 239–240
Private coast stations, 79–80
Proportional response, autopilots,
213

Radar, 197–211
antennas, 202–204
components of unit, 198
display unit, 204–205
electronic bearing line, 206
electronic variable range
marker, 206
features of radar set, 206–207
guard zones, 206
information on screen display,
207
installation of, 210–211
maintenance of, 211
navigation within harbor, 209
operating procedures,
208–210
power-saving modes, 199–200
pulse repetition, 200–201
ranges of, 201–202
raster scan radars, 205
targets with racon devices, 209
transmitting power, 199
workings of, 197–205
Radiobeacon network, 120
Radio direction finders, 119–131
accuracy of readings, 124–125
antenna, 122–123

automatic direction finder,
123, 129–131
buying guidelines, 127–128
federal plan for, 119–120
maintenance of, 128–129
Radiobeacon network, 120
receivers, 120–122
types of, 125–127
workings of, 122–125
Raster scan radars, 205
Receivers, radio direction finders,
120–122
Routing systems, in electronic plotters, 193–194
Rudder-feedback unit, 218

Satellite communications, 67–73
future view, 73
INMARSAT equipment,
68–72
voice quality, 72
workings of, 68, 72–73
Security systems, 258–264
closed-loop system, 260–261
control center, 261–262
installation of, 262–263
open-loop system, 260
Selective Availability, global positioning system, 168
Shoreside marine telephone stations, 78–79
Single sideband radio, 74–99
allocated frequency bands, 76
antenna, 82–83
antenna tuners, 83–85
going on the air, 95–99
grounding, 85–93
groundwave of, 76
international voice channel
designators, 98–99
licensing, 95
noise elimination, 94–95
range, 77–78
registration of station with
marine telephone operators, 97
services/broadcasts, 78–80
skywave of, 76–77
transceiver installation, 93–94
transceivers, 80–82
weak signals, 96–97
workings of, 75–78
Skywaves, 76–77, 125
Speedometers, 231–235
features of, 232
maintenance of, 234–235
paddlewheel, 233–234
readouts for, 231
transducers, disadvantages of,
233
Steering graphics, loran, 146

Technician class license, 102

Transceivers
single sideband radio, 80–82
VHF radio, 47–51
Transducers, depthsounders
elements of, 11–15
installation, 15–18
Transit, compared to global posi-
tioning system, 178
Trim, 218–219
Tru-Chart, 191
True wind angle, 248
True wind direction, 245–246

Vector digitization, electronic chart
plotters, 185–186
Velocity made good, 246–247, 248
Velocity prediction program,
193–194, 248
VHF radio, 32–60
antennas, 41–45
buying guidelines, 60
channels, 33–40
coaxial cable, 45–47
handheld units, 54–56
installation of, 51–54
licensing, 57–58
maintenance of, 59–60
operating procedures, 58–59
range, 40–41
transceivers, 47–51
Video sounders, 24–28
features of, 25–28

Warranties, 6–7
Waypoints
cautions about, 174
loran, 145
Weather facsimile reception,
111–118
computer system require-
ments, 115–116
drum recorders, 114–115
list of stations, source for, 112
NAVTEX receiver, 117–118
shortwave receiver for,
116–117
updates of weather charts, 112
workings of, 111–114
Wind instruments, 235–240
anemometers, 236
apparent wind functions and,
235
installation of, 237–239
masthead units, 236–237
vane sensor, 239
wind angle indicator, 235,
239–240
Windvane, autopilots, 215–216

Zoom function, electronic chart
plotters, 186